Guide to the EC Block Exemption for Vertical Agreements

International Competition Law Series

Volume 4.

The titles published in this series are listed at the end of this volume

Guide to the EC Block Exemption for Vertical Agreements

by

Martin Mendelsohn

and

Stephen Rose

KLUWER LAW INTERNATIONAL

THE HAGUE / LONDON / NEW YORK

blished by:
uwer Law International
). Box 85889, 2508 CN The Hague, The Netherlands
les@kli.wkap.nl
:p://www.kluwerlaw.com

ld and Distributed in North, Central and South America by:
uwer Law International
1 Philip Drive, Norwell, MA 02061, USA
uwerlaw@wkap.com

ld and Distributed in all other countries by:
uwer Law International
stribution Centre, P.O. Box 322, 3300 AH Dordrecht, The Netherlands

CIP Catalogue record for this book is available from the Library of Congress

inted on acid-free paper.

BN 90-411-9813-X

luwer Law International incorporates the imprint of Martinus Nijhoff Publishers

CONTENTS

INTRODUCTION

This book considers the "super block exemption" for vertical agreements which came into effect on 1 June 2000 and is referred to in this book as the Block Exemption Regulation.

The aim of the book is to put the Block Exemption Regulation in context for non-competition law specialists and for business people. Early chapters therefore explain the objectives of the European Treaties and the way in which competition law and policy have been applied to vertical agreements. Chapter 3 goes a step further in explaining the European Commission's far-reaching plans for the modernisation of European competition law.

Having laid these foundations, the book focuses in chapters 4 & 5 on the detailed provisions of the new law, including a clause by clause analysis of the Block Exemption Regulation.

As the book is intended as a practical handbook, the remaining chapters examine how some specific types of agreement are likely to be treated under the new rules, and highlight differences from the previous position. Chapter 10 is a checklist for application of the Block Exemption Regulation.

We have tried to avoid repetition by cross referencing or providing signposts to relevant sources.

The Block Exemption Regulation marks an important change in Commission policy and introduces a new methodology for applying the competition rules to vertical restraints. Inevitably there will be uncertainties and teething problems. We have tried to identify these and suggest possible interpretations or answers.

We thank our colleagues for their help, and encouragement. In particular we thank our respective secretaries, Julie Woods and Ginette Sargeant, for their assistance and for putting up with us and our handwriting.

Martin Mendelsohn
Stephen Rose

CHAPTER 1

EUROPEAN COMPETITION LAW

INTRODUCTION

This chapter summarises the aims and scope of European competition law and explains the key Treaty Articles which lay the foundation for the competition rules. The institutions charged with formulating and implementing competition law are also described.

THE BASIS OF EUROPEAN LAW

The European Economic Community has been in existence since the signing of the Treaty of Rome in 1957 (The EEC Treaty).[1] The EEC Treaty was designed to create a Common Market based on a full economic union between the Member States. It is the EEC Treaty which sets out the main European competition rules with which this work is primarily concerned. The six original EEC Member States were: France, Germany, Italy, Belgium, The Netherlands, and Luxembourg. In 1973 the UK, Denmark and Ireland acceded to the EEC. Greece joined with effect from 1981 followed by Spain and Portugal in 1986.

In 1986 the 12 Member States of the EEC signed the Single European Act, designed to eliminate remaining barriers to the single internal market by 31 December 1992. The Single European Act extended Community competencies, implemented a harmonisation programme and made changes to the Community decision making process to facilitate the creation of the single market.

---

1 The Treaty of Paris (The ECSC Treaty) and the Euratom Treaty also aimed at establishing greater co-operation within Europe but are not relevant to this work. The ECSC Treaty signed in 1951 was the first European Treaty aimed at economic integration and regulates certain coal and steel products. The ECSC Treaty is to expire in 2002 when the scope of the EEC Treaty will be extended to former ECSC products. The Euratom Treaty was signed at the same time as the EEC Treaty and co-ordinates the development of the nuclear industries of the Member States.

In 1992, the EEC Member States and the EFTA Member States[2] signed the Treaty as an European Economic Area (the "EEA Treaty"). That Treaty aims, inter alia, at ensuring free movement of goods, persons and services within the EEA and setting up a system of undistorted competition. To that end the EEA Treaty contains equivalent competition rules to those of the EEC Treaty.

In 1992 the EEC Member States signed the Treaty of the European Union (TEU) at Maastricht which came into force on 1 November 1993. This amended the EEC Treaty which was renamed the European Community Treaty (EC Treaty). The significance of this is to remove the word "economic" from the title reflecting the broadening of the scope of the Treaty to include social, monetary, policy, defence and other matters. The TEU provided for the creation of a full economic and monetary union by 1999 (with the UK and Denmark opting out). The TEU made further changes to the Community Institutions, in particular, enhancing the role of the European Parliament.

The TEU created a wider political union – the European Union to which Austria, Finland and Sweden acceded in 1995 bringing the number of Member States to 15. The scope of the EC competition rules will be further extended in the next few years with the anticipated accession of the first wave of countries from Central and Eastern Europe. Discussions are well advanced to enable the accession of Hungary, Czech Republic, Poland, Estonia & Slovenia. In the meantime a number of these countries have concluded so-called Europe agreements with the Commission which broadly speaking require them to change their laws to conform to the EC Treaty and other provisions having legal effect in the EU so that the path to accession will be smoother.

In October 1997 the Member States signed the Amsterdam Treaty which entered into force on 1 May 1999. The Amsterdam Treaty removed a number of redundant Articles in the TEU and the EC Treaty and reorganised aspects of the TEU. One of the consequences of the Amsterdam Treaty is the renumbering of most of the Articles of the EC Treaty with the effect that the key competition Articles of the EC Treaty, Articles 85 and 86 were renumbered Articles 81 and 82 respectively. For

---

2 The European Free Trade Association (EFTA) Members are Austria, Finland, Iceland, Liechtenstein, Norway, Sweden and Switzerland. Of these Austria, Finland and Sweden subsequently acceded to the European Union. Switzerland did not ratify the EEA Treaty and is not covered by its provisions.

The Treaty of Nice was signed on 26 February 2001 and makes various amendments to the EU Treaties although it does not affect the competition rules. In particular, it amends the TEU to provide for enhanced co-operation in relation to a common foreign and security policy and certain other matters.

convenience in this text we will refer to EC competition law and policy rather then the EU since the competition rules derive from the EC Treaty rather than the TEU. We will also refer to former Article numbers when first used in the text (eg Article 81 (ex 85)).

AIMS OF THE EC TREATY

The general aims of the EC Treaty are the creation of a common market in which goods, services, labour and capital circulate freely and to promote the co-ordination of the economies of the Member States. Article 2 of the EC Treaty, as amended and broadened by the Amsterdam Treaty reads:

> "The Community shall have as its task, by establishing a Common Market and an economic and monetary union and by implementing common policies or activities referred to in Articles 3 and 4, to promote throughout the Community a harmonious balanced and sustainable development of economic activities, a high level of employment and of social protection, equality between men and women, sustainable and non-inflationary growth, a high degree of competitiveness and convergence of economic performance, a high level of protection and improvement of the quality of the environment, the raising of the standard of living and quality of life, and economic and social cohesion and solidarity among Member States."

Articles 3 and 4 list the activities of the Community. These include: the elimination of barriers to trade between Member States such as customs duties and quantitative restrictions; the creation of a common commercial policy; the creation of an internal market by the abolition of obstacles to the free movement of persons, services and capital between Member States; common policies in the sphere of agriculture and transport.

Article 3 (g) (as amended) specifically requires *"the institution of a system ensuring that competition in the internal market is not distorted."* Article 3 (g) is implemented by the rules on competition set out in Articles 81-89 later in the EC Treaty. It is important to appreciate that the EC competition rules are very much part of the overall objective of promoting a single common market. As a result in addition to the objective of ensuring that competition is open and free, the rules are also used as a tool to promote a single market and prevent artificial barriers to trade between Member States. The reader should also be aware of the EC Treaty articles concerning the free movement of goods as these have a significant impact on distribution systems and other vertical agreements operating in Europe. A discussion of those articles is however beyond the scope of this work.

EUROPEAN INSTITUTIONS

The main European institutions are the European Parliament, the Council, the Commission and the European Courts.

European Parliament

The Members of the European Parliament (MEPs) are directly elected every 5 years. The Parliament is becoming increasingly important in the operation of the Community and now has a substantive legislative role in certain areas. As well as the main plenary body there are important committees including the Economic and Monetary Affairs Committee and the Legal Affairs Committee which discuss and review the Commission's activities. The Parliament adopts an annual resolution on the Commission Report on Competition policy and its debates often concern matters directly involving competition policy.

Council

The Council of the European Communities is charged with ensuring that the objectives of the Treaty are met and must ensure co-ordination of the general economic policies of the Member States. The Council consists of one representative from each Member State. One Member State holds the presidency which is rotated every 6 months. The Council is the principal legislature of the Community, and the Council adopts Regulations and Directives that have been proposed by the Commission including in the area of competition policy. For example, the Council adopted Council Regulation 17/62/EEC and Council Regulation 19/65 EEC which are the key implementing regulations for Articles 81 and 82. A necessary first step in introducing the Block Exemption Regulation and its associated reform was the adoption by the Council of amendments to these two regulations.

Commission

The Commission comprises 20 Commissioners who are nominated by the Member States and supported by a permanent staff of around 10,000. It is split into separate departments termed Directorates-General. The Commission is responsible for ensuring that the provisions of the Treaty are applied and for implementing decisions of the Council. The Commission makes proposals for legislation to the Council. The Commission also has the power to take its own decisions.

There are 23 Directorates-General, each of which reports to one of the

Commissioners. The Commission is also assisted by the Legal Service. The Commission has special competence in enforcing European competition law.

The Directorate-General for Competition ("DG Comp" (formerly DGIV)) reports to the Commissioner for Competition, who at the time of writing is Mario Monti. Former Competition Commissioners include Karel Van Miert, Sir Leon Brittan and Peter Sutherland.

DG Competition is split into distinct Directorates which deal with different sectors of the economy. The different Directorates are:

A General Competition Policy and co-ordination

B Merger Task Force

C Information, communication and multimedia:

- (1) Post and telecommunications and information society co-ordination
- (2) Media and music publishing
- (3) Information industries and consumer electronics

D Services

- (1) Financial services (banking, insurance)
- (2) Transport
- (3) Distributive trades, tourism and other industries

E Basic Industries

- (1) Steel, non-ferrous metals, non-metallic mineral products, construction, timber, paper and glass industries
- (2) Basic and processed chemical products and rubber industries
- (3) Energy (coal, oil and gas, electricity)
- (4) Cartels and inspection

F Capital and consumer goods industries:

- (1) Mechanical and electrical engineering and other manufacturing industries
- (2) Motor vehicles and other means of transport, and associated mechanical manufactured products
- (3) Agricultural, food and pharmaceutical products, textiles and other consumer goods industries.

G State aids

DG Comp has extensive powers to investigate infringements of competition law and to devise and implement competition policy. DG Comp is responsible for all stages of a case from initial investigation and fact-finding to prosecution. Its decisions are subject to appeal to the European Courts.

It is DG Comp which instigated the policy review which culminated in the adoption of the Block Exemption Regulation pursuant to Council Regulation 19/65/EEC.

European Courts

There are two tiers of judicial decision making: the Court of First Instance (CFI) and the European Court of Justice (ECJ). The CFI has jurisdiction to hear certain categories of cases including actions under Article 230 [ex 173] for the annulment of Commission decisions on competition law. Grounds for annulment are lack of competence, infringement of an essential procedural requirement, infringement of the Treaty, or misuse of powers. Decisions of the CFI can be appealed to the ECJ on the grounds of lack of competence, breach of procedure before the CFI or infringement of EC law. The ECJ also gives rulings on points of interpretation of the EC Treaty referred to it from national courts under Article 234 [ex 177].

SOURCES OF EC COMPETITION LAW

EC competition law derives from four main sources:

(i) Articles of the EC Treaty

(ii) Regulations and Directives issued under the authority of the EC Treaty

(iii) Decisions and Notices issued by the Commission

(iv) Judgments of the CFI and the ECJ

(i) Articles of the EC Treaty

Articles 81-92 (ex 85-98) of the Treaty contain the rules governing competition (including state aid) within the EC and implement Article 3(g) of the Treaty.

The key Articles are Articles 81 and 82 (ex 86) which have direct effect in the EC Member States and can be invoked before national courts.

Article 81(1) prohibits all agreements between undertakings, decisions by associations and concerted practices which may affect trade between Member States and which have as their object or effect the prevention, restriction or distortion of competition within the Common Market. Article 81(3) provides for the prohibition of Article 81(3) to be disapplied in certain circumstances.

Article 82 prohibits the abuse by one or more undertakings of a dominant position within the common market or in a substantial part of it which affects trade between Member States.

that exemption shall take effect no earlier than the date of notification. This is the general rule and Article 4(2) sets out the exceptions to that rule. Article 4(2)(2) benefits vertical agreements and was introduced as part of the reform package with the Block Exemption Regulation. Exemption of a vertical agreement can be backdated to the start of the agreement regardless of when notification is made. This amendment and its consequences are described in Chapter 5. Article 8 provides that an exemption decision shall be time limited and may be renewed on application by the parties or revoked in certain circumstances.

The procedure for notification and the relevant form (Form A/B) are set out in Commission Regulation 2576/95 EEC.

Article 3 gives the Commission the power to take a decision finding an infringement of Article 81 or 82. Article 9 is important because it reserves to the Commission the exclusive right to take an exemption decision under Article 81(3). The Member State authorities therefore have no right to grant an exemption[3]. They may however apply the prohibitions of Article 81(1) and Article 82 unless the Commission has already initiated a procedure. Article 10 sets out the obligations of the Commission to liaise with Member States, in particular through the medium of an Advisory Committee.

Articles 11 and 14 gave the Commission powers to request information and documents. In particular Article 14 enables the Commission to enter premises and examine books and business records of companies (so called dawn raids). Articles 15 and 16 give the Commission the power to impose fines (including periodic penalties) on companies which breach the rules. The maximum level of a fine is 10% of the worldwide group turnover of the company concerned (Article 15(2)). The Commission's policies for setting fines are set out in Commission Notice 98/ C9/03)[4]. Heavy fines have been imposed in a number of cases concerning vertical agreements, particularly where the companies concerned have attempted to restrict parallel imports.[5]

---

3 For a discussion of the consequences of this and options for reform see Chapter 3.

4 Commission Notice: Guidelines on the method of setting fines imposed pursuant to Article 15(2) of Regulation No. 17 and Article 65(5) of the ESCS Treaty. (98/C9/03)

5 In case VW, OJ 1998, L124/60, [1998] 5 CMLR 33 Volkswagen AG was fined 102 million Euros (reduced on appeal to 90 million Euros) for attempts to restrict reimports of cars from Austria and Italy.

Block exemptions
Council Regulation 19/65 EEC empowers the Commission to exempt *en bloc* under Article 81(3) certain categories of agreements and is of general application. Pursuant to Regulation 19/65 the Commission has adopted the following relevant block exemptions in relation to vertical agreements, which are discussed in this book:

Regulation 1983/83 exclusive distribution

Regulation 1984/83 exclusive purchasing

Regulation 4087/88 franchising

Regulation 1475/95 motor vehicles

Regulation 240/96 technology transfer agreements

Regulation 2790/99 vertical agreements and concerted practices (the Block Exemption Regulation)

In order to enable the Commission to adopt the Block Exemption Regulation. Regulation 19/65 was amended by Council Regulation 1215/99 EC in June 1999 to give the Commission greater scope to exempt all types of vertical agreements.

The first three of these block exemption regulations have expired and effectively been replaced by the Block Exemption Regulation. However they remain relevant for a transition period to 31 December 2001 (see Article 12 of the Block Exemption Regulation discussed in Chapter 4). The Motor Vehicle Regulation remains in force and motor vehicles and parts covered by that regulation are excluded from the Block Exemption Regulation as are any other subject specific block exemption regulations (see Article 2.5 of the Block Exemption Regulation below and paragraph 45 of the Guidelines). The Technology Transfer Regulation also remains in force and agreements whose principal objective is the licensing of patents and/or know-how many benefit from its terms. "Pure" intellectual property licenses are excluded from the scope of the Block Exemption Regulation (see Chapter 4).

(iii) Decisions and Notices issued by the Commission
The Commission is the source of EC competition policy. It communicates this policy through block exemption regulations, decisions, other announcements (eg Annual Report and Quarterly Newsletter) and Notices. The DG Comp website contains all relevant policy documents as well as press releases, speeches and some decisions of the Commission. The address is http//:europa.eu.int/comm/competition.

The Commission issues decisions in individual cases pursuant to its powers under Regulation 17 and the procedures of Commission Regulation 2576/95. The decision making procedure is in fact very cumbersome with the consequence that the Commission only issues decisions in about 20 cases each year, which are deemed to be of special economic, political or legal importance. The process to reach a full decision in practice takes many months or years and involves consultation of third parties and the Advisory Committee. A Commission decision is binding on the parties to whom it is addressed. Commission Decisions are generally published and act as an indicator of Commission policy for other parties.

The Commission receives on average about 200 notifications of agreements annually. At the end of 1999 it had 1,013 unclosed cases. It is impractical to deal with this volume of cases by decision and so the Commission adopted the administrative device of the "comfort letter" to enable it to dispose of the growing back log of cases. There are a number of forms of comfort letters but the essence of all positive comfort letters is the statement by the Commission that on the basis of the information provided to it, it has decided to close the file. In practice the effect of a comfort letter is that the Commission will not re-open the case unless material new facts emerge or it transpires that the information on which it based its decision was inaccurate or incomplete. A comfort letter is not legally binding on the national courts of the Member States and does not therefore exclude the risk that the agreement in question may be challenged. The Commission has attempted to address this risk in its Notice on cooperation between national competition authorities and the Commission.[6]

In addition the Commission publishes from time to time Notices providing guidance as to its enforcement policy. Notices are not binding and may be varied or withdrawn. Also subsequent Commission decisions may deviate from the general view expressed in a prior Notice. Notices must be treated with caution but in practice are widely used by the Commission to indicate policy. In addition to the Notice on cooperation with National Authorities, there are three further Notices which are crucial to the application of the competition rules to vertical agreements.

Commission Notice of agreements of minor importance which do not fall under Article 81(1) of the Treaty establishing the European Community (1997)[7] – This is set out in Appendix F. The purpose of the Notice is to provide guidance to business as to the categories of agreements which the Commission considers will fall outside

---

6 Commission Notice on cooperation between national competition authorities and the Commission in handling cases falling within the scope of Articles 85 and 86 of the Treaty (97 C313/03)

7 OJ 1997 C372/5

the scope of Article 81(1) because they have only an insignificant effect on competition. The Notice and its proposed replacement are discussed further in Chapter 2.

Commission Notice on the definition of relevant market for the purposes of Community Competition Law (1997)[8] – This is set out in Appendix G and provides guidance as to how the Commission applies the concept of relevant product market and geographical market in its enforcement of Community competition law. The definition of the relevant market is a crucial first step in any analysis under the Block Exemption Regulation and so this Notice is essential reading. The Notice is discussed in detail in Chapter 5 in the context of the Guidelines on Vertical Restraints.

Guidelines on Vertical Restraints[9]
The Guidelines are an integral part of the new Commission policy on vertical restraints and should be read in conjunction with the Block Exemption Regulation. The Guidelines are set out in Appendix C and they are discussed in more detail in Chapter 6.

(iv) Judgments of the CFI and ECJ
Judgments of the CFI and the ECJ are also crucial in the interpretation of EC competition law. Many of the most important Court judgments in relation to Articles 81 and 82 concern vertical agreements and are discussed in later chapters.

---

8 OJ 1997 C372/5

9 OJ 2000 C291/1

CHAPTER 2

EC COMPETITION RULES

INTRODUCTION

This chapter sets out an overview of Articles 81 and 82 of the EC Treaty. The Block Exemption Regulation exempts agreements from the prohibition of Article 81(1). The chapter therefore focuses on the elements of Article 81 and the way that Article has been applied to vertical agreements. There is no possibility of exemption from Article 82 and the Block Exemption Regulation does not affect the applicability of Article 82 to vertical agreements. However, Article 82 remains just as relevant for those companies in a dominant position (or those who are victims of abuse of a dominant position) and the way Article 82 applies to vertical agreements is also summarised.

ARTICLE 81

Article 81 provides:

1. The following shall be prohibited as incompatible with the Common Market; all agreements between undertakings, decisions by associations of undertakings and concerted practices which may affect trade between Member States and which have as their object or effect the prevention, restriction or distortion of competition within the Common Market, and in particular those which:
   a. directly or indirectly fix purchase or selling prices or any other trading conditions;
   b. limit or control production, markets, technical development, or investment;
   c. share markets or sources of supply;
   d. apply dissimilar conditions to equivalent transactions with other trading parties, thereby placing them at a competitive disadvantage;
   e. make the conclusion of contracts subject to the acceptance by the other parties of supplementary obligations which, by their nature or according to commercial usage, have no connection with the subject of such contracts.

2. Any agreements or decisions prohibited pursuant to this Article shall be automatically void.

3. The provisions of paragraph 1 may, however, be declared inapplicable in the case of:

   - any agreement or category of agreements between undertakings;
   - any decision or category of decisions by associations of undertakings;
   - any concerted practice or category of concerted practices;

   which contributes to improving the production or distribution of goods or to promoting technical or economic progress, while allowing consumers a fair share of the resulting benefit, and which does not:

   a. impose on the undertakings concerned restrictions which are not indispensable to the attainment of these objectives;
   b. afford such undertakings the possibility of eliminating competition in respect of a substantial part of the products in question.

ARTICLE 81(1)

In deciding whether an agreement falls within Article 81 (1), the following elements must be present:

"Agreement between one or more undertakings"

There must be an agreement (in writing or oral) between two or more undertakings. The term "undertaking" is viewed in the broadest sense, covering any entity engaged in economic or commercial activities and will range from small shops to large industrial conglomerates. An individual such as a sole trader or a consultant can be an undertaking, although an employee is not an undertaking for these purposes. The ECJ held[1] that the term "undertaking" in competition law indicates an economic unit even if in law that unit consists of several legal or natural persons (it could include shareholders and directors).

Undertakings under common control (eg a parent and subsidiary) are regarded as a single undertaking for the purposes of Article 81 and so in principle, intra-

---

1 *Hydrotherm Gerätebau GmbH v. Compact de Dott. Ing Mario Andreoli & CSAS 170/83* [1984] ECR 2999; [1985] 3 CMLR 224

group agreements will fall outside Article 81[2]. The rationale for this is that a true subsidiary has no ability to adopt its own commercial strategy independent of its parent and so should be viewed as a single economic entity with its parent[3]. Where a shareholding link of 50% or less exists, the presumption will be that the affiliated companies are not part of a single economic entity and so Article 81 may apply to relations between such affiliates. Above a 50% link, the issue will turn on the facts. In *Gosmé/Martel – DMP* the Commission decided that a 50/50 joint venture was not a single undertaking because it was subject to control by more than one parent.[4]

In the context of vertical agreements, a number of cases suggest that apparently unilateral conduct by a supplier in the context of an ongoing relationship with dealers in fact constitutes an "agreement". In *AEG Telefunken v. Commission*[5] AEG argued that a consistent refusal to supply dealers operating on narrow margins in order to maintain resale prices constituted unilateral conduct on its part outside of Article 81. The Court held that:

> *"On the contrary it forms part of the contractual relations between the undertaking and resellers. Indeed, in the case of the admission of a distributor, approval is based on the acceptance, tacit or express, by the contracting parties of the policy pursued by AEG which requires, inter alia, the exclusion from the network of all distributors who are qualified for admission but are not prepared to adhere to that policy".*

In *Sandoz*,[6] the Court held that conditions stamped on invoices formed part of the long term contract on which sales were regularly made to a dealer. In that case, Sandoz had stamped the words "export prohibited" on the invoices and the Court held that this was not a unilateral act outside Article 81 because the invoices contained other important terms which were tacitly accepted by dealers and formed part of the overall framework of the commercial relationship between the parties.

The *Adalat*[7] case appears to set the limit on how far the Commission may go in

---

2 *Viho v. Commission* (C-73/95P) [1996] ECR I-5457

3 A similar rationale is applied in the case of principal and agent. Agency is discussed in detail in chapter 6.

4 (91/335/EEC) [1992] 5 C.M.L.R. 586, para. 30

5 (107/82) [1983] ECR 3151

6 (277/87)[1990] ECR I-45

7 Case T 41/96 Judgment of the Court of First Instance of 26 October 2000. The Commission has appealed against this judgment to the ECJ (Case C-2 & 3/01 *Commission v. Bayer*, not yet decided).

interpreting an apparently unilateral action by a supplier as an agreement between the supplier and the dealer within the meaning of Article 81(1). In that case Bayer's heart drug, Adalat, was sold much more cheaply in Spain and France than in the UK with the result that dealers in the cheaper countries exported to the UK and Bayer's sales in the UK were halved by the impact of parallel trade. Bayer identified the exporting wholesalers and progressively reduced the quantity of Adalat supplied to them. Bayer denied imposing an export ban on its dealers although it admitted that the purpose of rationing was unilaterally to restrict exports to the UK. The Commission found that a continuous commercial relationship existed between Bayer and its dealers based on regular orders placed by telephone, electronic mail or ordinary mail. The Commission further found that the dealers were fully aware of what Bayer doing and that the evidence "demonstrates that the wholesalers were aware of the real motives of Bayer... to thwart parallel imports; they adapted to the system established by their supplier so as to comply with its requirements. This behaviour thus demonstrates their compliance with the export ban."

Bayer appealed the Commission decision. On the grounds, inter alia, that the Commission had not established the existence of an agreement between Bayer and its wholesalers to prevent exports.

The CFI annulled the Commission's decision on the basis that the Commission had incorrectly assessed the facts and made an error in the legal assessment of the facts ie by finding the existence of a common interaction between Bayer and its dealers to prevent exports.

The CFI held that the concept of an agreement within the meaning of Article 81(1) centres around the "existence of a concurrence of wills between at least two parties." The CFI concluded that :

> *"the Commission cannot hold that apparently unilateral conduct on the part of a manufacturer, adopted in the context of the contractual relations which he maintains with his dealers, in reality forms the basis of an agreement between undertakings within the meaning of Article [81 (1)] of the Treaty if it does not establish the existence of an acquiescence by the other parties, express or implied, in the attitude adopted by the manufacturer."*

On the facts the Commission had failed to establish such acquiescence. The CFI found that the Commission had not established that Bayer had adopted a systematic policy of monitoring the final destination of products; nor that it applied threats or penalties to dealers who exported; nor that supplies were made conditional on compliance with the alleged export ban. Importantly there was no evidence that Bayer required any particular conduct from dealers regarding export policy nor that Bayer had sought the agreement or acquiescence of dealers to the implementation of the policy. Finally the CFI held that the mere fact that dealers did not interrupt their commercial relations with Bayer is not a sufficient ground to hold the existence of an agreement to implement an acquiescence to the implementation of the alleged export ban.

"Decisions by associations of undertakings"

This phrase typically covers agreements and recommendations made by trade associations to their members, even if not binding. As such it is typically relevant to horizontal arrangements between member companies rather than vertical agreements.

"Concerted practices"

The concept of a concerted practice is used to describe collusion between undertakings which falls short of an agreement (although the distinction between "agreement" and "concerted practice" is blurred). The concept is typically relevant to a cartel situation involving collusion between competitors rather than to vertical relationships.

"Effect on trade between Member States"

This phrase represents the jurisdictional limit of Article 81 (and also Article 82). The Court of Justice has held that an agreement may affect trade between Member States on the following basis:

> *"it must be possible to foresee with a sufficient degree of probability on the basis of a set of objective factors of law or fact that it may have an influence, direct or indirect, actual or potential, on the pattern of trade between Member States, such as might prejudice the aim of a single market in all the Member States".*[8]

In practice this is a low jurisdictional hurdle and an agreement even if confined to a single Member State may be caught if it has the potential to restrict imports or exports, is part of a wider distribution system or is entered into between companies in different Member States.

---

8 Case 42/84 *Remia v. Commission* [1985] ECR 2545

Société Technique Minière[11]

The case concerned an agreement whereby a French company STM was given an exclusive right to sell in France machinery manufactured by a German company and agreed not to sell competing machines. The Court held that in deciding whether to apply Article 85 (1) (as it then was) the first step is to consider the "object" of the agreement. The grant of an exclusive right of sale does not by its nature have the "object" of restricting competition, at least where the exclusive right is necessary for the penetration of a new territory. If the "object" of the agreement does not by its nature restrict competition, it is necessary to consider the "effect" of the agreement on competition taking into account the full economic context. The effect on competition must be shown to be "appreciable" and relevant factors will include the market share of the parties; whether the agreement is part of a network of similar agreements and whether the agreement prevents parallel imports.

The case therefore demonstrates the need to consider whether an agreement has the effect of appreciably restricting competition, taking into account its economic context and the effects on the relevant market.

Consten and Grundig [12]

The approach adopted in technique in *Société Technique Minière* can be contrasted with the *Consten and Grundig* case which was decided at more or less the same time. In that case, Consten was appointed exclusive distributor in France of Grundig products and undertook not to deliver any Grundig products directly or indirectly outside France. Grundig agreed not to deliver its products directly or indirectly to anyone within France except Consten. Grundig assigned to Consten the relevant trademarks enabling it to sue any third party importing Grundig products into France. Grundig also imposed on all its other distributors in Europe obligations not to deliver products outside their respective territories. The object and effect of the Grundig system was therefore to protect its dealers (including Consten) from competition from imports of Grundig products (ie "parallel imports"). By imposing export bans in this way Grundig conferred "absolute territorial protection" on Consten so that consumers in France could not obtain Grundig products from anyone other than Consten. The Court established that agreements such as the one outlined above which prohibit exports within the EC by their nature restrict competition within the meaning of Article 81(1) irrespective of their actual effects.

The apparent inconsistency between the two cases can be explained by the fact

11 *Société Technique Minière v. Maschinenbau Ulm* Case 56/65 [1966] ECR 235

12 *Consten and Grundig v. Commission* Cases 56 & 58/64 [1966] ECR 299

that Consten and Grundig concerned "absolute territorial protection". Such total export bans were perceived by the Court as contrary to the fundamental objective of market integration under the Treaty and therefore "by their nature" prohibited by Article 81. In contrast in *Société la Technique Minière* the Court was considering an exclusive dealing agreement which did not grant absolute territorial protection. In other words, consumers in France could obtain the relevant machinery by placing orders with other distributors outside France for re-import into France. On these facts the Court was able to apply a rule of reason analysis to assess the effect of the exclusivity in the market context.

"Appreciable effect"

The effect of an agreement will only cause it to restrict competition within the meaning of Article 81 if that effect is deemed to be "appreciable". The question of what is appreciable is a question of fact and degree in each case. The requirement relates mainly to the size of the parties concerned, their market share and the structure of the market. Some guidance as to the meaning of "appreciable" can be taken from previous decisions. The Court in *Völk v. Vervaecke*[13] held that "an agreement falls outside the prohibition in Article [85] when it has only an insignificant effect on the market, taking into account the weak position which the persons concerned have on the market of the product in question." In that case the share of the supplier of the relevant products was less than 0.5% and in that case even a total export ban was, exceptionally, held to fall outside Article 85 (now Article 81). On the other hand, in *Miller v. Commission*[14] the principle was established that a company with 5% of the relevant market can be of sufficient importance for its behaviour to be caught by Article 81.

In the context of vertical agreements, the assessment of appreciable effect must also take into account the existence of networks of similar agreements in the relevant market. In *Stergios Delimitis v. Henninger Brau AG*,[15] the Court identified that the key question to ask is whether the existence of a network of agreements created barriers to entry or growth for participants in the market. If the market is found to be inaccessible as a result of such a network of agreements and all other relevant factors, it is then necessary to assess the extent to which the agreement in question contributes to that foreclosure. If the contribution of the particular supplier is

13 Case 5/69 [1969] ECR 295

14 Case 19/77 [1978] ECR 131

15 Case C-234/89 [1991] ECR 935

insignificant then the agreements in question will still fall outside Article 81(1).

The Commission Notice on Agreements of Minor Importance[16] (currently being revised – see below) provides guidance as to the approach the Commission takes to the issue of appreciability. In the Notice the Commission purports to establish quantitative criteria to enable undertakings to assess appreciability and so judge for themselves whether their agreements fall within Article 81(1) without the need for notification to the Commission.

In respect of agreements benefitting from the Notice, the Commission will not institute any proceedings either upon or on its own initiative (point 5). The Notice is without prejudice to the competence of national courts to apply Article 81 but it is a relevant factor for national courts to take into account (point 7).

The Notice states at point 9 that agreements between undertakings engaged in the production or distribution of goods or in the provision of services do not fall under the prohibition in Article 81 if the aggregate market share held by all of the participating undertakings does not exceed 10% on any of the relevant markets where the agreement is made between undertakings operating at different economic levels (in other words, a "vertical agreement"). However, point 11 of the Notice provides that with regard to vertical agreements which have as their object to fix resale prices or to confer territorial protection on the participating undertakings or third undertakings, the applicability of Article 81 cannot be ruled out even where the aggregate market share is less than 10%. The Commission considers, however, that it is in the first instance for national authorities to take action with respect to this category of agreement. It will only intervene in such cases where it considers that the interests of the Community so demands and in particular if the agreements impair the proper functioning of the internal market.

Point 19 of the Notice states that:

"Agreements between small and medium sized undertakings[17]*, as defined in the*

---

16 A copy of the Notice is at Appendix G

17 Small and medium sized enterprises (SMEs) are defined for these purposes as enterprises which:

- have fewer than 250 employees, and
- have either,

  an annual turnover not exceeding ECU 40 million, or

  an annual balance-sheet total not exceeding ECU 27 million,
- conform to the criterion of independence as defined in paragraph 3.

Where it is necessary to distinguish between small and medium-sized enterprises, the "small enterprise" is defined as an enterprise which:

Annex to Commission Recommendation 96/280/EC are rarely capable of significantly affecting trade between Member States and competition within the common market. Consequently as a general rule they are not caught by the prohibition in Article 81(1). In cases where such agreements exceptionally meet the conditions for the application of that provision they will not be of sufficient Community interest to justify any intervention. This is why the Commission will not institute any proceedings upon request or on its own initiative to apply the provisions of Article 81 (1) to such agreements even if the thresholds set out in points 9 and 10 above [ie 10% market share for vertical agreements] are exceeded."

At point 20 the Commission nevertheless reserves the right to intervene where the agreements in question impede competition in a substantial part of the relevant market or where competition is restricted by the cumulative effect of networks of similar agreements.

The Notice also needs to be read in conjunction with the Guidelines on Vertical Agreements. The Guidelines are expressed to be without prejudice to the Notice or its successors but they do elaborate on certain statements in the Notice. For example, in paragraph 11 of the Guidelines in relation to SMEs the Commission restates its

---

- has fewer than 50 employees and
- has either,

  an annual balance-sheet total not exceeding ECU 7 million, or

  an annual balance-sheet total not exceeding ECU 5 million,
- conforms to the criterion of independence as defined in paragraph 3.

Independent enterprises are those which are not owned as to 25% or more of the capital or the voting rights by one enterprise, or jointly by several enterprises, falling outside the definition of an SME or a small enterprise, whichever may apply. This threshold may be exceeded in the following two cases:

- if the enterprise is held by public investment corporations, venture capital companies or institutional investors, provided no control is exercised either individually or jointly,
- if the capital is spread in such a way that it is not possible to determine by whom it is held and if the enterprise declares that it can legitimately presume that it is not owned as to 25% or more by one enterprise, or jointly by several enterprises, falling outside the definitions of an SME or a small enterprise, whichever may apply.

(Commission recommendation 96/280/EC)

policy that agreements amongst SMEs generally fall outside Article 81. The Commission will normally refrain from opening proceedings for lack of sufficient continuing interest unless these undertakings collectively or individually hold a dominant position in a substantial part of the common market. This approach appears more relaxed than that set out in point 20 of the Notice.

The Notice is in practice of limited use because of the uncertainty of calculating market share and also because it is not clear on the face of the Notice what is meant by "territorial protection". A literal interpretation would mean any territorial protection including, for example, the grant of exclusive territory permitting passive sales by the dealer. It should not be assumed that the Commission intends only absolute territorial protection to be outside the scope of the Notice.

In the light of the revised thinking on vertical agreements, the Commission published for consultation a revised draft Notice in May 2001. A copy of the revised draft is included at Appendix G. Whilst the proposed draft Notice broadly follows the structure of the current Notice it differs in some important respects.

First, different market share thresholds are used. Where the agreement is made between undertakings which are not actual or potential competitors on any affected relevant markets (agreements between non-competitors) the market share threshold is 15%. This will be the case for the majority of vertical agreements. However, if the agreement is made between competitors, even if it is a vertical agreement, then the market share threshold will be 10%. Also, where in an affected relevant market competition is restricted by the cumulative effect of parallel networks of agreements which have similar effects on the market, the market share threshold is reduced to 5%. There is no guidance as to when cumulative effect will be present.

Second, the Notice includes the same list of hard core restrictions as appears in the Block Exemption Regulation in respect of all vertical agreements.

Third, agreements between small and medium sized undertakings are treated differently. The only reference to SMEs in the proposed draft Notice is to state that agreements between SMEs are rarely capable of affecting trade between Member States.

The proposed draft Notice is only a draft and further changes may be made following consultation with Member States and business. As it stands, the inclusion of the same blacklist in both Block Exemption Regulation and the proposed draft Notice would appear to send the signal that companies with market shares of up to 30% are likely to be subject to the same constraints on their business freedom. The only real difference for vertical agreements is that for businesses with a market share between 15% and 30% there is the additional constraint of the non-exempted restrictions in Article 5 of the Block Exemption Regulation.

as valid even though a number of other elements of the Agreement were arguably infringements of Article 85(1). The basis for the decision appears to be that valid consideration supported the relevant clause as the licensee had clearly received the know how in question. Each case will be considered on its facts to assess whether the deletion of the offending words or provision is possible whilst preserving a valid contract and not altering entirely the scope and intention of the agreement.

ARTICLE 81(3)

If an agreement falls within Article 81(1), the next question is whether the agreement benefits or could benefit from an exemption pursuant to Article 81 (3) since if it does the prohibition of Article 81(1) will be disapplied. Article 81(3) declares the prohibition of Article 81(1) inapplicable in the case of

> *"Any agreement or category of agreements between undertakings, any decision or category of decisions by associations of undertakings, any concerted practice or category of concerted practices which fulfils all the following four conditions:*
>
> *(a) contributes to improving the production or distribution of goods or to promoting technical or economic progress; and*
>
> *(b) allows consumers a fair share of a resulting benefits; and*
>
> *(c) imposes on the undertakings only restrictions which are indispensable to the attainment of those objectives; and*
>
> *(d) does not afford such undertaking the possibility of eliminating competition in respect of a substantial part of the product in question."*

Exemption under Article 81(3) may be granted either by a block exemption regulation – such as the Block Exemption Regulation – or by an individual decision addressed to the parties to the agreement. An agreement which benefits from an exemption is valid and enforceable under Article 81 and the parties to it cannot be subject to fines for the period of the exemption.

The policy of the Commission in granting individual block exemptions is explained in the Guidelines. In particular paragraphs 134-136 explain in general terms the Commission's interpretation of the four criteria for exemption of Article 81(3) in relation to agreements outside the Block Exemption Regulation. The last criterion – the elimination of competition – is related to dominance. In many ways it is the most important since if it is not satisfied exemption is not possible whatever benefits might be claimed for the agreement.

In claiming benefits to satisfy the first two criteria it is important that notifying parties substantiate any efficiencies and cost savings and demonstrate that the agreement will have a net positive effect (paragraph 136).

The application of Article 81(3) to particular types of agreements is discussed in Chapters 7, 8 and 9 in respect of agency, franchising and distribution respectively. The Guidelines in paragraphs 137-229 also explain enforcement in relation to different types of vertical restraints and are covered in the relevant chapters.

ARTICLE 82

Article 82 outlaws the abuse of monopoly power. Article 82 provides:

"Any abuse by one or more undertakings of a dominant position within the Common Market or in a substantial part of it shall be prohibited as incompatible with the Common Market in so far as it may affect trade between Member States.

Such abuse may, in particular, consist in:

a. directly or indirectly imposing unfair purchase or selling prices or other unfair trading conditions;

b. limiting production, markets or technical development to the prejudice of consumers;

c. applying dissimilar conditions to equivalent transactions with other trading parties, thereby placing them at a competitive disadvantage;

d. making the conclusion of contracts subject to acceptance by the other parties of supplementary obligations which, by their very nature, or according to commercial usage, have no connection with the subject of such contracts."

"Dominant position"

For Article 82 to apply there must be a dominant position enjoyed by one or more undertakings. For an undertaking to be dominant it must be capable of acting independently on the market without having seriously to take into account the actions of its competitors, purchasers or suppliers. The ECJ in *United Brands v. EC Commission* [20] defined dominance in the following terms:

---

20 Case 27/76 [1978] ECR 207

"Abuse"

For Article 82 to be infringed, there must be an abuse of a dominant position. The mere existence of a dominant position is not unlawful. The dominant player must take advantage of that dominant position in a way that causes injury to third parties or undermines the competitive structure of the market.

In the context of vertical agreements, examples of conduct which could constitute an abuse include:

- refusal to supply dealers without an objective reason. An objective reason might be poor creditworthiness or a genuine capacity shortage. An unacceptable reason might be to enforce minimum resale maintenance or to impose absolute territorial protection;
- imposition of an exclusive purchase obligation. For example *in Hoffman La Roche v. Commission*[23] the Court held that exclusive purchase obligations can be designed to deprive the purchaser or restrict his possible choices of sources of supply and to deny other producers access to the market;
- application of excessive prices;
- application of predatory prices;
- application of discriminatory prices. Price discrimination involves charging one customer more than another for equivalent transactions (or customers in a different position the same prices) without objective justification. *In United Brands*[24] the Court held that the pricing structure of United Brands constituted an abuse since the price at the point of dispatch differed according to the country of destination without objective justification;
- discount policies which are not objectively justifiable. Discounts based on cost savings for the supplier in supplying a particular customer will not be an abuse. For example, early settlement discounts will generally be permissible where the discount reflects the cost of not having to extend credit to the dealer. However, where the discount is not justified by savings made in supplying that customer, then there may well be an abuse. For example, discounts granted only when the dealer buys all or a specified (and significant) percentage of its requirements from a dominant supplier are likely to be an

23 Case 85/76 [1979] ECR 461

24 OJ [1076] L95/1

abuse. Similarly, the Court in *Michelin v. Commission*[26] condemned a "target" discount arrangement under which Michelin, which was in a dominant position, granted discounts in respect of all sales above a specific sales target assigned to its dealer. Other sorts of discounts which may well give rise to issues include rebates for not purchasing competing products and rebates based on the dealer buying other products from a supplier;

- tying or bundling. It will be an abuse if a dominant company is prepared to supply a product in respect of which he has a dominant position only if the customer agrees to buy another product.

"Effect on trade between Member States"

The same tests apply as for Article 81. (See above).

25 Case 322/81 [1983] ECR 3461

CHAPTER 3

HISTORY AND REFORM

INTRODUCTION

This chapter describes the circumstances and policies which led the Commission to adopt the BER and the related reforms. The drivers for reform were identified in a Green Paper published in early 1997 which was followed by over two years of consultation and drafting. The chapter also puts the new policy on vertical restraints in the context of the more wide ranging modernisation of EC competition law enforcement instigated by the Commission and set out in a white paper published in Spring 1999 and a proposal for a Council Regulation published in September 2000. If implemented this Council Regulation will transform the practice of EC Competition law.

THE GREEN PAPER

The Commission published the Green Paper on Vertical Restraints in EC Competition Policy in January 1997[1]. The Paper runs to over eighty pages divided into eight chapters covering:

- Chapter 1: Structure of Distribution;
- Chapter 2: Economic Analysis of Vertical Restraints on the Internal Market;
- Chapter 3: Current Procedures and Institutional Framework;
- Chapter 4: Current Rules for Vertical Restraints;
- Chapter 5: Advantages of the Present System;
- Chapter 6: Comparison of Community Law with Member State and Third Country Laws applicable to Vertical Restraints;

1 The full text of the Paper is available on the Commission web site at www.europa.eu.int/comm/competition/antitrust/96721en_en.pdf

- Chapter 7: Results of Fact Finding;
- Chapter 8: Options.

The Green Paper set out four basic options for reform on which it sought the comments of business, its advisers and the Member States.

REASONS FOR REFORM

In the Green Paper the Commission identified three key reasons why a review of its policy on vertical restraints was necessary:

- the single market legislation for the free movement of products is now largely in place;
- the existing block exemption regulations governing vertical restraints were due to expire[2];
- the major changes in methods of distribution in Europe over the last thirty years.

Whilst the Commission asserts in the Paper that the way in which it has applied the competition rules to vertical agreements has been successful, it also notes a number of criticisms made by third parties and these no doubt also contributed to the pressure for a fundamental review. Criticisms include:

- the current block exemptions lacked flexibility, having a "straitjacket" effect and being over regulatory.
- block exemptions should be less dirigiste. For example, one non-exemptable clause should not necessarily cause the nullity of the whole exemption;
- too much emphasis is put on an analysis of clauses and not enough on the economic impact of agreements;
- the coverage of the block exemptions was patchy with no economic or legally rational explanation for what is covered and what is not;
- the comfort letter system was unsatisfactory in failing to deliver the legal certainty which companies require;

---

2 Regulations 1983/83 (exclusive distribution), Regulation 1984/83 (exclusive purchasing) and Regulation 4087/88 (franchising) all expired at the end of 2000 (with Regulations 1983/83 and 1984/83 having already been renewed once).

- competition policies should not discriminate between different forms of distribution and should promote plurality of distribution techniques.

The Green Paper notes that the distribution sector has grown hugely in recent years and encompasses a very wide range on distribution techniques which may vary considerably from sector to sector. Considerable differences also exist in market structures between Member States even in the same sector. One of the drivers for change is the evolution of the distribution techniques, notably just-in-time and related refinements which have generated significant efficiency savings.

Unfortunately the Green Paper does not really anticipate the impact which e-commerce has had in distribution systems in Europe. One of the greatest challenges facing the Commission's new policy on vertical restraints is how it deals with internet sales. The Block Exemption Regulation itself is silent on internet sales. The Guidelines, however, set out the Commission's policy approach. This is described in Chapter 5 and also specifically in relation to franchising (Chapter 7) and selective distribution (Chapter 8) and is sure to be refined as the Commission gains greater experience of e-commerce.

Economic Analysis of Vertical Restraints and the Single Market

One of the most important aspects of the reforms is the Commission's analysis will in future be based on an economic assessment of the effect of vertical restraints in the relevant market. The Green Paper recognises that the fiercer the interbrand competition the more likely the pro-competitive and efficiency effects are to outweigh any anti-competitive effects of vertical restraints. Anti-competitive effects are only likely where interbrand competition is weak and barriers to entry exist.

The Commission draws the following specific conclusions:

- individual clauses in an agreement or different types of vertical restraints cannot be considered per se as having a negative or positive effect on competition or integration.
- the combination of several vertical restraints does not necessarily increase the probability of any anti-competitive outcome but in some circumstances may make the outcome more favourable;
- analysis should concentrate on the impact on the market rather than the form of the agreement. For example, whether entry is foreclosed by a network of agreements or whether the vertical agreement coupled with market power

permits producers or distributors to practice price discrimination between Member States;

- given the risk associated with either entry into new markets or significant market expansion, consideration should be given to a more favourable treatment of vertical restraints where this is accompanied by significant investment.

These observations are welcome but should be considered in the light of the terms of the BER finally adopted. For example, early drafts of the BER, and to a limited extent the final draft, can still be criticised for being too formalistic and for including an over-long technical list of per se prohibited restrictions in Article 4 (hard-core restrictions).

PROCEDURE AND INSTITUTIONAL FRAMEWORK

The Green Paper notes that Commission policy has been to apply Article 81(1) relatively expansively to vertical restraints. The introduction of Regulation 17/62 setting out the system of individual notification resulted in over 30,000 notifications in the early 1960s the majority of which concerned vertical agreements. Even though the numbers have reduced considerably since then, individual notifications to the Commission were still running at approximately 200 per annum in the 1990s. As explained in Chapter 2, Regulation 17/62 provides for a lengthy and cumbersome procedure for adopting individual decisions with the result that the Commission simply did not have the resources to deal with this level of notifications. Only about 20 formal decisions are adopted each year and only about 150 or so cases are closed by informal comfort letters. In the light of this, block exemptions certainly have a role to play.

Not surprisingly, the Commission states that "its competition policy towards vertical restraints has been largely successful. Its advantages can be characterised both in terms of substance and procedure." Substantive advantages, according to the Commission, include:

- The analysis of vertical restraints being primarily focused on exemptions under Article 81(3) allow the full economic assessment of an agreement, the impact on the structure of competition and consumer welfare.

- A response to this would be that much of this analysis is unnecessary as the Commission has interpreted Article 81(1) much too widely in catching far too many agreements which do not restrict competition significantly. For these agreements a benefits analysis under Article 81(3) is misplaced and a waste of resources.

- Market integration has been promoted by the current policy which prohibits absolute territorial protection. Thus, even though the pro-competitive gains from granting territorial exclusivity are permitted, vertical agreements must still leave the possibility of alternative sources of supply.

- The policy allows freedom to establish new and innovative forms of distribution since agreements not already covered by block exemptions can be notified individually. This is, in the authors' opinion, a disingenuous assertion. One of the most common criticisms of the existing system is that historically the block exemptions tended to reduce innovation since companies tend to take the easy option of drafting within the "straitjacket" because the alternative of falling outside those regulations exposed companies to the uncertainty of whether or not their restrictions would be unenforceable. The individual notification system does not remove this uncertainty.

The Commission identifies some procedural advantages:

- The notification system has been successful in providing the Commission with information about the many types of vertical agreements and the businesses and markets in which these agreements operate. This is certainly true although, whether it is the only or the most efficient way of obtaining this information is open to debate.

- The block exemptions provide basic legal certainty for the vast bulk of vertical agreements in the EU. Again this is disingenuous. If Article 81(1) were not interpreted so widely, these uncertainties would not exist in the first place. Also, legal certainty is only afforded to those agreements which are drafted within the often formalistic terms of the block exemption regulations when it may be more efficient to operate on different terms. Finally, the range of the block exemption regulations has rightly been criticised as being patchy. For example, intermediate goods and services were not covered by the block exemptions. There was no block exemption for selective distribution or for agreements involving more than two parties.

- Comfort letters have successfully dealt with any "mass problem" for cases not already covered by block exemptions. Time and again, industry has stated that it does not regard the comfort letter system as being adequate in providing legal certainty.

- The role of national courts and authorities improves the efficiency and speed of enforcement in this area. This assertion is again open to challenge since the involvement of national authorities varies greatly between Member States. However, it is in line with the theme of the white paper on modernisation which aims to delegate routine enforcement responsibility on to national authorities.

  The Green Paper sought comments on four options:

  - option 1 – maintain current system;
  - option 2 – wider block exemptions: this option would consist of maintaining the current approach with a number of block exemptions covering different types of agreement. A block exemption for selective distribution would also be considered. The block exemptions would be made more flexible, would cover more situations and be made less regulatory in response to criticisms made of them;
  - option 3 – more focused block exemptions: option 3 would propose a market share limit of 40% for each of the current block exemptions. Below this level option 2 would apply;
  - option 4 – reduce scope of Article 81(1): option 4 would reduce the number of agreements caught by Article 81(1) by introducing a rebuttable presumption that agreements between parties with a market share of less than 20% would be compatible with Article 81(1) (the negative clearance presumption). Above the 20% threshold there would be the option of two variants. Variant 1 would be the wider block exemption as described in option 2. Variant 2 would follow option 3.

The 4 options were stated to be non-exhaustive and indeed further consultation resulted in 3 further options being added to the list:

Option 5 – an umbrella block exemption : a single wide block exemption based on a blacklist approach and without market shares.

Option 6 – guidelines: no block exemption only guidelines indicating how the Commission would apply Article 81 in individual cases.

Option 7 – a control of abuse system: all vertical restraints would be presumed lawful with the Commission having the power to suspend a positive presumption only with prospective effects.

FOLLOW-UP TO THE GREEN PAPER ON VERTICAL RESTRAINTS

The Commission published a communication of the application of EC competition rules to vertical restraints in 1998[3].

The communication summarised the comments received on the Green Paper; provided further economic assessment of vertical restraints and their effects; discussed issues of market share thresholds and legal security; set out a proposed new policy; and described the procedural steps which would be followed to adopt the new policy.

The Commission received over 200 written submissions, a statistical breakdown of support for various options is set out below:

Options	*In favour*	*Not in favour*	*No comment*
1. Option I (maintain current system):	16.6%	51.6%	31.8%
2. Option II (wider block exemptions without a market share cap):	46.2%	23.3%	30.5%
3. Option III (more focused block exemptions with a market share cap of [40%]:	6.7%	59.6%	33.7%
4. Option IV-I (negative clearance presumption up to [20%] and above wider block exemptions without a market share cap):	20.2%	59.5%	20.3%
5. Option IV-II (negative clearance presumption up to [20%] and above wider block exemptions with market share cap of [40%]:	8.1%	82.4%	9.5%
6. Umbrella Block Exemption without market shares	17%	4.9%	78.1%
7. Guidelines only	1.8%	10.8%	87.4%
8. Control of Abuse system	10.8%	6.3%	82.9%

3 This Paper is also known as the follow-up to the Green Paper on vertical restraints and is available on the web site at www.europa.eu.int/comm/competition/antitrust/com1998544_en.pdf

The Commission also held public hearings in October 1997 and consulted the Community institutions and the Member States.

It is ironic that the consultation exercise revealed the greatest support (nearly 50%) in favour of option 2 (wider block exemptions but without a market share cap). The solution adopted by the Commission is a single umbrella block exemption with a market share cap – an option which elicited no support in the consultation process.

Option 1 of the Green Paper was rejected as having 3 major shortcomings: form based straightjacket regulation, neglect of market power and block exemptions which are too narrow. Options 2 and 4 (variant 1) reduced straightjacket effect but were rejected because they did not pay any attention to market power. Similarly the idea of an umbrella block exemption without market shares was rejected because it ignores market power. Option 3 and option 4 (variant 2) were found to take account of market power but to be too narrow so as to maintain a straightjacket effect. The option of moving to a control of abuse system which presumed that vertical agreements are not anti-competitive within the meaning of Article 81(1) was rejected because it was supported neither by economic thinking nor enforcement experience and would result in increased legal uncertainty for industry.

The eventual Commission proposal was therefore a single umbrella block exemption regulation covering all vertical restraints based mainly on a blacklist approach (now called hard-core) and using market share caps. Although the Commission's initial preference was for two market share caps, it did note that the majority of Member States preferred the simplicity of a single market share cap.

The safe harbour of the block exemption regulation would be complemented by additional "flanking" measures, being: the extension of Article 4(2) of Regulation 17 to all vertical agreements (ie creating the possibility of retrospective exemption by the Commission and removing the need for pre-emptive and protective notification): greater de-centralisation with national courts and national competition authorities being able to apply the block exemption and to apply Article 81(1) outside the block exemption: guidelines detailing the policy above the threshold and possible withdrawal of the block exemption.

LEGISLATIVE CHANGES

In order to implement the new policy, two Council regulations were made. Council Regulation 1215/99/EC of 10 June 1999[4] extended the Commission's powers under

---

4 The full text of the Regulation is available at www.europa.eu.int/eur-lex/en/lif/dat/1999/en_399R1215.html

Regulation 19/65 by broadening the scope of the Commission's powers to adopt new block exemption regulations to all the vertical restraints rather than specific categories of agreements[5].

Council Regulation 1216/99/EC of 10 June 1999[6] was introduced to amend Article 4(2) of Council Regulation 17/62 to enable the Commission to grant retrospective exemption to vertical agreements.[7]

The Block Exemption Regulation itself was finally adopted as Commission Regulation (EC) 2790/1999 on 22nd December 1999.

The Commission's Guidelines were somewhat delayed and were adopted in May 2000 published in the Official Journal on 13 October 2000.

ONGOING MODERNISATION – THE COMMISSION WHITE PAPER

On 28th April 1999 the Commission adopted a White Paper on modernisation of the rules implementing Articles 81 and 82 of the EC Treaty[8]. In many ways the reforms in relation to vertical agreements represent the first moves in a much wider revolution of competition law enforcement in the Community.

That White Paper proposed a root and branch reform of the way in which EC competition law is enforced. The Paper was a response not only to the way in which the competition rules have been enforced as discussed in relation to the Green Paper above but also to the more general challenges which will face the Commission in the future including:

- completion of economic and monetary union and continuing globalisation of the European economy;
- enlargement of the EU. Following the agreement on Agenda 2000, the first wave of accessions of countries from Central and Eastern Europe have come closer and a Union of 20-25 Member States is a realistic prospect.

The conclusion reached in the White Paper is that Regulation 17 and the notification system which it introduced is no longer suited to business nor to an enlarged Community in which many markets are extensively integrated. The radical solution

5 The amended text of Regulation 19/65 is attached as Appendix E.

6 The Regulation is available at www.europa.eu.int/eur-lex/en/lif/dat/1999/en_399R1216.html

7 The amended text of Regulation 17/62 is attached at Appendix D.

8 Commission programme No 99/027

proposed by the White Paper is to abandon a centralised authorisation system. The proposed new system would have three elements:

- a "directly applicable exception" system would replace centralised authorisation (notification)
- development of decentralised application of the competition rules; and
- intensified "export" control

By "directly applicable exception" system, the Commission is referring to a system whereby the Commission and national competition authorities and courts would apply Article 81(3) in all proceedings in which they are called upon to apply the prohibition rule to Article 81(1) which is already directly applicable. In other words the Commission would abandon its monopoly of Article 81(3).

The White Paper attracted support from both Community institutions and business for its more efficient and less bureaucratic approach. Many observers, however, raised grave concerns about the need to ensure reform does not lead to inconsistent application and "renationalisation" of Community competition law.

In September 2000, the Commission published a Proposal for a Council Regulation on the implementation of the EC Competition Rules.[9]

There is no fixed timetable for the implementation of this proposed Regulation. If it is adopted, it will have far reaching consequences for the application of competition law to vertical agreements. The key elements of the proposed Regulation include:

- direct applicability of Article 81(3). Agreements falling within Article 81(1) but outside Article 81(3) will be void ab initio; agreements falling within Article 81(1) and within Article 81(3) will be valid ab initio without the need for any prior administrative decision. National authorities and courts will have the power to take decisions under Article 81(3).
- disapplication of national competition rules to agreements which are capable of affecting trade between Member States. In other words, national competition authorities and courts will have to apply Articles 81 and 82 to all cases affecting trade between Member States. This is undoubtedly a bold

9 Proposal for a Council Regulation on the implementation of the rules on competition laid down in Articles 81 and 82 of the Treaty and amending Regulations (EEC) No 1017/68, (EEC) No 2988/74, (EEC) No 4056/86 and (EEC) No 3975/87 (COM (2000) 582 final of 27.9.2000) available at www.europa.eu.int/eur-lex/en/com/dat/2000/en_500PCO582.html)

step which will attract considerable debate. The obvious concern is that the "effect on trade between Member States" is not a "bright line text" for determining jurisdiction between national and EC competition rules.

- national competition authorities will gain the power to withdraw EC block exceptions in their Member States in certain circumstances.
- extensive co-operation between the Commission and the competition authorities of the Member States. The system will be based on the "decentralised but consistent" application of the EC competition rules. To promote this the aim is to achieve a network between all competition authorities comprising information and consultation mechanisms. Other measures will also be put in place to promote consistent decision taking by national authorities. Clearly the need for uniform application of the competition rules is paramount and whatever system is implemented must be able to secure this goal which is after all embodied in the EC Treaty.

CHAPTER 4

UMBRELLA BLOCK EXEMPTION

INTRODUCTION

In any consideration of the Regulation it is useful to consider what went before. In exclusive distribution and exclusive purchasing there have been block exemption regulations since 1967 as well as a number of European Court of Justice (ECJ) and Commission decisions. In the case of selective distribution there has not been any regulation but there have been decisions by the Commission and the ECJ. In franchising there has only been one ECJ decision[1], five Commission decisions and a block exemption regulation which came into force on 1st February 1989.

THE PREAMBLE TO THE REGULATION

The Regulation follows the usual pattern which the Commission has established with a preamble which seeks to justify and explain what the regulation contains.

The preamble is in some respects unhelpful.

Paragraph (2) relies on "experience acquired to date (which) makes it possible to define a category of vertical agreements which can be regarded as normally satisfying the conditions laid down in Article 81(3)". While undoubtedly the Commission has considerable experience of distribution and selective distribution techniques as Commission officials admitted to the authors in a meeting it has not had any experience of franchising since the 1988 block exemption regulation had been adopted. Where it obtained the experience to reach the conclusion expressed in this preamble is a matter of speculation so far as franchising is concerned. The outcome has led to a substantial change in the rules applicable to franchising for which no justification is given except that the Commission wanted to treat all agreements containing vertical restraints in the same way regardless of the market differences between the distribution systems affected by the regulation and the

---

1 *Pronuptia de Paris GmbH v. Pronuptia de Paris Irmgard Schillgalis* (Case 161/84) 1986 CMLR 414 (hereinafter "the Pronuptia Case").

European Court's judgment which contrasted franchising with other distribution systems, particularly selective distribution.[2]

In paragraph (8) there is reference to certain agreements "which do not contain certain types of severely anti-competitive restraints" as generally leading to an improvement in production or distribution and allowing consumers a fair share of the resulting benefits"[3] presumably a reference to the restraints mentioned in paragraph (10). Since, for example, the new regulation bans restraints which were formerly permitted in franchise agreements and the Commission admit that they have had no experience of franchising, or indeed so it is understood, any complaints about franchising since the 1988 regulation came into force, one is inclined to wonder what is the justification for this assertion so far as concerns franchising.

Paragraph (10) is the key to the provision in Article 4 identifying as unacceptable for exemption vertical agreements containing restrictions which are not indispensible to the attainment of the "positive effects mentioned above", presumably a reference to paragraph (8).

Paragraph (11) seeks to justify the restrictions on product ties, post termination restraints and a ban on provisions which prohibit sales by the members of a selective distribution system of named competing brands by asserting that this is necessary in order to ensure access to or to prevent collusion on the relevant market. Given the Commission's blanket approach to distribution it is perhaps understandable that in order to be consistent it has taken this stance. However, in many respects the first two of these restrictions are fundamental and inherent in many franchise systems which serves to underline the dangers which are inevitable in the blanket treatment of different distribution systems which the Commission has chosen to adopt.

THE REGULATION

The Regulation comprises 13 Articles:

Article 1: contains definitions

Article 2: contains the exemption

Article 3: sets a cap on the market share to which the exemption will apply

Article 4: contains a list of hardcore restrictions. If one of these restrictions is found in a vertical agreement it will not benefit from the exemption

---

2 *Ibid.* paragraph 15

3 See more on this aspect in Chapter 7 (Franchising)

at premises X would be considered interchangeable with or substitutable for the very same goods obtained from the same supplier sold by Buyer B at premises Y as well as those goods sold by competing suppliers and their competing buyers.

It is necessary to decide what are the contract goods or services. Invariably the contract will be between the supplier and the buyer and, in the case of distribution arrangements other than franchising the contract goods will be the goods or services purchased by the buyer from the supplier. The approach in relation to franchising is more complex and the issues are discussed in Chapter 7. The treatment of services in this definition serves to emphasis the problems created by the Commission by regarding services as analagous to goods. Clearly goods can pass down the production to consumer chain without much, if any, change being made to their constitution. However, where services are provided there will invariably be a different service provided at each level calculated to assist or prepare each lower level to provide a different service culminating in the finally delivered service to the end user. A simple two level example would be where service provider at level one teaches service provider at level two how to deliver a service to its customers.

> *"(b) 'non-compete obligation' means any direct or indirect obligation causing the buyer not to manufacture, purchase, sell or resell goods or services which compete with the contract goods or services, or any direct or indirect obligation on the buyer to purchase from the supplier or from another undertaking designated by the supplier more than 80% of the buyer's total purchases of the contract goods or services and their substitutes on the relevant market, calculated on the basis of the value of its purchases in the preceding calendar year;"*

This definition deals with two issues. The first deals with what most would normally regard as a non-compete obligation concentrating as it does on a prohibition against making, purchasing, selling or reselling goods or services which compete with the contract goods or services. The second is really directed at product ties. Anything which requires the buyer to purchase from the supplier or a nominated supplier more than 80% of the buyer's total purchases the contract goods or services is also a non-compete obligation.

> *"(c) 'exclusive supply obligation' means any direct or indirect obligation causing the supplier to sell the goods or services specified in the agreement only to one buyer inside the Community for the purposes of a specific use or for resale;"*

This is a very limited definition relating to an obligation to supply one buyer inside the Community on an exclusive basis. It clearly refers to an arrangement where the buyer is granted the exclusive rights for the whole European Union. It is to be noted that there is a reference to the "goods or services specified in the agreement" and not to the "contract goods or services". The expression used in this definition could well have resolved the issue relating to services discussed above. As it stands the use of this expression in this definition is just one example of how the Commission's approach to drafting can cause confusion.

> *"(d) 'Selective distribution system' means a distribution system where the supplier undertakes to sell the contract goods or services, either directly or indirectly, only to distributors selected on the basis of specified criteria and where these distributors undertake not to sell such goods or services to unauthorised distributors;"*

In order for there to a selective distribution system, there must be two questions to be answered positively. First – Does the supplier undertake to sell the contract goods and services directly or indirectly only to those distributors who have been selected on the basis of specified criteria? Assuming that that element is satisfied the second question has to be considered – Do those distributors undertake not to sell such goods or services to unauthorised distributors? If the answer to both questions is "yes" there is a selective distribution system. If the answer to either question is "no" there is not a selective distribution system. The reference to "distributor" rather than "buyer" indicates that the two expressions are interchangeable. (see Article 4).

> *"(e) 'intellectual property rights' includes industrial property rights, copyright and neighbouring rights."*

The use of the word "includes" shows the intention that the list should not be regarded as exhaustive. The expression "neighbouring rights" relates to a form of copyright. It is somewhat surprising that specific reference has not been made to trade marks given their importance although most would consider them to be industrial property rights.

> *"(f) 'know-how' means a package of non-patented practical information, resulting from experience and testing by the supplier, which is secret, substantial and identified: in this context "secret" means that the know-how as a body or in the precise configuration and assembly of its components*

> *is not generally known or easily accessible; "substantial" means that the know-how includes information which is indispensible to the buyer for the use, sale or re-sale of the contract goods or services; "identified" means that the know-how must be described in a sufficiently comprehensive manner so as to make it possible to verify that it fulfils the criteria of secrecy and substantiality".*

This definition follows the pattern of the definitions of know-how in Regulation 4087/88 (franchising) and Regulation 240/96 (technology transfer) with subtle differences. The most significant difference is found in the description of the meaning of "substantial" which could amount to very little or with imaginative interpretation almost whatever one would like it to mean. Given the meaning of interchangeability or substitutability of goods and services (see definition of "competing undertakings" above) the logical meaning should be that there must be some know-how without which the contract goods and services could not be sold at all although resaleability of contract services remains an issue. This test of the substantiality of the know-how would be so difficult to satisfy that very few would be able to benefit from establishing that it applied to their goods and services. There must be very few instances of goods where the supplier had a magic formula without which the goods could not be sold. Unfortunately, neither the preamble or the guidelines provide any clues about the Commission's views on this issue. The broadest possible interpretation could be that the know-how has to be indispensable for the buyer to sell the contract goods or services in the manner specified by the supplier but such an interpretation would be a quantum leap although it could clearly be argued that if it does not mean that it means nothing at all. The Courts and the Commission are to be expected to try to give meaning rather than accept provisions are meaningless. While they may be able to cross that hurdle in relation to goods it is difficult to see how they can do so in relation to services for reasons already given.

> *"(g) 'buyer' means an undertaking which, under an agreement falling within Article 81(1) of the Treaty, sells goods or services on behalf of another undertaking."*

This definition clearly covers agency arrangements. However in the guidelines the Commission has made it plain that they do not intend to bring within this definition a genuine agency where the agent is merely the alter ego of the principal with power to contract in his name and on his behalf. Such agency arrangements are not regarded as falling within Article 81(1) (see Chapter 6). This definition could well lude commercial agency arrangements which are themselves the subject of the nmercial agents directive which has been brought into effect in the laws of all mber states.

Article 2 – The Exemption

"1. Pursuant to Article 81(3) of the Treaty and subject to the provisions of this Regulation, it is hereby declared that Article 81(1) shall not apply to agreements or concerted practices entered into between two or more undertakings each of which operates, for the purposes of the agreement, at a different level of the production or distribution chain, and relating to the conditions under which the parties may purchase, sell or resell certain goods or services ('vertical agreements').

The exemption shall apply to the extent that such agreements contain restrictions of competition falling within the scope of Article 81(1) ('vertical restraints')."

: the exemption to apply there must be a number of elements present:

1. There must be an agreement or concerted practice;
2. to which there must be two or more undertakings – that excludes contracts between an undertaking and a consumer although there could be an agreement between two undertakings and a consumer which could qualify for exemption. In Paragraph 24 of the Guidelines the Commission suggests that vertical agreements with final consumers not operating as a business are not covered as they would not be undertakings.
3. Each of the undertakings which are parties to the agreement or concerted practice must (subject to 4) operate at a different level in the production or distribution chain.
4. In considering whether the parties operate at such different levels regard is had only to the purposes of the agreement. If therefore there is an agreement between a distributor who operates at wholesale and retail levels and a retailer, one should disregard the distributors' own retail operations unless they are relevant to the purposes of the agreement.
5. The agreements or concerted practices must relate to the conditions under which the parties may purchase, sell or re-sell certain goods or services. This means that if the parties operate at different levels there does not need

to be a seller/buyer relationship between them; if there is to be a vertical agreement; there need only be conditions in the agreement relating to the purchase, sale or resale or goods or services. It is not clear why the word "certain" appears.[4]

6. The agreements must contain restrictions of competition falling within the scope of Article 81(1). There is no explanation of why a reference to concerted practices is omitted from the second paragraph of Article 2(1).

There is one other point to consider. The exemption refers to "two or more undertakings each of which operates at a different level of the production or distribution chain". If there are three undertakings to the parties to the agreement, one can see that each may operate at a different level, that is manufacturing, wholesaling, retailing. If there are four undertakings which are parties to the agreement, it is difficult to see how each of them could operate at a different level.

"2. *The exemption provided for in paragraph 1 shall apply to vertical agreements entered into between an association of undertakings and its members, or between such an association and its suppliers, only if all its members are retailers of goods and if no individual member of the association, together with its connected undertakings, has a total annual turnover exceeding EUR 50 million; vertical agreements entered into by such associations shall be covered by this Regulation without prejudice to the application of Article 81 to horizontal agreements concluded between the members of the association or decisions adopted by the association.*"

This applies the exemption also to vertical agreements between associations of undertakings and its members or suppliers but there are two conditions to be satisfied:

1. All members must be retailers of goods;
2. No member of the association together with its connected undertakings can have a total annual turnover exceeding EUR.50m. (See below under Article 11 for definition of connected undertakings.)

---

4 One explanation may be that the automobile sector is excluded from the ambit of the Regulation as that sector remains subject to Regulation 1475/95. (See "Motor Vehicles" in Chapter 8.)

Any horizontal agreements between members of the association and the decisions adopted by the association will not be exempted by the Regulation if they infringe Article (81)(1). (See paragraph 29 of the Guidelines.)

It appears that an association whose members are providers of services will not benefit from this provision.

> *"3. The exemption provided for in paragraph 1 shall apply to vertical agreements containing provisions which relate to the assignment to the buyer or use by the buyer of intellectual property rights, provided that those provisions do not constitute the primary object of such agreements and are directly related to the use, sale or resale of goods or services by the buyer or its customers. The exemption applies on condition that, in relation to the contract goods or services, those provisions do not contain restrictions of competition having the same object or effect as vertical restraints which are not exempted under this Regulation."*

This confirms that agreements which relate to the use by the buyer of intellectual property rights which are ancillary, to the use, sale or resale of goods or services are permitted. Paragraphs 30-44 of the Guidelines identify the five conditions which must be satisfied for a vertical agreement containing intellectual property right provisions to qualify for exemption under the Regulation. In summary these are:

The IPR provisions

- must be part of a vertical agreement
- must be assigned to or for the use of the buyer
- must not constitute the primary object of the agreement
- must be directly related to the use, sale or resale of the goods or services by the buyer to his customers
- must not contain restrictions of competition, which would have the same object or effect as vertical constraints not exempted under the Regulation.

> *"4. The exemption provided for in paragraph 1 shall not apply to vertical agreements entered into between competing undertakings; however, it shall apply where competing undertakings enter into a non-reciprocal vertical agreement and:*
>
> *(a) the buyer has a total annual turnover not exceeding EUR 100 million, or*
>
> *(b) the supplier is a manufacturer and a distributor or goods, while the buyer is a distributor not manufacturing goods competing with the contract goods, or*

the sales by distributors or franchisees". Before considering this issue it is useful to refer to Article 9 of the Regulation.

> "9. *The market share of 30% provided for in Article 3(1) shall be calculated on the basis of the market sales value of the contract goods or services and other goods or services sold by the supplier, which are regarded as interchangeable or substitutable by the buyer, by reason of the products' characteristics, their prices and their intended use;"*

In paragraph 91 of the Guidelines the Commission state:

> "91. *For the application of the Block Exemption Regulation, the market share of the supplier is its share on the relevant product and geographic market on which it sells to its buyers. In the example below, this is market A. The product market depends in the first place on substitutability from the buyers' perspective. When the supplied product is used as an input to produce other products and is generally not recognisable in the final product, the product market is normally defined by the direct buyers' preferences. The customers of the buyers will normally not have a strong preference concerning the inputs used by the buyers. Usually the vertical restraints agreed between the supplier and buyer of the input only relate to the sale and purchase of the intermediate product and not to the sale of the resulting product. In the case of distribution of final goods, what are substitutes for the direct buyers will normally be influenced or determined by the preferences of the final consumers. A distributor, as reseller, cannot ignore the preferences of final consumers when it purchases final goods. In addition, at the distribution level the vertical restraints more often do not only concern the sale of products between supplier and buyer, but also their resale. As different distribution formats usually compete, markets are in general not defined by the form of distribution that is applied. Where suppliers generally sell a portfolio of products, the entire portfolio may determine the produce market when the portfolios and not the individual products are regarded as substitutes by the buyers. As the buyers on market A are professional buyers, the geographic market is usually wider than the market where the product is resold to final consumers. Often, this will lead to the definition of national markets or wider geographic markets."*

This appears to support the literal meaning of the Article.

Paragraph 93 however, suggests that the market share of a manufacturer and wholesaler should both be below the 30% market share.

> *"93. Where a vertical agreement involves three parties, each operating at a different level of trade, their market shares will have to be below the market share threshold of 30% at both levels in order to benefit from the Block Exemption Regulation. If for instance, in an agreement between a manufacturer, a wholesaler (or association of retailers) and a retailer, a non-compete obligation is agreed, then the market share of both the manufacturer and the wholesaler (or association of retailers) must not exceed 30% in order to benefit from the Block Exemption Regulation."*

Paragraph 95 of the Guidelines potentially adds confusion in the case of franchising and this is discussed in more detail in Chapter 7.

> "2. *In the case of vertical agreements containing exclusive supply obligations, the exemption provided for in Article 2 shall apply on condition that the market share held by the buyer does not exceed 30% of the relevant market on which it purchases the contract goods or services."*

This sets a cap of a 30% share of the relevant market held by the buyer where there is an exclusive supply obligation.

Article 4

> *"The exemption provided for in Article 2 shall not apply to vertical agreements which, directly or indirectly, in isolation or in combination with other factors under the control of the parties, have as their object:"*

Article 4 contains the list of so-called hardcore restrictions which lead to the exclusion of the whole agreement from the scope of the Regulation. This wording is somewhat puzzling. It seems clear that the words "containing vertical restraints" should have been inserted after the words "vertical agreements". It is also surprising that the words "or effect" are not added to the end of this clause. On the face of the wording the omission of the words "containing vertical restraints" and the expression "have as their object" raises an interesting issue.

There must surely be a difference between the object of a vertical agreement and, any of the restrictions which are referred to in this list of hardcore restrictions. The objects of the agreements normally would be to set up an exclusive distribution system, an exclusive purchasing arrangement or franchise arrangement. None of those agreements would have these hardcore restrictions as their object because the restrictions deal with some mechanisms which may or may not be introduced by the parties in order to give efficacy and strength to the network of arrangements which they are establishing. Presumably reliance must be placed on paragraph (10) in the preamble to the Regulation which in justifying Article 4 states *"This Regulation should not exempt vertical agreements containing restrictions which are not indispensible to the attainment of the positive effects mentioned above ..."*.

> *"(a) the restriction of the buyer's ability to determine its sale price, without prejudice to the possibility of the supplier's imposing a maximum sale price or recommending a sale price, provided that they do not amount to a fixed or minimum sale price as a result of pressure from, or incentives offered by, any of the parties;"*

The supplier cannot restrict the buyer from fixing its own prices, however, the supplier can impose a maximum sale price or recommend a sale price. This is a departure from previous practice although it could always clearly have been argued that fixing a maximum sale price is not within Article 81(1) since in many circumstances it does not restrict or distort competition. This is the first time that the Commission has recognised and approved the practice. However, such arrangements need to be structured with care to ensure that there could be no suggestion of any maximum or recommended price amounting to a fixed or minimum sale price. Paragraph 47 of the Guidelines identifies those practices on the part of the supplier which may be regarded as pressure or incentives on the buyer to impose a fixed or minimum price. The reference to "a fixed price" is somewhat puzzling because surely imposing a maximum sale price could amount to a fixed price. However, in the absence of pressure or incentives a maximum sale price would not be regarded as a fixed price unless what results is maximum prices set at such a low level that there are in reality disguised minimum prices.

> *"(b) the restriction of the territory into which, or of the customers to whom, the buyer may sell the contract goods or services, except:"*

This part of the article contains a prohibition against restricting territories into which or the customers to whom the buyer may sell goods or services.

There then follow four exceptions to what otherwise appears to be a prohibition against establishing exclusive territorial rights. The first exclusion reads as follows:

> "• *the restriction of active sales into the exclusive territory or to an exclusive customer group reserved to the supplier or allocated by the supplier to another buyer, where such a restriction does not limit sales by the customers of the buyer,"*

It will be possible to restrict active sales into the exclusive territory or to an exclusive customer group subject to two elements being satisfied.

The first element is an either/or and concerns exclusive territories or customer groups reserved to the supplier or, alternatively, allocated by the supplier to another buyer. The words "reserved to the supplier" were added to acknowledge that it would always be likely that there would be unallocated territories or customer groups since very few systems, whether they be distribution systems or franchise systems allocate all potential customer groups or territories in the early stages of their development. Only one of these alternatives need be satisfied. The second element is that there must not be a restriction which limits sales by customers of the buyer. This may be thought to present a difficulty for a system operating at wholesale level but that is dealt with in the next bullet point. This clause in fact voices one of the more difficult issues raised by the Regulation: how to treat sales by buyers over the internet. This is because paragraph 50 of the Guidelines treats sales over the internet as "passive sales". Paragraph 51 of the Guidelines states that:

> *"(51) Every distributor must be free to use the Internet to advertise or to sell products. A restriction on the use of the Internet by distributors could only be compatible with the Block Exemption Regulation to the extent that promotion on the Internet or sales over the Internet would lead to active selling into other distributors' exclusive territories or customer groups. In general, the use of the Internet is not considered a form of active sales into such territories or customer groups, since it is a reasonable way to reach every customer. The fact that it may have effects outside one's own territory or customer group results from the technology, i.e. the easy access from everywhere. If a customer visits the web site of a distributor and contacts the distributor and if such contact leads to a sale, including delivery, then that is considered passive selling. The language used on the website or in the communication plays normally no role in that respect. Insofar as a web site is not specifically targeted at customers primarily inside the territory or customer group exclusively allocated to another distributor, for instance with the use of banners or links in pages of providers specifically available to these exclusively allocated customers, the website is not considered*

a form of active selling. However, unsolicited e-mails sent to individual customers or specific customer groups are considered active selling. The same considerations apply to selling by catalogue. Notwithstanding what has been said before, the supplier may require quality standards for the use of the Internet site to resell his goods, just as the supplier may require quality standards for a shop or for advertising and promotion in general. The latter may be relevant in particular for selective distribution. An outright ban on Internet or catalogue selling is only possible if there is an objective justification. In any case, the supplier cannot reserve to itself sales and/or advertising over the Internet."

This is most likely to be a problem in relation to franchising and selective distribution and is further discussed in Chapter 7 and 8 respectively.

"• *the restriction of sales to end users by a buyer operating at the wholesale level of trade,"*

This enables the supplier, where the buyer is operating as a wholesaler, to require the the buyer to continue as a wholesaler and to prevent it from operating at retail level.

"• *the restriction of sales to unauthorised distributors by the members of a selective distribution system, and"*

This enables an operator of a selective distribution system to prevent its distributors from selling to unauthorised resellers (ie. others who are not members of the selective distribution system). If this were possible it would destroy one of the main raisons d'être of a selective distribution system. Indeed, without this provision the definition of a selective distribution system would not make sense.

"• *the restriction of the buyer's ability to sell components, supplied for the purposes of incorporation, to customers who would use them to manufacture the same type of goods as those produced by the supplier;"*

This is to prevent a buyer from selling components to a manufacturer who would use them in making its manufactured products which would compete with the supplier's products.

Having excluded these practices from the fundamental prohibition, in the case of selective distribution the next paragraph imposes further restrictions:

"(c) the restriction of active or passive sales to end users by members of a selective distribution system operating at the retail level of trade, without prejudice to the possibility of prohibiting a member of the system from operating out of an unauthorised place of establishment;"

For this paragraph to take effect, there would need to be two elements. Firstly, there must be a selective distribution system and secondly, the restriction must be imposed on those members of the system who operate at the retail level of trade. The first issue is a question of determining whether or not the system which is being operated meets the definition requirements of a selective distribution system which has been discussed above. If the arrangements are structured so that they do not amount to a selective distribution system, this restriction will have no implications. In addition, if it is a selective distribution system, for the restriction to take effect the members of the system on whom these restrictions cannot be imposed would need to be operating at retail level of trade. Whether or not this is so will be a question of fact to be determined in each case. Basically it could be said that those operating at the retail level of trade deal with end user consumers, that is to say those who are making their purchase otherwise than for the purpose of a business operated or to be operated by them. In the guidelines the Commission state "The hardcore restriction of Article 4(c) of the BER concerns the restriction of active or passive sales to end users, whether professional end users or final consumers, by members of a selective distribution network".

"(d) the restriction of cross-supplies between distributors within a selective distribution system, including between distributors operating at different level of trade;"

This provision is not surprising. It has certainly featured in decisions on selective distribution and Regulation 4087/88 (franchising).

"(e) the restriction agreed between a supplier of components and a buyer who incorporates those components, which limits the supplier to selling the components as spare parts to end-users or to repairers or other service providers not entrusted by the buyer with the repair or servicing of its goods."

A manufacturer of spare parts must remain free to supply these parts to all end users, independent repairers or service providers.

Article 5

"The exemption provided for in Article 2 shall not apply to any of the following obligations contained in vertical agreements:"

This contrasts with the introductory paragraph in Article 4 in that the exemption will not be available for any of the obligations described. This effectively means that an Article 5 clause can be struck out of the agreement while the rest of the agreement benefits from the exemption while if the agreement contains any of the prohibited clauses in Article 4 the whole agreement would not be exempt.

"(a) any direct or indirect non-compete obligation, the duration of which is indefinite or exceeds five years. A non-compete obligation which is tacitly renewable beyond a period of five years is to be deemed to have been concluded for an indefinite duration. However, the time limitation of five years shall not apply where the contract goods or services are sold by the buyer from premises and land owned by the supplier or leased by the supplier from third parties not connected with the buyer, provided that the duration of the non-compete obligation does not exceed the period of occupancy of the premises and land by the buyer;"

This article contains a number of issues which need to be considered. It should be remembered that a non-compete obligation is either an obligation causing the buyer not to manufacture, purchase, sell or resell goods or services which compete with the contract for goods or services or a tied buying arrangement which applies to more than 80% of the buyer's total purchases of the contract goods or services.

The first prohibition in Article 5(a) is against either of those obligations during the term of an agreement exceeding five years or being of indefinite duration. Any Agreement could well exceed five years so long as the non-compete obligations contained in it do not. This may effectively mean that agreements will not in practice be entered into for a period exceeding five years. The Guidelines offer hope of a longer term for franchise and exclusive distribution (see paragraphs 157 and 159) and for more on this issue see Chapter 7 and 8 under Franchising and Exclusive Distribution.

So far as tied buying is concerned, following the line of petrol station solus agreements decisions commencing with *Esso Petroleum Co Ltd. v. Harpers Garage (Stourport) Ltd*[6] tied buying arrangements are regarded as being an unlawful

6 [1968] AC 296 [1967] All ER 699

restraint of trade at common law and thus void if they exceed five years. In one later case seven years was permitted[7]. It is for this reason that many franchise agreements which have tied buying arrangements in England and Wales are expressed to be for five years with the franchisee having a right to renew.

This brings us to the second issue raised in this Article which is that a tacitly renewable non-compete obligation beyond five years is deemed to be indefinite in duration. Tacit basically means silent, unspoken or not openly expressed or stated but implied, understood or inferred. One can conclude that the intention is to prohibit gentlemen's agreements, understandings, nods and winks but to require that any renewal obligation is expressly granted. A renewal obligation which provides the franchisee with the option to decide whether or not to enter into a further agreement for a period of five years would not offend against this provision provided the agreement was not expressed in the future to be *automatically* renewable for further periods and there are no undertakings that it will be. It would be wise to ensure that a new agreement is entered into. (See paragraph 58 in the Guidelines).

The third point is somewhat curious and, presumably is in response to the brewing industry's lobbying efforts, has the effect of extending the period beyond five years if the term of the lease under which the buyer occupies the premises and land from which he trades, lasts longer than five years. The period is then extended to the period of the lease provided the buyer's immediate landlord is the seller. In the Guidelines the Commission explain "*The ratio legis of this exception is that it is unreasonable to expect competing products being sold from the premises and land owned by the supplier without his permission*".

"*(b) any direct or indirect obligation causing the buyer, after termination of the agreement, not to manufacture, purchase, sell or resell goods or services, unless such obligation:*

- *relates to goods or services which compete with the contract goods or services, and*
- *is limited to the premises and land from which the buyer has operated during the contract period, and*
- *is indispensable to protect know-how transferred by the supplier to the buyer,*

and provided that the duration of such non-compete obligation is limited to a period of one year after termination of the agreement; this obligation

[7] *Alec Lobb Garages Ltd v. Total Oil Great Britain* [1985] 1 WLR 173; [1985] All ER 303; [1983] 1 WLR 87

is without prejudice to the possibility of imposing a restriction which is unlimited in time on the use and disclosure of know-how which has not entered the public domain;"

The terms of this post term restraint against competition appear so narrowly drafted as to be of no practical value. There are four elements to be satisfied if this provision is to be relied upon:

- the restraint must relate to goods or services which compete with the contract goods or services.
- it is limited to the premises and land from which the buyer has operated.
- it must be indispensable to protect know-how transferred; and
- it should be limited to a period of one year after termination.

There are two important issues, firstly limiting the geographical scope to the trading premises affords no protection whatever to the supplier against unfair competition. Secondly, given the definition of know-how (see above) with its limited scope, no-one is likely to be able to satisfy the indispensability test. In fact, the combination of this provision and the definition of know-how means there are two indispensability tests to be satisfied. The Commission seeks to offer a sop by permitting a restraint which is unlimited in time on the use and disclosure of know-how which has not entered the public domain but, again, given the way in which know-how is defined, this is scarcely of comfort and would benefit few.

"(c) any direct or indirect obligation causing the members of a selective distribution system not to sell the brands of particular competing suppliers."

This article seems to have limited application. Apparently the supplier can ban all competing brands but not Brand X and/or Brand Y and/or Brand Z. This may have limited impact on some selective distribution systems but is unlikely to affect most distribution or franchising systems.

Article 6

"The Commission may withdraw the benefit of this Regulation, pursuant to Article 7(1) of Regulation No 19/65/EEC, where it finds in any particular case that vertical agreements to which this Regulation applies nevertheless have effects

The Commission offers no guidance as to how often it expects to involve the withdrawal procedure. It is hoped for the sake of legal certainty that it will do so rarely. Paragraph 73 of the Guidelines identifies some circumstances (eg. cumulative effects of parallel networks) where it would consider withdrawal. Elsewhere in the Guidelines, the Commission identifies circumstances in relation to specific types of agreement. (See, for example, Chapter 8 on exclusive and selective distribution.)

Article 8

"1. Pursuant to Article 1a of Regulation No 19/65/EEC, the Commission may by regulation declare that, where parallel networks of similar vertical restraints cover more than 50% of a relevant market, this Regulation shall not apply to vertical agreements containing specific restraints relating to that market.

2. A regulation pursuant to paragraph 1 shall not become applicable earlier than six months following its adoption."

As an alternative to individual withdrawal, the Commission (but not the Member States) may, pursuant to Article 8, disapply the Regulation to a category of agreement containing specific restrictions relating to the market in question. Article 8 only applies to markets in which parallel networks of similar vertical restraints cover more than 50%. Action under Article 8 is likely only where access to the market is appreciably restricted (paragraph 83 of the Guidelines). The authors assume that the Commission would invoke Article 8 only rarely, especially as it requires a reasoned Regulation to be enacted. If invoked, the effect of disapplication of the Regulation is to leave the relevant agreements open to challenge under Article 81(1) without the benefit of exemption. The Regulation must, however, allow a transitional period of at least six months before it comes into effect. During this time, the exemption of the Regulation will continue to benefit affected agreements. (See generally paragraphs 80-81 of the Guidelines.)

Article 9

"1. The market share of 30% provided for in Article 3(1) shall be calculated on the basis of the market sales value of the contract goods or services

and other goods or services sold by the supplier, which are regarded as interchangeable or substitutable by the buyer, by reason of the products' characteristics, their prices and their intended use; if market sales value data are not available, estimates based on other reliable market information, including market sales volumes, may be used to establish the market share of the undertaking concerned. For the purposes of Article 3(2), it is either the market purchase value or estimates thereof which shall be used to calculate the market share.

2. *For the purposes of applying the market share, threshold provided for in Article 3 the following rules shall apply:*
   - (a) *the market share shall be calculated on the basis of data relating to the preceding calendar year;*
   - (b) *the market share shall include any goods or services supplied to integrated distributors for the purposes of sale;*
   - (c) *if the market share is initially not more than 30% but subsequently rises above that level without exceeding 35%, the exemption provided for in Article 2 shall continue to apply for a period of two consecutive calendar years following the year in which the 30% market share threshold was first exceeded;*
   - (d) *if the market share is initially not more than 30% but subsequently rises above 35%, the exemption provided for in Article 2 shall continue to apply for one calendar year following the year in which the level of 35% was first exceeded;*
   - (e) *the benefit of points (c) and (d) may not be combined so as to exceed a period of two calendar years."*

There is a discussion above of "market shares" and "relevant markets". It should be remembered that Article 3(1) of this Regulation refers to "30%" of the relevant market on which it (the supplier) sells the contract goods or services".

The principal guidance for definition of the relevant market is the Commission Notice on market definition (Appendix H). The Guidelines also contain additional guidance on specific issues at paragraphs 88-95 (discussed above).

This Article introduces marginal relief for two years in cases where the market share rises above 30% but not above 35% and for one year where it rises above 35%.

Article 10

"1. For the purpose of calculating total annual turnover within the meaning of Article 2(2) and (4), the turnover achieved during the previous financial year by the relevant party to the vertical agreement and the turnover achieved by its connected undertakings in respect of all goods and services, excluding all taxes and other duties, shall be added together. For this purpose, no account shall be taken of dealings between the party to the vertical agreement and its connected undertakings or between its connected undertakings.

2. The exemption provided for in Article 2 shall remain applicable where, for any period of two consecutive financial years, the total annual turnover threshold is exceeded by no more than 10%."

There are two references in the Regulation to "turnover". In Article 2(2) its purpose is to set a gap on the turnover level permitted to a retail member of an association. In Article 2(4) its purpose is to set a cap on the turnover of a buyer where the parties to the agreement are competing undertakings.

Article 10(2) provides marginal relief for a two year period during which the turnover threshold is exceeded by no more than 10%.

Article 11

"1. For the purposes of this Regulation, the terms 'undertaking', 'supplier' and 'buyer' shall include their respective connected undertakings.

2. 'Connected undertakings' are:

(a) undertakings in which a party to the agreement, directly or indirectly:
- *has the power to exercise more than half the voting rights, or*
- *has the power to appoint more than half the members of the supervisory board, board of management or bodies legally representing the undertaking, or*
- *has the right to manage the undertaking's affairs;*

(b) undertakings which directly or indirectly have, over a party to the agreement, the rights or powers listed in (a);

(c) undertakings in which an undertaking referred to in (b) has, directly or indirectly, the rights or powers listed in (a);

(d) undertakings in which a party to the agreement together with one or more of the undertakings referred to in (a), (b) or (c), or in which two or more of the latter undertakings, jointly have the rights or powers listed in (a);

(e) undertakings in which the rights or the powers listed in (a) are jointly held by:

- *parties to the agreement or their respective connected undertakings referred to in (a) to (d), or*
- *one or more of the parties to the agreement or one or more of their connected undertakings referred to in (a) to (d) and one or more third parties.*

3. For the purposes of Article 3, the market share held by the undertakings referred to in paragraph 2(e) of this Article shall be apportioned equally to each undertaking having the rights or the powers listed in paragraph 2(a)."

This Article confirms that the terms undertaking, supplier and buyer include all connected undertakings as defined. This means that for calculating market share or turnover of an undertaking for the purposes of the Regulation, the position of group companies needs to be taken into account. The position of group companies also needs to be taken into account when considering whether two undertakings are competing undertakings.

Article 12

"1. The exemptions provided for in Commission Regulations (EEC) No 1983/83[9]*, (EEC) No 1984/83*[10] *and (EEC) No 4087/88*[11] *shall continue to apply until 31 May 2000.*

2. The prohibition laid down in Article 81(1) of the EC Treaty shall not apply

9 Regulation 1983/83 (exclusive distribution)

10 Regulation 1984/83 (exclusive purchasing)

11 Regulation 4087/88 (franchising)

during the period from 1 June 2000 to 31 December 2001 in respect of agreements already in force on 31 May 2000 which do not satisfy the conditions for exemption provided for in this Regulation but which satisfy the conditions for exemption provided for in Regulations (EEC) No 1983/83, (EEC) No 1984/83 or (EEC) No 4087/88."

This extended the validity of the regulations which would otherwise have expired on 31 December 1999 until the new regulation came into force.

Article 13

"This Regulation shall enter into force on 1 January 2000."

It shall apply from 1 June 2000, except for Article 12(1) which shall apply from 1 January 2000.

This Regulation shall expire on 31 May 2010.

CHAPTER 5

THE GUIDELINES

INTRODUCTION

The Guidelines are intended to fulfil a number of functions but basically as the Commission point out in paragraph 1, "these Guidelines set out the principles for the assessment of vertical agreements under Article 81 of the EC Treaty. It is made plain that the Guidelines have been issued by the Commission to help companies make their own assessment of vertical agreements under the EC competition rules". The Commission expect companies to evaluate their circumstances in the light of the relevant facts when applying the standards set out in the Guidelines. The Commission also make it plain that they will apply the Guidelines reasonably and flexibly[1]. The Guidelines are without prejudice to any interpretation which might be given by the Court of First Instance and the Court of Justice and to the possible application of Article 82.

Given that the Block Exemption Regulation is relatively short and is intended to cover nearly all vertical agreements, it would be difficult to apply the "one size fits all" policy without detailed explanation. In practical terms, the Guidelines should enable the parties to an agreement to decide whether or not the Block Exemption Regulation exempts their agreement but if it does not, how they should assess their position in order to avoid notification. The Guidelines replace other notices, e.g. the 1962 Notice on Commercial Agents but are complementary to some notices, e.g. Notice on Minor Agreements and Notice on Market Definition.

The Commission issued a notice giving guidance on interpretation of Regulations 1983/88 and 1984/83 (exclusive distribution and purchasing). However, the Guidelines are much more ambitious offering not just a commentary on Articles in the Regulation but also on economic justification and explanation of its approach generally to vertical restraints and also how they might be treated beyond the safe harbour of the Regulation. Whilst the Guidelines might be criticised as being

---

[1] See paragraph 3

inaccessible at times, they are extremely important for lawyers and businessmen working out where they stand.

The Guidelines are also consistent with the Commission's new role as described in the White Paper where they make it plain they intend to be a policy setter which will concentrate on serious and substantial cases rather than being a notification vetter. It should be appreciated that the Guidelines are the Commission's views and policy. As explained above, they are not necessarily law, that is a matter for the Court. They have also made it plain that the Guidelines can be expected to change and that they intend to keep them under review.

HOW TO APPROACH THE GUIDELINES

The Guidelines are divided into six sections as follows:-

1. introduction (with which we have dealt above);
2. vertical agreements which generally fall outside Article 81(1);
3. application of the Block Exemption Regulation;
4. withdrawal and disapplication of the Block Exemption Regulation;
5. market definition and market share calculation issues; and
6. enforcement policy in individual cases.

We shall consider sections 2-6.

2. Vertical agreements which generally fall outside Article 81(1)

This section deals with agreements which are not infringing Article 81(1). It deals with such issues as agency which is referred to in Chapter 7 and agreements of minor importance including agreements with small medium sized enterprises which are dealt with in Chapter 2.

3. Application of the Block Exemption Regulation

It is important to bear in mind this section of the Guidelines when considering the terms of the Regulation which is dealt with in Chapter 4 and the relevant paragraphs are discussed in that chapter.

Paragraphs 62-65 of the Guidelines explain the effect of the associated reforms to Regulation 17 which are a key element of the so-called flanking measures which complement the Regulation itself. Paragraph 62 states:

> *"Vertical Agreements falling outside the Block Exemption Regulation will not be presumed to be illegal but may need individual examination. Companies are encouraged to do their own assessment without notification. In the case of an individual examination by the Commission, the latter will bear the burden of proof that the agreement in question infringes Article 81(1)."*

Under the predecessor block exemption regulations, in practice it was often presumed that an agreement outside the terms of the relevant regulation would infringe Article 81(1) if it contained any restrictions. This paragraph corrects that presumption, going forward. It will be for the Commission to establish an infringement of Article 81(1), although it will be for the parties claiming exemption to show that the agreement in question fulfills the criteria of Article 81(3).

There is no need for precautionary notification of vertical agreements – according to paragraph 63 of the Guidelines. This paragraph notes the consequence of the important amendments to Article 4(2) of Regulation 17.

Article 63 states that in practice no precautionary notification needs to take place *"if a dispute arises an undertaking can still notify, in which case the Commission can exempt vertical agreements with retroactive effect from the date of entry into force of the agreement if all four conditions of Article 81(3) are fulfilled. A notifying party does not have to explain why the agreement was not notified earlier and will not be denied retroactive exemption simply because it did not notify earlier. Any notification will be reviewed on its merits."*

Precautionary notifications will not be welcomed. The Commission make it quite plain that unless there is litigation in National Courts or complaints, notifications of vertical agreements will not be given priority in the Commission's enforcement policy (paragraph 65).

The onus is placed on National Courts for assessing the likelihood of the applicability of Article 81(3) when they should suspend proceedings pending a position by the Commission. However, "no suspension is necessary in respect of injunction proceedings where National Courts themselves are in power to assess the likelihood of the application of Article 81(3)" (paragraph 64).

While all these explanations are fine in enabling the Commission to achieve its objective in determining notifications and companies seeking comfort, there may well be cases where notification is legitimate in order to obtain legal certainty (e.g. high cost ventures; ventures involving major disruption or risk of challenge). In these latter cases, the Guidelines may not provide sufficient comfort or guidance to convince companies that there is no need to notify. It would be disappointing to say the least if the Commission were to deny such companies the opportunity of clarifying their situation by insisting that they will not give priority to notifications. One would hope that the statement in paragraph 3 of the Guidelines that the Commission will apply the Guidelines reasonably and flexibly will extend to such circumstances.

Paragraphs 71-87 deal with withdrawal and disapplication and are discussed in the preceding chapter. There is a distinct risk that there will be inconsistent application by National Authorities despite the Commission's assurance in paragraph 79 that "the Commission considers that the consultation mechanism provided for in the notice on co-operation between National Competition Authorities and the Commission should be used to avert the risk of conflicting decisions and duplication of procedures".

4. Withdrawal and disapplication of the Block Exemption Regulation

It seems that it is not likely that withdrawal and disapplication by the Commission would occur in more than a handful of cases in any event, and this section of the Guidelines is discussed in the preceding chapter.

5. Market definition and market share calculation issues

The Guidelines cross-refer to the Commission notice on the definition of relevant market which will be found in Appendix H. The Commission confirm *"this notice will not be further explained in these Guidelines and should serve as the basis for market definition issues. These Guidelines will only deal with specific issues that arise in the context of vertical restraints and that are not dealt with in the general notice on market definition"* (paragraph 88). Paragraphs 88-95 discuss the relevant market for calculating the 30% market share threshold. There is discussion of this issue in Chapter 4 where it will be seen that at least in the case of franchising there could be at least two relevant markets. Consideration will have to be given in the case of each agreement and the structure of the arrangements as to whether or not there is more than one market. Chapter 4 and the Guidelines will need to be read together when considering this issue.

6. Enforcement policy in individual cases

This section, which occupies about one half of the Guidelines (paragraphs 100-229), is concerned with individual assessment of vertical restraints. Although the Regulation is a safe harbour there will still be a number of agreements which will fall outside the Regulation. It is this section which guides businesses as to how to analyse those agreements.

The section is therefore of crucial importance to those businesses or their advisers who find their agreements for whatever reason outside the safe harbour of the Regulation. The Guidelines attempt to clarify vertical restrictions by type of restriction (eg. (i) single branding group, (ii) limited distribution group, (iii) resale price maintenance group, and (iv) market partitioning group (see paragraphs 103-114)). This approach reinforces the Commission's change in tack in focusing on restrictions and their effect rather than the type of agreement.

In the next section headed *"General rules for the evaluation of vertical restraints"* (paragraph 119), the Commission attempts to identify the general rules to be applied in evaluating vertical restraints. However, even these Guidelines suffer from being of general application and it may be hard for the businessman or his adviser to assess how much weight to attach to a particular factor. The Guidelines neither offer clear legal rules nor quantitative measures of economic effect. For example, paragraph 119(8) states that *"the more the vertical restraint is linked to the transfer of know-how, the more reason there may be to expect efficiencies to arise and the more a vertical restraint may be necessary to protect the know-how transferred or the investment costs incurred"*. This general rule appears to tie in with the statement made earlier in paragraph 116(5) that *"in as far as the know-how was not readily available to the buyer, is substantial and indispensible for the operation of the equipment, such a transfer may justify a non compete type of reduction. This would normall fall outside Article 81(1)."* (See also statement at paragraphs 134, 157 and 158.) Yet these statements appear hard to square with the specific treatment of non-compete clauses in Article 5 of the Regulation which limits non-compete clauses to 5 years and permits post term non-compete only on absurdly narrow terms. In the face of the Regulation, it may be hard for business to gauge how significant the know-how must be in order to permit a wider non-compete. The Guidelines do not give specific help.

Perhaps of more practical use is paragraph 121 which provides a list of the factors which the Commission considers the most important to establish whether a vertical agreement contains an appreciable restriction of competition under Article 81(1):

"(a) market position of the supplier

(b) market position of competitor

(c) market position of the buyer

(d) *entry barriers*

(e) *maturity of the market*

(f) *level of trade*

(g) *nature of the product*

(h) *other factors".*

It is somewhat interesting to note that although products are mentioned, services are not although they feature in the Regulation.

Paragraphs 123-133 provide a narrative explaining the Commission's approach to these issues. Subsequent sections of the Guidelines which address different types of verical agreements and restraints also follow this methodology. (See for example paragraphs 161-175 on exclusive distribution and Chapter 8.)

As these sections make clear, it is very important to appreciate that by applying the Guidelines and making the case by case assessment in accordance with the guidance provided, one may be able to conclude that Article 81(1) does not apply at all. Since the Commission have said that they will adopt a realistic, reasonable and flexible approach there may well be some comfort to be found in many cases.

It is also possible that an agreement which falls outside the Regulation because it involves a market share above 30% but which clearly on the basis of the Guidelines may benefit from an individual exemption if ever notified makes the full economic assessment exercise a worthwhile (if not altogether certain) project in which to engage.

It should be appreciated in this context that if the agreement does end up being challenged before a National Court it will be necessary to conduct such an assessment supported by the underlying evidence either to convince the Court or to secure a favourable fast track decision from the Commission granting negative clearance or retroactive exemption. If the proceedings involve an application for an injunction having the economic assessment as supporting evidence to assist the Court in reaching the conclusion that Article 81(3) could be relevant and applied may become an essential part of such proceedings.

By way of conclusion, in applying the Guidelines one should however not lose sight of three factors:

1. Much of the guidance is academic, difficult to follow and general in nature. In some respects it appears contradictory. Businessmen looking for a clear answer may not find them easy.

2. Only parts are helpful. Some parts will involve a novel approach for business and advisers and there may well be quite a period of adjustment for business people, advisers and the Commission in applying these rules.

3. One can of course take some comfort from the fact that it seems to be a fairly clear factor that the Commission really do not expect or want to be involved in the vast majority of vertical agreements.

In Chapters 6, 7 and 8 there is an analysis by reference to the most common types of distribution agreements and an explanation of how the Regulation may apply.

Chapter 5

CHAPTER 6

AGENCY AGREEMENTS

INTRODUCTION

In principle EC competition law adopts a permissive approach to the relationship between a principal and an agent.

Genuine agency agreements will therefore fall outside Article 81(1) altogether and indeed the Guidelines discuss agency agreements in paragraphs 12-21 under the general heading *"Agreements Falling Outside Article 81(1)"*. This tolerant approach derives from the fact that agency situations involve a much closer business relationship than might be the case for independent distributors and that therefore the principal and agent are so closely related that the agent is to be regarded as merely an auxiliary organ forming an integral part of the principal's activities. This principle may sound straightforward but has proved difficult to apply in practice. The guidelines restate the Commission's approach but in the authors' opinion are unlikely to result in greater clarity.

THE RELATIONSHIP OF "AGENCY"

The term "agency" can have different meanings under the various EC national legal systems. For the purposes of EC law the most commonly adopted definition is that contained in Council Directive 86/653 on commercial agents[1].

> *"For the purposes of this Directive, 'commercial agent' shall mean a self employed intermediary who has continuing authority to negotiate the sale or the purchase of goods on behalf of another person hereinafter called the 'principal', or to negotiate and conclude such transactions on behalf of and in the name of that principal."*

---

1 Council Directive (86/653/EEC) OJ [1986] L382/17 on the co-ordination of the laws of the Member States relating to self-employed commercial agents. (The Directive was implemented in the UK by the Commercial Agents (Council Directive) Regulations 1993, SI 1993/3053 (as amended).

'he Commercial Agents Directive only applies to agreements for the sale of goods, owever. EC competition law applies equally to goods or services and so in aragraph 12 of the guidelines agency agreements are defined as follows:

> *"Agency agreements cover the situation in which a legal or physical person (the agent) is vested with the power to negotiate and/or conclude contracts on behalf of another person (the principal), either in the agent's own name or in the name of the principal, for the:*
>
> - *purchase of goods or services by the principal, or*
>
> - *sale of goods or services supplied by the principal."*

n practice, commercial agents play an important part in the distribution chain for oods and services in the EC. An agent will typically perform a marketing function n behalf of a manufacturer or supplier and have little or no responsibility for the oods or services being sold. The agent will generally be remunerated by means of ommission based on a percentage of sales made by the agent. The position of the gent is therefore to be contrasted with that of a distributor whose remuneration 'ill depend on the margin achieved between the purchase from the supplier and esale by the distributor. Often the distributor will be entrusted with additional asks such as maintenance of extensive stocks within the contract territory, extensive fter sales service, providing local marketing intelligence and generally local legal nd market knowledge. As a result the distributor will often receive a higher reward n absolute terms reflecting the greater economic risks accepted compared to an gent.

The advantage to a manufacturer or supplier of an agency relationship is that it an exert much greater control over how its goods or services are sold by the gent. In a genuine agency relationship, the supplier and manufacturer is able to et the prices and terms on which products are sold and still fall outside of Article 1(1).

GENUINE AGENCY AGREEMENTS FALLING OUTSIDE ARTICLE 81(1)

'or a full understanding of how EC competition law has been applied to agency greements, the starting point is the Commission's Notice on exclusive dealing contracts with commercial agents published in 1962[2]. That Notice stated that Article 81(1) does not apply to an agreement between a principal and an agent in which the latter agrees, in relation to a specified part of the common market, to procure business, or to close transactions in the name and on behalf of the principal, in circumstances where the agent is not acting as an independent trader on his own account. The Notice further states that the *"characteristic feature which all commercial agents have in common is their function as auxiliaries in the negotiation of business deals"*. The Notice provides that Article 81(1) would nevertheless be likely to apply where the agent in fact acted as more in the role of an independent trader by assuming responsibility for maintaining considerable stocks of the product, for providing free, substantial customer services or for fixing prices or business terms.

The general approach of the Commission in the 1962 Notice was confirmed by the European Court in the *Sugar* case[3]. In that case the Court held that Article 85 did not apply to clauses in an agreement between an agent and a principal only in circumstances where the agent is to be regarded merely as an auxiliary organ forming an integral part of the principal's undertaking. This would not be the case where the agent in question in fact accepts the financial risks of the sales or performance of contracts with third parties[4].

In *Bundeskartellamt v. Volkswagen AG and VAG Leasing GmbH*[5] the European Court held that Volkswagen dealers could not be regarded as an integral part of the business of Volkswagen and its leasing company because the dealers in fact bore part of the financial risks of leasing vehicles and carrying out their sales and after sales business independently.

It is also clear from the cases that Article 81 may apply if an agent in fact operates as an independent trader vis a vis its principal. Whether or not an agent is regarded as an independent trader is a question of fact in each case and must be assessed in the overall commercial context and not by reference to the legal nature of the relationships. The mere fact that an agent acts for more than one principal does not of itself cause Article 81 to apply (see paragraph 13 of the Guidelines). However, in *VVR v Sociale Dienst*[6] the European Court held that where travel agents regularly

---

2 Commission Notice of 24 December 1962 on exclusive dealing contracts with commercial agents.

3 *Suiker Unie v. Commission* [1975] ECR 1663.

4 See also *ARG/Unipart* OJ 1988 L45/34.

5 [1996] ECR 1-3477.

6 Case 311/85 [1987] ECR 3801.

Corning case[10]. At least in the eyes of the Commission, the fact that an agent carries on considerable business on its own account or acts for a number of other principals are not material factors in determining the applicability of Article 81(1) to a particular agency agreement.

TYPES OF FINANCIAL AND COMMERCIAL RISK

Not all risk will be relevant. Paragraph 14 states that:

> *"There are two types of financial or commercial risk that are material to the assessment of the genuine nature of an agency agreement under Article 81(1). First there are the risks which are directly related to the contracts concluded and/or negotiated by the agent on behalf of the principal, such as financing of stocks. Secondly, there are the risks related to market-specific investments. These are investments specifically required for the type of activity for which the agent has been appointed by the principal, i.e. which are required to enable the agent to conclude and/or negotiate this type of contract. Such investments are usually sunk, if upon leaving that particular field of activity the investment cannot be used for other activities or sold other than at a significant loss."*

It will be a question of fact in each case whether a risk should be regarded as "market specific". In paragraph 16 the Commission refers to the example of a petrol storage tank in the case of petrol retailing or specific software to sell insurance policy in case of insurance agents as examples of market specific investment. On the other hand, investment in a warehouse or investment in non bespoke computer hardware or software may in other circumstances presumably not be regarded as market specific. Each case must be considered on its merits and there is clearly scope for uncertainties.

An agency agreement falls outside Article 81(1) if the agent does not bear any or only "insignificant" risks in relation to relevant contracts and/or market specific investments. There is no guidance as to when a particular investment will be regarded as "insignificant". Is the assessment solely by reference to the allocation of risk as between principal and agency in relation to that particular contract or is it by reference to the absolute level of investment or by reference to potential reward available to the agent?

The fact that each assessment must be made on a case by case basis is reiterated in paragraph 16 of the Guidelines which states that:

---

10 *Ibid.*

"The question of risk must be assessed on a case-by-case basis, and with regard to the economic reality of the situation rather than the legal form. Nonetheless, the Commission considers that Article 81(1) will generally not be applicable to the obligations imposed on the agent as to the contracts negotiated and/or concluded on behalf of the principal where property in the contract goods bought or sold does not vest in the agent, or the agent does not itself supply the contract services and where the agent:

- *does not contribute to the costs relating to the supply/purchase of the contract goods or services, including the costs of transporting the goods. This does not preclude the agent from carrying out the transport service, provided that the costs are covered by the principal;*
- *is not, directly or indirectly, obliged to invest in sales promotion, such as contributions to the advertising budgets of the principal;*
- *does not maintain at its own cost or risk stocks of the contract goods, including the costs of financing the stocks and the costs of loss of stocks and can return unsold goods to the principal without charge, unless the agent is liable for fault (for example, by failing to comply with reasonable security measures to avoid loss of stocks);*
- *does not create and/or operate an after-sales service, repair service or a warranty service unless it is fully reimbursed by the principal;*
- *does not make market-specific investments in equipment, premises or training of personnel, such as for example the petrol storage tank in the case of petrol retailing or specific software to sell insurance policies in case of insurance agents;*
- *does not undertake responsibility towards third parties for damage caused by the product sold (product liability), unless, as agent, it is liable for fault in this respect;*
- *does not take responsibility for customers' non-performance of the contract, with the exception of the loss of the agent's commission, unless the agent is liable for fault (for example, by failing to comply with reasonable security or anti-theft measures or failing to comply with reasonable measures to report theft to the principal or police or to communicate to the principal all necessary information available to it on the customer's financial reliability)."*

The checklist is an innovation and similar checklists were not included in the 1962 or draft 1990 Notice. Some of the elements, for example maintenance of stocks or operation of after-sale service do, however, feature in the 1962 Notice.

The first example of risk is that of the risk of transport costs. It is not clear why this is a relevant factor since in many cases transport will merely be a cost to be allocated as between principal and agent without significant bearing on the risk allocation in the relationship. It is hard to see that an agent who receives a slightly higher level of commission whilst assuming responsibility for arranging transport is in a materially different position in competition terms from an agent receiving a slightly lower level of commission reflecting the fact that the principal bears responsibility for transport.

The second example refers to promotional costs. It is common for agents to be obliged to contribute to promotional activities conducted by the principal. Again, presumably this cost is reflected in the level of commission and exactly how it is accounted for will not have a material bearing on the relationship between the principal and the agent in competition terms.

The third example relates to stocks and it is important to note a difference in the 1962 which referred to "considerable stocks" whereas the Guidelines refer simply to "stocks".

The fourth example concerns after-sales service. It is relatively common for agents to carry out some level of after-sales service in accordance with the principal's instructions and for a specified price. This might be reflected in the level of commission rather than being specifically reimbursed by the principal. However, on its face this after-sales function would potentially cause Article 81(1) to apply where it might not otherwise have done so.

The fifth example refers to market specific investments and is discussed above.

The sixth example concerns product liability and does not appear to be controversial.

The seventh example concerns customers' non performance of the contract and again appears not to be controversial. Del credere agents who guarantee the payments of third parties would appear to fit within this.

It should be borne in mind that this list is not exhaustive. There may be other factors which in the particular circumstances of the principal/agent relationship, might cause Article 81(1) to apply.

Paragraph 17 affirms that where the agent incurs one or more of the risks or costs identified in paragraph 16 then Article 81(1) may apply. The Article 81 assessment will turn not only on the significance of the particular risk or cost in the overall commercial context but also the nature of the restrictions adopted and the market position of the parties and the market context in which they are operate. So

AGENCY AGREEMENTS WITHIN ARTICLE 81(1)

Where the agent incurs one or more of the risks identified in paragraph 16, the Guidelines state that Article 81(1) may apply as with any other vertical agreements. Assuming therefore that the agency agreement has an appreciable effect on competition, the restrictive clauses in it may be unenforceable under Article 81(2) unless they can benefit from an exemption under Article 81(3). In considering the availability of an exemption, an agency agreement will be considered under the Verticals Regulation and the Guidelines in a similar way to any other vertical agreement. In practice, the biggest stumbling block is likely to be the degree of control which the principal may exert over the prices and terms on which the agent sells its products.

Article 4(a) of the Verticals Regulation provides that the setting of fixed or minimum resale prices is a blacklisted clause and, as such, will be unlikely ever to benefit from an exemption.[11]

Paragraph 48 of the Guidelines specifically addresses price setting in the context of agency agreements. That paragraph provides:

> *"In the case of agency agreements, the principal normally establishes the sales price, as the agent does not become the owner of the goods. However, where an agency agreement falls within Article 81(1) (see paragraphs 12-20), an obligation preventing or restricting the agent from sharing its commission, fixed or variable, with the customer would be a hardcore restriction under Article 4(a) of the BER. The agent should thus be left free to lower the effective price paid by the customer without reducing the income for the principal."*[12]

It would seem therefore that the Commission regards the establishment of the sales price by the principal as acceptable but only in circumstances where the agent may pass on some or all of its commission to the customer. Presumably, the agent's freedom to give away his commission could be a significant commercial issue in a market in which the manufacturer appoints a number of non-exclusive agents potentially targeting the same customers.

Similarly, if an agency agreement potentially falls within Article 81(1) Article 4(b) will blacklist any attempts by the manufacturer to impose absolute territorial

---

[11] See paragraph 46 of the Guidelines.

[12] See for instance the Commission Decision of 18 October 1991 relating to a proceeding pursuant to Article 85 of the EEC Treaty (IV/32.737 – Eirpage), OJ L 306, 7.11.1991, p. 22, in particular point (6).

CHAPTER 7

FRANCHISING

An examination of the *Pronuptia* decision[1] provides some useful guidance and as will be seen below, some scope for confronting some of the issues which arise under the Regulation which many franchise systems need to avoid if they are to continue their operations without significant adverse consequences.

The Court had something relevant to say in relation to three issues which impact the effect of the Regulation on franchise systems:

THE DEFINITION OF "SELECTIVE DISTRIBUTION SYSTEM"[2]

It should be noted that in its Green Paper the Commission described selective distribution in the following way[3]

> *"In selective distribution a manufacturer usually agrees to supply only to dealers satisfying certain professional or technical requirements, while the approved dealers undertake not to purchase or sell the contract goods from wholesalers or retailers outside the official network. As a general rule the establishment of a selective distribution system is motivated by the nature of the product."*[4]

In its description of Franchising Agreements in the Green Paper the Commission makes no mention of selective distribution as being a feature or component of franchising. However, in its follow-up to the Green Paper on vertical restraints[5]

1 *Ibid.*

2 In Article 1(d) of the BER.

3 Paragraph 127 Green Paper on Vertical Restraints in EC Competition Policy.

4 See also paragraph 15 of the *Pronuptia* case *"Rather than a system of distribution it (franchising) concerns a way of exploiting financially, without committing its own capital, a collection of skills"*.

5 See p.27 of the Green Paper.

the Commission asserts *"usually franchising is a combination of selective distribu-tion and non-compete obligations in relation to goods which are the subject matte of the franchise. Sometimes also exclusive distribution obligations are added"*. I should be noted that in its definition of a selective distribution system the Commis-sion refers to services although they were not previously mentioned in this contex in either the Green Paper or the follow-up[6].

Furthermore, in paragraph 199 of the Guidelines the Commission state ".. *Franchising may enable the franchisor to establish with limited investments a uniform network for the distribution of its products. In addition to the provision o the business method franchise agreements usually contain a combination of differen vertical restraints containing the products being distributed, in particular, selective distribution and/or non-compete and/or exclusive distribution or weaker form thereof ....".*

This passage indicates that selective distribution as well as the other restraint mentioned may be a feature of a franchise agreement.

In paragraph 200 we find *"As for the vertical restraints on the purchase, sale and re-sale of goods and services within a franchising arrangement, such a selective distribution, non-compete or exclusive distribution, the Block Exemption Regulation applies up to the 30% market share threshold ...".*

This confirms the line adopted in paragraph 199 namely that such vertica restraints may be found in franchise systems. There are many franchise system which do not have vertical restraints of the type described as "selective distribution" "non-compete" or "exclusive distribution".

The ECJ in paragraph 15 of the *Pronuptia* judgment contrasted franchising wit selective distribution in the following terms:

> *"distribution franchise agreements are thus different from either dealershi agreements or those binding approved re-sellers appointed under a system o selective distribution which involves neither use of a simple mark or applicatio of uniform commercial methods nor payment of royalties as consideration o the advantages thus conferred. Such a system which permits the franchisor t take advantage of this success is not by itself restrictive of competition".*

While it would have been better, had the Commission followed the ECJ reasoning they are making it clear that if franchising systems have any of the other element described (ie. selective distribution, non-compete or exclusive distribution) the

6 The definition is discussed below.

will be subject to the same treatment as are these elements. Thus in paragraph 200 of the Guidelines the Commission confirms "The guidance provided earlier in respect of these type of restraints applies also to franchising".

This issue is considered further below when considering the effect of the definition of a selective distribution system.

Know-How

The next issue arising from the *Pronuptia* decision to be addressed relates to know-how. There are two provisions in the Regulation which are relevant. The first is the definition of know-how (Article 1); the second the post term restraint (Article 5(b)).

The ECJ addresses the issue of know-how in franchising in paragraphs 15 and 16 of its decision in the following terms.

> "15. *In a system of distribution franchises such as this, a firm which is established in a market as a distributor and which is thus able to develop a scheme of commercial methods, grants independent business men – for consideration – the opportunity to establish themselves in other markets using its sign and its business methods on which its success has been based. Rather than a system of distribution, it concerns a way of exploiting financially, without committing its own capital, a collection of skills. Moreover, this system makes available to business men, who do not have the necessary experience, access to methods which they would have acquired only after long efforts of trial and error and allows them to benefit from the reputation of the sign. Distribution franchise contracts are in this respect different from sales concession contracts or from those which link the appointed retailer in a system of selective distribution which includes neither the use of the same sign nor the application of uniform business methods nor the payment of royalties in respect of agreed advantages. Such a system, which allows the franchisor to share the success, does not in itself jeopardise competition. To enable it to function, a double condition has to be fulfilled.*
>
> 16. *In the first place, the franchisor has to be able to communicate to franchisees his know-how and to provide them with the necessary help in implementing his methods, without running the risk that this know-how and this help benefit, however indirectly, his competitors. Consequently the clauses which are indispensable to avoid this risk do not constitute restrictions on competition in the sense of Article 85(1). From this follows the prohibition*

> *on the franchisee on opening, during the period of the contract or during a reasonable period after its expiration, a shop having a similar or identical purpose, in a region in which it could compete with members of the network. Similarly, from this flows the obligation imposed on the franchisee not to transfer his shop without the prior agreement of the franchisor; this clause helps to avoid the benefit of the know-how provided and the help given passing indirectly to a competitor."*

Paragraph 18 of the judgment is also relevant.

> *"Similar considerations apply to the obligation on the franchisee to apply the business methods developed by the franchisor and to make use of the know-how which has been provided".*

NON-COMPETE CLAUSES

Paragraphs 17 and 18 of the ECJ judgment are clearly relevant. Where considering the non-compete clauses the subject of Article 5(b). The ECJ also had the following comments to make in relation to the non-compete clauses the subject of Article 5(a).

> *"In the second place the franchisor must be able to take appropriate measures to preserve the identity and the reputation of the network symbolised by the sign. It follows from this that the clauses which institute controls indispensable for this purpose do not constitute restrictions of competition in the sense of Article 85(1)".*

To summarise; according to the ECJ judgment

- franchising is different from selective distribution
- appropriate indispensable measures to preserve the identity of the sign symbolised by the sign do not constitute an infringement of Article 81(1) and are not affected by any hard core restrictions under Article 4 or conditions under Article 5 of the regulation. This is confirmed by the Commission in paragraph 192(2) of the guidelines although the guidelines do not confirm that the application of this principle is not confined to non-compete clauses.
- clauses which are indispensable for the purpose of preventing the know-how provided and the help given by the franchisor from benefiting com-

petitors do not constitute an infringement of Article 81(1) and are not affected by any hard core restrictions under Article 4 or conditions under Article 5 of the regulation. Significantly the Commission stated in paragraph 6 of the Guidelines:

> "These are without prejudice to the view that may be taken of vertical agreements by the Court of first instance and the Court of Justice of the European Communities."

It is to be regretted that the Regulation does not reflect the issues referred to above with which the ECJ dealt in the *Pronuptia* judgment and that the Guidelines are silent about the extent to which the judgment affects the issues for franchising systems.

The Franchising Issues

How to define the relevant market for franchising

The first step is actually to identify what are the contract goods and services.

For example, the contract between a franchisor and a franchisee will comprise three relevant elements; the first will be the grant of the franchise which in itself is the provision of a service together with any goods and/or services which will initially be supplied or provided to the franchisee pursuant to the contract terms. The second element will be the goods and/or services to be supplied or provided to the franchisee on an ongoing basis throughout the contract term. The third element will concern the goods and services to be sold and supplied by the franchisee to his customers.

Where there is a Master Franchise arrangement one will also have to consider the sale of the Master Franchise and the continuing provision of services and goods which will or may flow between Franchisor and Master Franchisee to enable it to perform its functions in sub-franchising. This adds to the range of contract goods and services since those provided under the Master Franchisee Agreement will differ from those provided by the Master Franchisee to sub-franchisees which are analogous to those provided by a franchisor to its franchisees.

Goods purchased from the franchisor may be resold in exactly the same form as they were when received. They may have to be dealt with in some way; for example in fast food they will have to be cooked or processed in some way. The goods may be sold to the franchisee by a third party supplier (see further on this issue below). If there is a service to be provided by the franchisee to his customers, that service may require goods (which may flow from the franchisor or from a third party supplier) to be used in the provision of the service. Certainly the services to be provided by the franchisor to the franchisee will be different from those which the

showed a failure to recognise the difference between services and goods in the 1988 Regulation which they have carried through to the Regulation.

Since a franchise agreement will invariably contain conditions under which the franchisee has to purchase, sell or resell certain goods or services, the agreement would clearly be a vertical agreement which is exempt subject to compliance with the Regulation but are those goods or services the contract goods or services? If so, why not use that expression. If not then do the references elsewhere in the Regulation to contract goods or services include the goods or services referred to in Article 2(1).

The 30% market share cap relates to the relevant market on which the supplier sells the contract goods or services. Those goods or services in the franchise example could well be different from those sold or provided by the franchisees. Does this mean that the 30% cap applies only to the goods or services sold by the franchisor and that the franchisee is the supplier under contracts with customers which may or may not contain vertical restraints. Invariably, they will not contain such restraints.

To the extent that those agreements contain vertical restraints they can benefit from the exemption only if one views them as separate vertical agreements from the supplier agreements and the argument that there are two relevant markets, at least, in franchising assists in giving meaning to the Regulation where otherwise it would be difficult to understand.

There is some more assistance when one refers to the definition of "know-how" and in particular the meaning of the element "substantial" in that definition. This issue is discussed in Chapter 7 when considering the franchising issues. The conclusion reached there is that there are indeed at least three categories of contract goods or services.

One is thus driven to the conclusion in franchising that there are at least two (possibly three) relevant markets and one 30% market share cap for each provided there are vertical agreements in each containing vertical restraints which are infringing Article 81(1) of the Treaty. This conclusion is supported by paragraph 95 of the Guidelines despite the otherwise confusing nature of its assertions which are discussed below in relation to Article 3(1).

> *"95. Where the vertical agreement, in addition to the supply of the contract goods, also contains IPR provisions – such as a provision concerning the use of the supplier's trademark – which help the buyer to market the contract goods, the supplier's market share on the market where it sells the contract goods is decisive for the application of the Block Exemption Regulation. Where a franchisor does not supply goods to be resold but provides a bundle of services combined with IPR provisions which together form the business method being*

franchised, the franchise needs to take account of its market share as a provider of a business method. For that purpose, the franchisor needs to calculate its market share on the market where the business method is exploited, which is the market where the franchisees exploit the business method to provides goods or services to end users. The franchisor must base its market share on the value of the goods or services supplied by its franchisees on this market. On such a market the competitors may be other franchised business methods but also suppliers of substitutable goods or services not applying franchising. For instance, without prejudice to the definition of such market, if there was a market for fast food services, a franchisor operating on such a market would need to calculate its market share on the basis of the relevant sales figures of its franchisees on this market. If the franchisor, in addition to the business method, also supplies certain inputs, such as meat and spices, then the franchisor also needs to calculate its market share on the market where these goods are sold."

Paragraphs 42 and 43 of the Guidelines also refer to the different categories of goods and services which merit consideration:

"42. Franchise agreements, with the exception of industrial franchise agreements, are the most obvious example where know-how for marketing purposes is communicated to the buyer. Franchise agreements contain licences of intellectual property rights relating to trade marks or signs and know-how for the use and distribution of goods or the provision of services. In addition to the licence of IPR, the franchisor usually provides the franchisee during the life of the agreement with commercial or technical assistance, such as procurement services, training, advice on real estate, financial planning etc. the licence and the assistance are integral components of the business method being franchised."

"43. Licensing contained in franchise agreements is covered by the Block Exemption Regulation if all five conditions listed in point 30 are fulfilled. This is usually the case, as under most franchise agreements, including master franchise agreements, the franchisor provides goods and/or services, in particular commercial or technical assistance services, to the franchisee. The IPR's help the franchisee to resell the products supplied by the franchisor or by a supplier designated by the franchisor or to use these products and sell the resulting goods or services. Where the franchise agreement only or primarily concerns licensing of IPR's, such an agreement is not covered by the Block Exemption Regulation, but it will

be treated in a way similar to those franchise agreements which are covered by the Block Exemption Regulation."

There can also be difficulties where the supplier of the goods and some services may not be a party to the vertical agreement (see Article 2). An example is of a franchise agreement where the franchisor provides services in assisting the franchisee in opening the business and on-going support in the running of the business while the franchisee purchases goods and/or raw materials from a third party supplier which has no continuing interest after the sale is completed. Since the supplier is not a party to the vertical agreement although it may be designated as a supplier, to preserve the identity and reputation of the system, the reference to the contract goods would appear to have limited application in these circumstances which are not unusual in franchising arrangements. Unfortunately neither the preamble nor the guidelines provide much assistance on this issue. The following is the outcome:

1. If the supplier is a third party nominee it may not enter into a contract with the buyer which is a vertical agreement containing vertical restraints.

2. If the supplier is a third party nominee and there is an agreement between the nominator and the third party's customer it may well be suggested that there is a vertical agreement containing vertical restraints but to meet the definition of a vertical agreement it would need to contain conditions relating to the purchase, sale or resale of certain goods or services which fall within the scope of Article 81(1).

3. If the supplier is not a third party nominee or one of the other parties to the agreement there could still be a vertical agreement containing conditions relating to the sale or resale of certain goods or services which fall within the scope of Article 81(1).

4. There can be a vertical agreement containing conditions relating to the sale of services which fall within the scope of Article 81(1) but the question to be answered will require an assessment of the meaning of "contract goods or services" in the context of the agreement and the reference to that phrase in the provision in the Regulation under consideration.

Having identified the goods and services one must then identify those goods and services which are regarded as substitutable or interchangeable by the buyer. (See the discussion of Article 3 of the Regulation in Chapter 4.) Paragraph 95 of the Guidelines attempts to address the issue in relation to franchising.

> *"95. Where the vertical agreement, in addition to the supply of the contract goods, also contains IPR provisions – such as a provision concerning the use of the supplier's trademark – which help the buyer to market the contract goods, the supplier's market share on the market where it sells the contract goods is decisive for the application of the Block Exemption Regulation. Where a franchisor does not supply goods to be resold but provides a bundle of services combined with IPR provisions which together form the business method being franchised, the franchisor needs to take account of its market share as a provider of a business method. For that purpose, the franchisor needs to calculate its market share on the market where the business method is exploited, which is the market where the franchisees exploit the business method to provide goods or services to end users. The franchisor must base its market share on the value of the goods or services supplied by its franchisees on this market. On such a market the competitors may be other franchised business methods but also suppliers of substitutable goods or services not applying franchising. For instance, without prejudice to the definition of such market, if there was a market for fast food services, a franchisor operating on such a market would need to calculate its market share on the basis of the relevant sales figures of its franchisees on this market. If the franchisor, in addition to the business method, also supplies certain inputs, such as meat and spices, then the franchisor also needs to calculate its market share on the market where these goods are sold."*

According to this paragraph, the Commission's view of the market initially assumes that so far as the "contract goods" (no mention of services at that point)[7] the suppliers market share on the market where *it sells* the contract goods is decisive for the application of the Regulation. This immediately begs the question discussed in more detail above as to what are "contract goods or services" and with which of the two, three or more markets this paragraph is dealing.

The next issue with which the paragraph deals recognises that there is a market for the franchisor in its role as the provider of a business method. That may raise issues of whether that market which clearly exists should be segmented according to the nature of the underlying system or the financial means of those who wish to take up franchises. The Commission does not say whether this market relates to "contract goods or services" but clearly it must accept that it does, otherwise the Article does not apply to this market on which it is clear that the franchisor sells (*sic*) the business method. Presumably the market on which a master franchisee

7 But see paragraph 2 of the Guidelines.

sells the franchised business method to individual franchisees is separate from the market on which the franchisors sells (*sic*) the business method to master franchisees. The services provided by the franchisor to a master franchisee differ from those provided by the master franchisee to its sub-franchisees. It would be difficult to argue in favour of their aggregation to qualify as the relevant market in which the franchisor sell the contract goods or services.

However, the Commission take a different line by asserting that *"the franchisor needs to calculate its market share on the market where the business method is exploited which is the market where the franchisees exploit the business method to provide goods or services to end users"*. This blurring of the different aspects of franchising produces a nonsensical outcome.

The next statement *"The franchisor must base its market share on the value of the goods or services supplied on this market"*. The franchisees are not exploiting the business method. Only the franchisor or a master franchisee do that. What the franchisees do is to use the business method in providing goods and/or services to their customers.

The implication that *"suppliers of substitutable goods or services not applying franchising"* compete with franchisors seeking franchisees who will "buy" the right to exploit a business using the business method is fundamentally flawed.

The Commission concludes paragraph 95 by providing an example by referring to a market for fast food services in which *"a franchisor would need to calculate its market share on the basis of the relevant sales figures of its franchisees on this market"* and adds that *"if the franchisor in addition to the business method also supplies inputs such as meat and spices, then the franchisor also needs to calculate its market share on the market where those goods are sold."*

The market for fast food services is different from that in which franchisees sell those services. If we look at Article 9 with its rules for the calculation of market share how can it be concluded that the goods or services which a franchisor provides in selling a franchise could be considered as "interchangeable or substitutable by the buyer" in any way, let alone by reason of the products characteristics, their prices and their intended use" with the goods or services sold by the franchisee to his customers. There are two entirely different buyers each with a totally different objective and perspective. The franchisee "buys" the right to establish and operate a business using the franchisor's business methods and IP rights. The franchisees' customer buys the product of the franchisees' business whether it be goods and/or services. Furthermore, the franchisor may not supply inputs, they may be supplied by third party manufacturers or wholesalers providing goods manufactured to the franchisors specifications.

Insofar as these guidelines clearly contradict the Regulation, the Regulation

of the distribution network must therefore be limited in number. Consequently, the Group can of its own accord choose the traders which seem to be most suitable for maintaining the cohesion of the network".

This reasonably accurately describes the reality which is that the franchisor's ultimate decision is more than likely to be a subjective judgment while with the benefit of hindsight a franchisor may be able to identify the factors which led to its choice of a particular individual franchisee that is a long way from having "specified criteria". Franchising uniquely and invariably requires a close working relationship and the parties to a franchise agreement have to be satisfied that they can develop and sustain that relationship.

Many franchisors explicitly reserve rights to sell in other ways and through other means and certainly it would be unusual for them to require their franchisees to undertake not to sell the goods or services to unauthorised distributors. Franchising is geared up on the whole to cope with relationships between a franchisor at one level and the franchisee at the next level dealing with his customer. There are some wholesale arrangements between manufacturers and wholesalers or wholesalers who franchise others to sell by wholesale but such undertakings would be rare even in those cases. There could be a case where there is a master franchise arrangement where the sub-franchisor would resell goods to sub-franchisees but, again, it is unlikely that one would find such undertakings in those arrangements.

There may however be cases where franchisors are inclined to enter into undertakings or require franchisees to give undertakings. It should be borne in mind that the definition requires both undertakings to be given which is unlikely to happen except in rare cases. The consequences of doing so will have to be considered. Even if the franchisor were to ask the franchisees to undertake not to sell goods or services to unauthorised distributors, if the franchisor has not given the undertaking required by the first element of the definition, there would not be a selective distribution system. Likewise, if the franchisor undertakes to sell the contract goods or services only to franchisees selected on the basis of specified criteria, that in itself does not require the franchisees to undertake not to sell goods or services to unauthorised distributors and in the absence of such an undertaking there would not be a selective distribution system.

Most franchisors will wish to avoid being regarded as involved in a selective distribution system and so avoid the more restrictive provisions which the Regulation applies to selective distribution. In many cases it should be possible to achieve that objective by a combination of contractual provisions and carefully controlled and monitored market behaviour. However, it is the economic reality of the situation which counts, not just the drafting of the contract, and so, if the reality is that the franchiser operates a system which meets the definition of a selective distribution system in the Regulation, then it will be treated as such.

Know-how

A last minute change to the "substantial" element of the definition of know-how, after the public consultation had taken place, renders the definition at odds with the description of know-how in the *Pronuptia* judgment and makes one wonder almost how anything could meet the test which requires to be satisfied to establish substantiality. The know-how must not merely be secret and identified but it must be substantial. Substantial means that it must include information which is "indispensable to the franchisee for the use, sale or resale of the contract goods or services". In this case it is clear that the know-how referred to refers to that provided by the franchisor to the franchisee to the extent, if that is possible, that it is indispensable for the use, sale or re-sale of the contract goods or services.

In Chapter 5 there is a discussion of contract goods or services. The wording in the definition of "substantial" is difficult to comprehend since the contract goods or services have to be sold, used or re-sold. This suggests that there has to be a movement of goods or services down the production to consumer chain. That may not occur in some franchise systems. As has already been explained, services will not be dealt with in that way – at each level they will be different although they will be provided at each level. Goods may not flow either. In order for this to mean something the contract goods or services referred to must be those to be sold or provided by the franchisee to his customers pursuant to the franchise agreement.

Franchise systems do not have any exclusivity of goods or services (save for their own trade marked products and services), they tend to be in competition in the market place with other sellers of similar goods or services. Clearly the franchisee cannot sell under the trademark of the franchisor without using the franchisor's know-how as required in the franchise agreement but could it really be said that that know-how is indispensable for the sale or resale of those goods or services?

If one considers the definition of competing undertakings which is similar to that dealing with the market sales value of contract goods or services contained in Article 9, the market include goods or services which are regarded by the buyer as interchangeable with or substitutable for the contract goods or services by reason of the products' characteristics, their prices and their intended use. If that is the way that the goods or services are to be regarded then it makes the indispensability test almost impossible to satisfy. The definition which was contained in the draft regulation which was published for consultation had some of the elements of franchise know-how although not as much as was in the *Pronuptia* judgment but the removal of those words in the final version makes it very difficult for any franchise system to rely with confidence on satisfying the substantiality test and thus having know-how which qualifies to regard it as such for the purposes of this regulation. If the meaning to be attached to the contract goods or services is as suggested above, it could be argued that since those goods or services are to be sold within the framework of the franchise system the franchisor's know-how is indispensable for that purpose, otherwise it would not be that franchise system without the use of the know-how. Franchise systems should consider the guidance in the *Pronuptia* judgment to show that the know-how and its treatment in the agreement is outside the scope of Article 81(1) and therefore there is no need to benefit from the exemption granted by the Regulation.

The Guidelines confirm in certain respects that the judgment of the ECJ in *Pronuptia* which described the sort of provisions which are outside the scope of Article 81(1), can be relied upon. In this respect paragraph 44 of the Guidelines acknowledge that certain IP related obligations may not fall within Article 81(1). Paragraph 119(8) of the Guidelines states: *"The more the vertical restraint is linked to the transfer of know-how the more reason there may be to expect efficiencies to arise and the more a vertical restraint may be necessary to protect the know-how transferred or the investment costs incurred"*. This issue is again referred to in paragraph 200(1) of the Guidelines. *"In line with general rule 8 (see point 119) the more important the transfer of know-how, the more easily the vertical restraints fulfil the conditions for exemption"*.

Since in many franchise systems the franchisees may have had no previous experience of self employment or running a business and may have had no previous experience of the type of business being franchised the degree of importance to them is very high or do the Commission intend that there should be a subjective test of importance regardless of the state of experience or knowledge of the franchisee?

Territorial Rights

The prohibition in Article 4 against active or passive sales to end-users (which means professional end users or final consumers[10]) effectively destroys the concept of exclusive territorial rights for those franchise systems which are selective distribution systems for the purposes of the Regulation. Since it will only affect those operating at the retail level of trade, the impact may not be as great for many of those systems as was feared before the expression "operating at the retail level

10 Guidelines paragraph 53.

of trade" was inserted after the consultation process was completed in the Autumn of 1999.

The reference to the prohibition of operation out of an unauthorised place of establishment was to meet the point raised by franchisors that as they invariably grant rights to franchisees only to conduct their business from approved premises it would not be right to allow a franchisee to have carte blanche to open wherever he wanted to do so. In paragraph 19 of the ECJ *Pronuptia* judgment when explaining what was not a restriction within Article 81(1) the ECJ said "This is also the case with the franchisee's obligation only to sell the merchandise covered by the agreement in premises set up and decorated according to the franchisor's specifications which have as their purpose to guarantee a uniform image corresponding to specified requirements. The same requirements apply to the location of the shop, the choice of which is apt to affect the reputation of the network." The permitting of such a prohibition is therefore following the ECJ judgment. The issue was also raised with the Commission, from the franchising point of view, of what would be the situation where the franchisee operates a mobile franchise. That is to say where he serves his customers at their place of business or home. This is not dealt with in the regulation but in paragraph 54 of the Guidelines the Commission state: "If the dealer's outlet is mobile ("shop on wheels") an area may be defined outside which the mobile outlet cannot be operated". The problem is that paragraph 54 applies only where there is selective distribution. There do not seem to be any adverse competitive issues if the "dealers" are franchisees and not selective distributors. See also below on page [17].

The Guidelines deal extensively with the Commission's views on active and passive sales. Paragraph 50 defines active sales in the following way:

> *"Active sales mean: (1) actively approaching individual customers inside another distributor's exclusive territory or exclusive customer group by for instance direct mail or visits, or (2) actively approaching a specific customer group or customers in a specific territory allocated exclusively to another distributor through advertisement in media or other promotions specifically targeted at that customer group or targeted at customers in that territory, or (3) creating a warehouse or distribution outlet in any other distributor's exclusive territory."*

Passive sales are also defined in the same paragraph as follows:

> *"Passive sales mean: responding to unsolicited requests from individual customers including delivery of goods or services to such customers. General advertisement or promotion in media or on the Internet that reaches customer*

> *in other distributors' exclusive territories or customer groups but which is a reasonable way to reach customers outside those territories or customer groups, for instance to reach customers in non-exclusive territories or in ones own Territories."*

Passive sales have never been a practical problem for franchise systems. Active sales outside the territory creates great difficulty. Indeed, it would adversely impact the effect which franchise systems have on inter brand competition. In its comments in the Guidelines on market partitioning the Commission state in paragraph 114 *"the main negative effect on competition is a reduction of intra brand competition that may help the supplier to partition the market and thus hinder market integration. This may facilitate price discrimination. When most or all of the competing suppliers limit the sourcing or resale possibilities of their buyers this may facilitate collusion, either at the distributors level or at the suppliers level."*

In a sense this could be regarded as critical of franchise systems but ignores the thrust of their impact in the market place. So far as the consumer is concerned, many franchise systems have all the appearance of a system comprising multiple outlets in single ownership which competes with other brands and other businesses offering competitive products. It is the ability of the franchise system to provide its franchisees with benefits which as individuals, they would lack, in terms of bulk purchasing power, marketing, promotional and advisory support which enables these businesses to offer competition in the market place coupled with the interested and concerned service provided by an owner which results in more choice for the consumer.

In paragraph 116(8) the paragraph dealing with *"positive effects of vertical restraints"* the Commission state *"the following reasons may justify the application of certain vertical restraints"* ... (8) *"Uniformity and quality standarisation. A vertical restraint may help to increase sales is by creating a brand image and thereby increasing the attractiveness of a product to the final consumer by imposing a certain measure of uniformity and quality standardisation on the distributors. This can for instance be found in selective distribution and franchising."*

And then again in paragraph 119 under the general heading of "General rules for the evaluation of vertical restraints" the Commission states

> *"In evaluating vertical restraints from a competition policy perspective, some general rules can be formulated:*
>
> *1) For most vertical restraints competition concerns can only arise if there is insufficient inter brand competition"*

and again in sub-paragraph 2:

> *"vertical restraints which reduce inter brand competition are generally more harmful than vertical restraints that reduce intra brand competition"*

and then again in sub-paragraph 3:

> *"Vertical restraints from the limited distribution group, in the absence of sufficient inter brand competition may significantly restrict the choices available to consumers."*

and finally in sub-paragraph 8:

> *"The more the vertical restraint is linked to the transfer of know-how the more reason there may be to expect efficiencies to arise and the more a vertical restraint may be necessary to protect the know-how transferred or the investment costs incurred".*

All these statements by the Commission reinforce the importance of interband competition. In fact, one of the main impacts on the market of franchising is to stimulate interbrand competition. However, that positive impact relies on a degree of "market sharing" which is an inherent and necessary feature of franchising. The product which the franchisor is selling is essentially a recipe for the successful way of carrying on business within a tried and tested framework. The franchisor cannot ethically, and possibly at the risk of legal action, offer the prospect of success to a franchisee if the franchisor cannot allocate the market in a way in which each franchisee will benefit from having a sufficient market to exploit to enable him to make a success of his business and to be able to compete with other brands in the market place on a more equal footing. The ECJ in the *Pronuptia* judgment recognised the issue in paragraph 24 *"It is certainly possible that a prospective franchisee may not want to take the risk of joining a chain and making his investment, paying a relatively high entry fee and agreeing to pay a considerable annual fee, if he were not in a position to hope that his business would be profitable thanks to a certain amount of protection from competition by the franchisor and other franchisees".*

The Court continued *"This consideration can, however, be significant only in the context of an examination of the agreement in the light of the conditions of Article 85(3)".*

The example which the Commission provides of a franchise system in paragraph

201 of the Guidelines has the following features *"In addition, the franchisees are only allowed to sell from the agreed premises, are only allowed to sell to end users or other franchisees and are not allowed to sell other sweets. The franchisor has the obligation not to appoint another franchisee nor operate himself a retail outlet in a given contract territory."*

Further on in the example, when explaining why this sort of franchise agreement is likely to fulfil the conditions for exemption under Article 81(3) the Commission state *"The restrictions on selling (contract territory and selective distribution) provide an incentive to the franchisees to invest in the colouring machine and the franchise concept and, if not necessarily for, at least help to maintain the common identity thereby offsetting the loss of intra brand competition. The non-compete clause excluding other brands of sweets from the shops for the full duration of the agreements does allow the franchisor to keep the outlets uniform and prevent competitors from benefiting from its trade name. It does not lead to any serious foreclosure in view of the great number of potential outlets available to other sweet producers".*

It is not clear, although the Commission assert, that there is "selective distribution" included in the restriction on selling, that the restrictions described amount to selective distribution at all and certainly not in the way in which that expression is defined in the regulation. This aspect of the example re-enforces the view expressed above. (See page 98.)

In its analysis it is also puzzling to read in paragraph 148 of the Guidelines "For final products, foreclosure is in general more likely to occur at the retail level given the significant entry barriers for most manufacturers to start retail outlets just for their own products". It is these significant entry barriers for most manufacturers which led those who have ventured into franchising to do so since franchising substantially reduces those barriers. By and large, it seems that the Commission presents a very convincing argument for the benefits of franchising. Given the Commission's policy statement and the guidance from the European Court of Justice it would seem that the Commission would be in considerable difficulty in denying franchise systems the benefit of exemption under Article 81(3) except in the most exceptional cases – for example where price fixing in breach of Article 4(a) is present.

The Guidelines also raise the issue of the use of the Internet. In paragraph 51 the Commission state *"Every distributor must be free to use the Internet to advertise or to sell products. A restriction on the use of Internet by distributors could only be compatible with the Block Exemption Regulation to the extent that promotion on the Internet or sales over the Internet would lead to active selling into other distributors' exclusive territories or customer groups."*

The Commission also acknowledges that *"the supplier may require quality standards for the use of the Internet site to resell its goods just as the supplier may require quality standards for a shop or for advertising and promotion in general"*.

At the end of paragraph 51 the Commission state *"An outright ban on Internet or catalogue selling is only possible if there is an objective justification"*.

The Internet issue raises problems for franchise systems arising not only from the points already discussed but also from the fundamental view point of what the franchise system is. A franchisee is only given the right to carry on the franchise business in accordance with the franchisor's system. In the example to which reference has already been made (it appears in paragraph 194 of the Guidelines) it is quite clear that the business there described could not be operated as required by the franchisor if the franchisee were to offer products for sale on the Internet.

This brings us to the basic issue of who controls the way in which the business presents itself to the consumer in the environment and creating the ambience in which the franchisor considers that its franchised businesses should be operated. A combination of the common identity and reputation and the use of IP rights need to be capable of protection. It is quite clear in the example in the Guidelines to which reference is made that the manufacturer has made a success of its operation *"through a number of its own retail outlets all operating under the same trade name and with the uniform fun image (style of layout of the shops common advertising etc) ... the franchisees are obliged to buy the sweets liquid and colouring machine from the manufacturer to have the same image and operate under the trade name pay a franchise fee, contribute to the common advertising ... the franchisees are only allowed to sell from the agreed premises"*.

The Commission state later in the example *"Most of the obligations contained in the franchise agreements can be assessed as necessary to protect the intellectual property rights or maintain the common identity and reputation of the franchise network and fall outside Article 81(1)."* Many franchise systems argue that they satisfy these criteria and that selling on the Internet would damage the common identity and reputation of the franchised network. Whether the Commission will take the same view remains to be seen. The common identity issue is almost self evident since if franchisees had a choice as to whether or not they sold on the Internet the common identity would be lost as selling methods would differ between those who had a web site and those who did not. Methods of presentation of the website could differ. The use of the franchisor's name would also have to be a feature of the website if the franchisee's business is to be so promoted. Quite apart from the fact that its use may not be authorised except at the trading premises and in a particular way the franchisor would not be in full control of its IP rights. Also, the reputation of the system which is associated with the quality of service and the standards of the products (including freshness where appropriate) and services provided could be at risk since it would not be structured to accommodate Internet sales (see example in Guidelines referred to above). The Commission acknowledge (see paragraph 31 *"In other words restrictions, concerning the assignment or use of IPRs can be covered when the main object of the agreement is the purchase or distribution of goods or services"*.

This must mean that the owner of the intellectual property rights must be in a position to supervise and control the quality of standards and the way in which products or services are sold using the IP rights. Otherwise, the reputation would be put substantially at risk. This is only possible where the IPRs are not the main object of the agreement which should always be the case in genuine franchise systems.

Non-Exclusive Territories

The exclusion of exclusive territories from the prohibition in Article 4(b) is to be welcomed but there are systems which operate with non-exclusive territories. The Guidelines give no assistance except in a reference to non-exclusive territories in the definition of "passive sales" in paragraph 50.

Clearly, the Commission regards non-exclusive territories as having the potential to involve market-sharing[11].

> "(22) *The combined effect of the clause which prohibits the franchisee from setting up further outlets outside his own territory, and the territorial protection clause which prevetns the franchisee from actively seeking customers outside his territory, results in a certain degree of market-sharing between the franchisees, thus restricting competition within the Service-Master network.*
>
> *This territorial protection is, however, limited by two elements: the franchisee holds a non-exclusive right only within his territory with regard to ServiceMaster itself and each franchisee is entitled to provide services to non-solicited customers outside his territory."*

A non-exclusive territory per se is not an infringement of Article 81(1) but if there is a vertical agreement which means one has to review what vertical restraints there are which infringe Article 81(1). If the restraint prevents the franchisee from actually selling outside the territory it cannot benefit from the exception to Article

11 ServiceMaster decision 88/604/EEC OJ [1988] L 332/38.

4(b) of the Regulation since the other territories will also be non-exclusive although, of course, the Franchisor could reserve the exclusive rights to all territories and customer group not granted to the individual franchisee. Since the effect of a non-exclusive territory is to allow the franchisor to operate within the territory itself or to appoint another franchisee to operate within the territory it is somewhat ironic to find that non-exclusive territories are not able to escape the blanket prohibition of Article 4(b) and thus not escape from Article 4(c) by not incorporating the elements of selective distribution.

It is interesting to read the Commission's analysis of the non-exclusive territorial clause coupled with a ban on active out of territory sales in the *ServiceMaster* decision[12].

"(24) *The ServiceMaster standard form franchise agreement contributes, through the combined effect of all its provisions, to improving the supply of the services concerned for the following reasons:*

- *it helps ServiceMaster rapidly to penetrate new markets with only limited investments, in this case the markets of all 12 Member States,*
- *this rapid development of a European-wide service network increases inter-brand competition with other service providers in the various markets concerned,*
- *it helps a great number of small undertakings to enter a new market by allowing them to set up outlets more rapidly and with a higher chance of success because they receive the benefit of ServiceMaster's name and reputation, and of its technical, commercial and administrative know-how,*
- *it permits an intensive servicing of customers through the personal commitment of independent traders.*

(25) *The ServiceMaster standard form franchise agreement allows consumers a fair share of the benefit resulting from the above improvements in the supply of services. First, the network as a whole is intended to provide a better an uniformly high-quality service to consumers. Secondly, as already mentioned in the preceeding paragraph, consumers will benefit from the efficient service which the franchisee will be encouraged to provide as an independent trader who has a personal an direct interest in the success of*

12 *Ibid.*

his business. Thirdly, the freedom which consumers enjoy to obtain services elsewhere in the network will force franchisees to pass on to consumers a reasonable part of the benefits of this intra-band competition. Finally, because of a strong inter-brand competition, the franchisees can be expected to offer better services and prices.

(26) *The provisions falling within Article 85(1) are indispensable to the establishment and existence of the franchise network: the limited territorial protection granted to the franchisees is necessary to obtain and protect their investment, comprising* inter alia *the cost of the establishment and maintenance of the business premises, the payment of the initial franchise fee, the acquisition of the necessary means of transport for the carrying out of the services at the customers' premises and the acquisition of special equipment. The limited territorial protection is also necessary to ensure that the franchisees will concentrate their service activity on their own territory. On the other hand, the franchisees retain passive service rights in other territories and remain free in the determination of their sales prices.*

(27) *The ServiceMaster standard form franchise agreement does not afford its members the possibility of eliminating competition in respect of a substantial part of the services concerned.*

The inter-brand competition in the market concerned is both very strong and open: the market for cleaning, housekeeping and maintenance service is highly competitive, with a large number of firms supplying similar or identical services. It is also a market with no barriers to entry, with the result that new suppliers can at any time challenge any attempt by ServiceMaster or its franchisees to increase their prices.

Intra-brand competition within the ServiceMaster network itself is also preserved: the limited territorial protection does not grant the franchisees any marketing or customer exclusivity. Franchisees are free to provide services to non-solicited customers resident outside their own territory. This brings about a certain degree of price competition between franchisees, who are free to determine their sales prices.

(28) *The notified agreement therefore meets all the requirements for an exemption under Article 85(3)."*

The same reasoning could well be applied to many systems unless there is a market without competition of any significance.

There are two other considerations. According to the Guidelines (paragraph 50) a mobile franchisee, if in a selective distribution system, can be prevented from using his vehicle outside his territory. If there is a mobile franchise with non-exclusive territories whose contract contains such a provision the franchisee cannot effectively service customers outside the territory and the problem does not exist. (See discussion on selective distribution on page 87).

Where there is not a mobile franchise the more likely category to have a problem is the business to business sector where franchisees would and do welcome the opportunity to try to pick up business wherever it may be available. National accounts are often a problem since individual franchisees can be incapable of coping with the volumes of business generated but many would not be deterred by their deficiencies.

A result of such selling efforts would result in individual franchisees operating under the same brand offering different terms of business to the same prospective customers. There are instances where such conduct results in no business for the system at all since the prospective customer does not understand how the same brand can offer different terms. This results in disbelief and damage to the reputation of the brand.

Franchisors placed in this position should examine whether they can institute controls to achieve their objective by relying on the *Pronuptia* judgment's conclusion that *"Clauses which institute controls indispensable for the preservation of the identity and reputation of the network symbolised by the sign do not constitute restrictions of competition within the meaning of Article 85(1) (now 81(1))"*.

One would expect that if the Commission is called upon to issue a decision or guidance in relation to non-exclusive territories it would place them in at least the same position as exclusive territories for the purposes of Article 4(b) of the Regulation (but see further Chapter 8).

Non-compete clauses

The non-compete clause is in two parts. The first part which includes being involved in a competing business and product ties applies during the term of the agreement and the second part which relates to post term restraints on competition by definition applies after the agreement has come to an end. We shall examine each.

The restriction on competition by involvement in a competing business during the term is limited to 5 years which on the face of it means that a franchise agreement should not exceed 5 years. However, given the decision of the ECJ in the Pronutpia case and its views on know-how (see discussion above) and the protection which it affords a franchisor, franchisors should rely on that judgment rather than seeking to rely on the exemption. If the *Pronuptia* judgment is followed the restrictions introduced into the contract should not be infringing Article 81(1) and the regulation would be irrelevant.

The issue does not end there. The permitted post term restraint on completion contained in Article 5(b) is worthless since it affords no protection against unfair competition. As if that were not bad enough, the reference to know-how sets a test which is difficult to follow.

The definition of substantial establishes an indispensability test. Assuming one can overcome that hurdle Article 5(b) states "thirdly, it (the restraint) must be indispensable to protect know-how transferred". So not only must the know-how be indispensable for the sale of the products or services, the restraint must be indispensable to protect the know-how. Given the uncertainty about what the first indispensability test means the second test makes it much more difficult, particularly given the reality that the Commissions own other parameters make it impossible to achieve.

One is inclined to the view that following the Commission's own Guidelines and the *Pronuptia* decision would enable franchisors to structure know-how restraints to ensure that they do not infringe Article 81(1).

Paragraphs 116 (5) and 119 (8) of the Guidelines which appear respectively under the headings "Positive effects of vertical restraints" and "General rules for the evaluation of vertical restraints" provide much useful guidance.

> *"The specific hold-up problem that may arise in the case of transfer or substantial know-how. The know-how, once provided cannot be taken back and the provider of the know-how may not want it to be used for or by its competitors. In as far as the know-how was not readily available to the buyer, is substantial and indispensable for the operation of the agreement, such a transfer may justify a non-compete type of restriction. This would normally fall outside Article 81(1)."*[13]

> *"The more the vertical restraint is lined to the transfer of know-how, the more reason there may be to expect efficiencies to arise and the more a vertical restraint may be necessary to protect the know-how transferred or the investment costs incurred."*[14]

Paragraph 157 supports the view we recommend.

---

13 Guidelines, paragraph 116(5).

14 Guidelines, paragraph 119(8).

> *"The transfer of substantial know-how (efficiency 5) usually justifies a non-compete obligation for the whole duration of the supply agreement, as for example in the context of franchising."*[15]

These three paragraphs combined with the principles laid down in the *Pronuptia* decision provide a powerful argument for justifying that a longer than 5 years in term restriction does not infringe Article 81(1) or, if it does, should benefit from exemption.

So far as the tied buying arrangement is concerned, as the Commission acknowledge in paragraph 200(2) of the Guidelines *"a non-compete obligation on the goods or services purchased by the franchisee falls outside Article 81(1) when the obligation is necessary to maintain the common identity and reputation of the franchised network. In such cases also the duration of the non-compete obligation is irrelevant under Article 81(1) as long as it does not exceed the duration of the franchise agreement itself."* Most franchise systems should be able to satisfy that requirement which would mean that their restrictions would not be within Article 81(1) and the Regulation would be irrelevant from that point of view. It should be borne in mind that this principle which flows from the *Pronuptia* decision is not limited to tied buying but to any other aspect of the franchise relationship where it is relevant. For a discussion of the other issues referred to in Article 5(1) see Chapter 4.

The post term restraint is discussed in Chapter 4 and in the comments above in this Chapter under the heading "know-how".

Generally

The regulation provides that agreements already in force on 31 May 2000 which satisfy the conditions for exemption provided in the 1988 regulation will remain exempt from Article 81(1) until 31 December 2001, assuming they do not satisfy the conditions for exemption provided for in the new regulation. This means that franchise systems with agreements which do not expire until after the 31 December 2001 will need to consider their strategy for introducing change if on an investigation of their contractual and business arrangements changes need to be made in order to comply with the new regulation and obtain the benefit of the exemption which it affords.

In developing their strategy franchisors should also bear in mind the following:

---

[15] Guidelines, paragraph 157.

- *"Companies are encouraged to do their own assessment without notification. In the case of an individual examination by the Commission the latter will bear the burden of proof that the agreement in question infringes Articles 81(1)"*[16]
- *"This means in practice that no precautionary notification needs to be made. If a dispute arises, an undertaking can still notify, in which case the Commission can exempt the vertical agreement with retroactive effect from the date of entry into force of the agreement if all four conditions of Article 81(3) are fulfilled. A notifying party does not have to explain why the agreement was not notified earlier and will not be denied retroactive exemption simply because it did not notify earlier. Any notification will be reviewed on its merits."*[17]
- *"In addition, the Commission considers that, subject to cumulative effect and hardcore restrictions, agreements between small and medium-sized undertakings as defined in the Annex to Commission Recommendation 96/280/EC are rarely capable of appreciably affecting trade between Member States or of appreciably restricting competition within the meaning of Article 81(1), and therefore generally fall outside the scope of application of Article 81(1). In cases where such agreements nonetheless meet the conditions for the application of Article 81(1), the Commission will normally refrain from opening proceedings for lack of sufficient Community interest unless these undertakings collectively or individually hold a dominant position in a substantial part of the common market."*[18]

Franchisors should take comfort from these guides. The last means that many franchise companies which are small or medium-sized undertakings are low risk, particularly if the totality of their arrangements result from an informed and careful consideration of the issues.

The same approach should also enable franchisors who need to notify for whatever reason to be able to provide the Commission with a convincing case for exemption and reduce or eliminate the risk of fines.

---

16 Guidelines, paragraph 62.

17 Guidelines, paragraph 63.

18 Guidelines, paragraph 11.

In some cases fundamental changes may have to be made. In other cases minimal adjustment may suffice. This exercise is best embarked upon sooner rather than later and the risks should not be ignored.

CHAPTER 8

EXCLUSIVE AND SELECTIVE DISTRIBUTION

INTRODUCTION

The agreements considered in this Chapter can be classified as:

- *exclusive distribution agreements* whereby a supplier appoints a distributor for a territory. The buyer buys the goods from a supplier on his own account and resells them. Typically the distributor agrees not to deal in competing products while the supplier agrees not to supply products in the territory himself or to appoint another distributor in that territory;
- *selective distribution agreements* whereby the supplier also sells goods to a distributor who resells on his own account. In a selective distribution agreement the supplier wants to control the outlets where its product is sold to the public. The supplier sells only to approved dealers and tells those dealers (usually retailers) to sell only to the public or other approved dealers. Selective distribution is used typically for prestige branded products and/or technically complex products.

Both exclusive distribution and selective distribution agreements potentially benefit from the Regulation. For both, the Regulation is likely to be the starting point for the competition analysis. This Chapter deals first with exclusive distribution (including exclusive customer allocation and non exclusive distribution) and then with selective distribution.

EXCLUSIVE DISTRIBUTION

Paragraph 161 of the Guidelines identify an exclusive distribution agreement as one in which *"the supplier agrees to sell its products only to one distributor for resale in a particular territory. At the same time the distributor is usually limited in its active selling into other exclusively allocated territories"*.

In an exclusive distribution relationship the potentially restrictive effect on competition stems first from the fact that the exclusive distributor is appointed as the only source of the products in the contract territory (except to the extent that parallel imports may occur) and second from the fact the distributor will typically agree not to deal in competing products. As noted in paragraph 161 of the Guidelines the possible competition risks are mainly reduced intra-brand competition and market partitioning resulting from the grant of an exclusive territory.

In practice, the anti-competitive potential of these restrictions may be outweighed by the positive benefits of achieving efficient distribution of products by incentivising the distributor to maximise sales in its contract territory. Nevertheless, the Commission in its early decisions on vertical agreements[1] consistently regarded exclusive dealing provisions as falling within Article 81(1) subject to the de minimis rules. The Commission perceived exclusive distribution agreements as potentially dividing the common market and so typically treated exclusive distribution agreements as infringing Article 81(1) but as candidates for exemption under Article 81(3)[2]. As noted above, this approach induced a flood of precautionary notifications prompting the Commission to adopt specific block exemptions benefiting exclusive distribution agreements, being Regulation 1967/67 which on expiry was replaced by Regulation 1983/83.

THE APPLICABILITY OF ARTICLE 81(1) TO EXCLUSIVE DISTRIBUTION

In assessing the application of Article 81(1) it is, as with other agreements, necessary to take into account not only the provisions of the exclusive distribution agreement but also the whole surrounding legal and economic context. The methodology as summarised in section 1.4 of the Guidelines is described in Chapter 6 above.

On a full economic analysis it may well be that the grant of an exclusive territory does not infringe Article 81(1) at all. The leading cases, *Société la Technique Minière* and *Consten and Grundig* are discussed in Chapter 2 above.

Other clauses which have been held to infringe Article 81(1) include:

- obligation on the distributor not to sell competing products;
- obligation on the distributor to purchase all or a proportion of its requirements of the contract goods from the supplier;

1 See, for example, *Consten and Grundig v. Commission* (56 and 58/64) [1966] ECR 299.

2 The approach of the Commission can be contrasted to some extent with that of the CFI and ECJ which appeared less likely to find that exclusivity required exemption. See for example *Société la Technique Minière* 56/65 (1966) ECR 235.

- obligation on the distributor not to engage in active sales promotion outside the territory;
- obligation on the distributor not sell outside the EC;
- restrictions on the customers to whom the goods may be sold or the channels through which they may be sold or the purposes for which they may be sold;
- resale price maintenance;
- obligations on the distributor not to advertise or promote the contract products outside the contract territory.

Other obligations and restrictions on advertising and promotion; packaging; maintenance of stocks; provision of ancillary services; provision of warranty services; purchase of complete range/minimum quantities will in most cases fall outside Article 81(1) although these would need to be assessed on their particular facts since certain restrictions on advertising or packaging, for example, may in practice have the effect of impeding parallel imports.

EXEMPTION UNDER ARTICLE 81(3)

In practice, the starting point for the analysis of an exclusive distribution agreement has been Regulation 1983/83 and in future will be the Regulation since the question of whether the agreement infringes Article 81(1) at all will not be relevant if in any event it benefits from the Regulation.

REGULATION 1983/83

By virtue of Article 12 of the Regulation agreements entered into before 31 March 2000 will continue to be exempt for a transitional period running until the end of 2001 as if the provisions of regulation 1983/83 were still in force.

The terms of Regulation 1983/83 therefore remain relevant for many pre-existing distribution agreements since in practice a very large number of ongoing distribution agreements will have been drafted to comply with that Regulation over the last 17 years.

It is outside of the scope of this work to include a detailed analysis of Regulation 1983/83 particularly as most of the specific case law on that Regulation will not be relevant to the interpretation of the Regulation. However, given that so many agreements have in practice been drafted within the terms of Regulation 1983/83 the

- to sell the contract goods under trade marks or packed and presented as specified by the other party (Article 2(3)(b));
- to make measures for promotion of sales, in particular: to advertise, to maintain a sales network or stock of goods, to provide customer a guarantee of services, to employ staff having specialised or technical training (Article 2(3)(c)).

Regulation 1983/83 does not exempt any other restrictions on competition and by implication therefore prohibits any form of resale price maintenance, absolute territorial protection or any restrictions which extend beyond the period of the agreement including a post term non compete.

THE REGULATION

The Checklist included in Chapter 9 sets out the questions to ask when determining whether the Regulation will benefit an agreement. In considering the list of hardcore restrictions, Article 4(b) is important for exclusive or sole[3] distribution agreements because it represents a change from the position under Regulation 1983/83.

Article 4(b) blacklists any restriction of the territory into which or of the customers to whom the buyer may sell the contract goods or services except:

- the restriction of active sales into the exclusive territory or to an exclusive customer group reserved to the supplier or allocated by the supplier to another buyer where such a restriction does not limit sales by the customers of the buyer.

Any other form of active sales ban will remove the benefit of the Regulation from the whole agreement. The key difference from the position under Regulation 1983/83 is the reference to a territory or customer group "reserved to the supplier or allocated by the supplier to another buyer". Presumably a ban on active sales which would have been permissible under Regulation 1983/83 will not benefit from the Regulation if the supplier cannot demonstrate that the relevant territory has been reserved to itself or allocated to an alternative dealer. This additional requirement

3 A sole distribution agreement is one in which the supplier appoints only one distributor for the contract territory but reserves the right himself to supply customers within the territory. In an exclusive agreement, the supplier agrees in addition that he will not supply into the territory.

should therefore be addressed in the drafting of exclusive distribution agreements although the supplier may, if challenged, be able to demonstrate that in fact the relevant territories have been reserved or allocated. In the absence of an express clause in the contract, the supplier could also seek to argue that by implication he has reserved to himself any territories not exclusively granted. The point could be problematic in the relatively common situation where a supplier wishes to roll out his product progressively through Europe by appointing a distributor in its home territory and once the product gains acceptance in the market then appointing other distributors in other EC countries. If the supplier wishes to ensure that the first distributor does not make active sales into other EC territories, then it should in the initial distribution agreement expressly reserve to itself the right to sell in territories other than that granted to the distributor.

In addition, the Regulation will not benefit any clauses listed in Article 5 (although the inclusion of such non exempted clauses will not remove benefit of the exemption from the rest of the agreement). Article 5(a) is of particular relevance to exclusive distribution. Article 5 provides:

> *"The exemption provided for in Article 2 shall not apply to any of the following obligations contained in vertical agreements:*
>
> *(a) any direct or indirect non-compete obligation, the duration of which is indefinite or exceeds five years. A non-compete obligation which is tacitly renewable beyond a period of five years is to be deemed to have been concluded for an indefinite duration. However, the time limitation of five years shall not apply where the contract goods or services are sold by the buyer from premises and land owned by the supplier or leased by the supplier from third parties not connected with the buyer, provided that the duration of the non-compete obligation does not exceed the period of occupancy of the premises and land by the buyer ..."*

For these purposes Article 1 provides that "non compete obligation" means both an obligation on the exclusive distributor not to manufacture, purchase, sell or resell goods or services which compete with the contract goods or services and an obligation on the exclusive distributor to purchase from the supplier or from another undertaking designated by a supplier more than 80% of the distributor's total purchases of the contract goods or services and their substitutes on the relevant market.

The Restriction is therefore more limited than Regulation 1983/83 since that Regulation permits a non compete obligation for the duration of the agreement and does not impose any limit on duration of the agreement. Also Regulation 1983/83 expressly permits an obligation on the distributor to purchase its requirements of the goods only from the supplier.

The rationale for making the Regulation stricter in this respect is not clear. Although paragraphs 57 to 59 of the Guidelines discuss this clause they do not offer any justification for it. Presumably the Commission took the view that for most agreements a five year non-compete would be sufficient bearing in mind the specific investments made in connection with the agreement. However, the approach could be criticised as being arbitrary and too restrictive. An alternative approach might have been to exempt product ties but expressly state in the Guidelines the circumstances in which a non-compete for longer than 5 years might justify withdrawal of the exemption. In particular, there would appear to be no justification in competition law terms for distinguishing between a situation where a supplier leases premises and one where it does not.

An exclusive distribution agreement which includes non compete restrictions which go beyond the terms of Article 5 will still benefit from the Regulation. However, the non compete restrictions themselves will not and, if challenged, must be exempted on an individual basis. Of course there is no presumption of illegality in respect of a clause outside the Block Exemption Regulation as is confirmed in para. 62 of the Guidelines. In this respect, para. 158 and para. 171 of the Guidelines gives some comfort. Paragraph 158 states:

> *"Below the level of dominance the combination of non compete with exclusive distribution may also justify the non compete obligation lasting the full length of the agreement. In the latter case, the non compete obligation is likely to improve the distribution efforts of the exclusive distributor in his territory."*

Paragraph 171 states:

> *"Therefore in the absence of [significant] foreclosure effect, the combination of exclusive distribution with non-compete is exemptable for the whole duration of the agreement, particularly at the wholesale level"*

The net result of this is that in practice, the position under the new rules may not diverge from that under Regulation 1983/83 in those cases where the market is not foreclosed by networks of similar agreements. Many non compete clauses will be justified by reference to the need to focus the distribution effort of the distributor in its territory and so are likely to be permissible.

The second type of non-exemptable clause identified in Article 5 is a post-term non-compete. The Regulation permits a post term non-compete in an exclusive distribution agreement but only on the strict conditions listed in Article 5(b). As noted in Chapter 4 the fact that the non-compete is permitted only in relation to the "premises and land from which the buyer has operated during the contract period" may make it commercially useless in many situations. Whilst there is room for debate as to what is meant by the "premises and land from which the buyer operated", the Guidelines at paragraph 60 seem to take a restrictive interpretation and refer to the "point of sale from which the buyer has operated". Presumably this means a shop or office rather than a territory.

Summary of the Changes for Exclusive Distribution

In summary, the Regulation adopts a more flexible approach in most respects compared to that under Regulation 1983/83. For example:

- the Regulation benefits services as well as goods;
- the Regulation is not limited to goods for resale and will cover a situation where goods are supplied for further processing, alteration or integration before being resold;
- the Regulations applies to agreements entered into between more than two parties;
- under the Regulation the supplier can allocate to the reseller the exclusive right to sell to a specified category of customers (albeit that the supplier cannot stop passive sales to these customers);
- finally, any obligations or restrictions not listed in Articles 4 or 5 of the Regulation are exempted automatically. In other words, it is not necessary to analyse any other restrictions to see if they restrict competition.

The Regulation is, however, stricter in the following respects:

- it only benefits agreements beneath the 30% market share test;
- a supplier can only prohibit active sales into an exclusive territory reserved to the supplier or allocated to another buyer;
- a non compete obligation (as defined in Article 1) is exempted only for a period of 5 years (or the period of a lease if the supplier leases premises to the buyer). That said in some circumstances a non compete obligation may be justified for the duration of the agreement on an individual basis.

AGREEMENTS OUTSIDE THE REGULATION

Paragraphs 161-183 of the Guidelines discuss the applicability of Article 81 to agreements outside the Regulation. These paragraphs principally cover the situation where the supplier will have a market share greater than 30% but does not include a blacklisted clause. If an exclusive distribution agreement includes a blacklisted clause then it is unlikely to benefit from individual exemption.

Where the market share threshold is exceeded the Guidelines state at para. 163 that the market position of the supplier and its competitors is of major importance as the loss of intra-brand competition can only be problematic if inter-brand competition is limited. The stronger the position of the supplier the more serious is the loss of intra-brand competition above the 30% market share threshold. In order to be exemptable, the loss of intra-brand competition needs to be balanced with real efficiencies.

The approach adopted by the Commission is to analyse in turn the key factors identified at para. 121 and to apply each to the situation of exclusive distribution.

- Market position of the supplier: is obviously of major importance (para. 163).
- Market position of competitors: can be two-edged. Strong competitors should lead to strong inter-brand competition and so outweigh loss of inter-brand competitors. However, a very concentrated market increases the risk of collusion. Also if two or more powerful suppliers appoint the same exclusive distributor, the risk of collusion may even justify withdrawal of the Regulation (para. 164).
- Entry barriers: a non-compete clause in an exclusive distribution agreement may foreclose opportunities for other suppliers to enter (para. 165). Foreclosure of distributors is likely to be a problem only where the exclusive distributor itself has buyer power across an important territory (e.g. a major supermarket has exclusive rights to a leading brand). In extreme cases this may lead to withdrawal of the Regulation (para. 166).
- Market position of buyer: buyer power may be problematic but only where "important buyers" impose the exclusive distribution arrangements as a result of which collusion between those buyers becomes a risk (para. 167).
- Maturity of the market: loss of intra-brand competition is likely to be more serious in a mature market (para. 168).
- Level of trade: at the retail level the Commission states that loss of intra-brand competition is especially likely if coupled with large territories since

consumer choice may be limited (para. 169). At the wholesale level, large territories are less likely to raise issues (para. 170).

The combination of exclusive distribution and exclusive purchasing (i.e. the exclusive distributor is required to buy from the supplier) precludes arbitrage between distributors. As a result this combination is unlikely to be exempted for suppliers with a market share above 30% and may even lead to withdrawal of the block exemption below 30% if clear and substantial efficiencies do not flow (para. 172).

- Nature of the product: is not a crucial factor in assessing the anti-competitive effect of exclusive distribution. In considering exemption, products which require significant investment such as branded products, new or complex products are more likely to generate efficiencies outweighing any competitive detriment (para. 174).

Three examples of exclusive distribution and included at paras 175-7. All deal with situations of concentrated markets where the supplier has significant market share. Given the importance of individual assessment of the market structure in such cases, the examples should be treated with some caution when seeking to apply them to potentially analogous real life situations. However, they may indicate the likely approach of the Commission in general terms.

EXCLUSIVE CUSTOMER ALLOCATION

"In an exclusive customer allocation arrangement, the supplier agrees to sell his products only to one distributor for resale to a particular class of customers. At the same time the distributor is usually limited in his active selling to other exclusively allocated classes of customers." (para. 178)

Exclusive customer allocation is treated in the same way as the allocation of exclusive territories and the above comments in relation to exclusive distribution broadly apply.

However, the Commission states at para. 180 that above the 30% market share threshold, exclusive customer allocation is unlikely to be exemptable unless there are clear and substantial efficiency effects.

A combination of exclusive customer allocation and selective distribution will fall foul of Article 4 and is unlikely to be exemptable.

NON-EXCLUSIVE DISTRIBUTION

ıon-exclusive distribution arrangement may benefit from the Regulation, uming of course that it infringes Article 81(1) in the first place. Many non-lusive distribution agreements will not be anti-competitive if they have no reciable effect on intra-brand or inter-brand competition. That said, the inclusion ıny of the "hard core provisions" in Article 4 of the Regulation will still bring a -exclusive agreement within Article 81(1) subject to de minimis and so, for mple, a ban on meeting unsolicited orders from outside the territory will not be mitted.

The wording of Article 4(b) which is replicated in paragraph 12(2)(b) in the ft Notice on Agreements of Minor Importance appears to pose a problem in ition to a prohibition on active sales outisde the allocated territory/customer up as well. This is because Article 4(b) permits such a restriction only where territory in question is exclusively reserved to the supplier or allocated to another er. If the supplier operates a network of non-exclusive distributors, this will be the case. This interpretation suggests that a prohibition on active sales outside territory in a non-exclusive agreement might be considered hard-core whereas same clause in an exclusive agreement would not.

SELECTIVE DISTRIBUTION

agraph 184 of the Guidelines contrast Selective Distribution Agreements with clusive Distribution Agreements:

> *'184 Selective distribution agreements, like exclusive distribution agreements, estrict on the one hand the number of authorised distributors and on the other hand the possibilities of resale. The difference with exclusive distribution is that he restriction on the number of dealers does not depend on the number of erritories but on selection criteria linked in the first place to the nature of the product. Another difference with exclusive distribution is that the restriction on esale is not a restriction on active selling to a territory but a restriction on any sales to non-authorised distributors, leaving only appointed dealers and final customers as possible buyers. Selective distribution is almost always used to distribute branded final products."*

the purposes of the Regulation, selective distribution has a specific meaning. ective distribution system is defined in Article 1(d) as:

> *"A distribution system where the supplier undertakes to sell the contract goods or services, either directly or indirectly, only to distributors selected on the basis of specified criteria and where these distributors undertake not to sell such goods or services to unauthorised distributors"*

This definition is interesting for a number of reasons. First, it may well be possible in practice to operate some sort of selective system of approved dealers without expressly including in the agreement with the dealer either or both of the restrictions identified in this definition of selective distribution system. Presumably a system which operates in practice as a selective distribution system will be treated as such whatever the specific wording of the agreement. But what of a system where only one of the two restrictions in the definition is applied in practice? In other words, the system bears many of the characteristics of a selective system but the supplier permits the possibility of some goods circulating outside the system. In such a case, presumably the system could not be regarded as a selective distribution system within the meaning of the Regulation. This may be important as the Regulation is in some important respects more restrictive of selective systems than of other distribution types.

Second, the definition in the Regulation does not differentiate between different types of selective distribution systems. Conventionally under EC law a distinction has been drawn between so called "qualitative" systems and "quantitative" systems[4]. Qualitative systems are those under which dealers are selected on the basis of predetermined and non-discriminatory qualitative criteria relating to their technical ability to handle the goods or the suitability of their premises. These "simple systems" generally fall outside Article 81(1) altogether. Under a quantitative system the numbers may be limited, for example by limiting the number of dealers in a given area or imposing minimum or maximum sales targets (unlike qualitative systems where all suitable qualified dealers are admitted.)

Whilst the Regulation does not expressly include the distinction, it remains important in any analysis of a selective system. Indeed this is expressly recognised at para. 185 of the Guidelines which states "To assess the possible anti-competitive effects of selective distribution under Article 81(1), a distinction needs to be made between purely qualitative selective distribution and quantitative selective distribution."

---

4 It is interesting to note that in early drafts of the Regulation the distinction between the two types of distribution was preserved and only removed relatively late in the consultation process.

A selective system can restrict competition for the obvious reason that non-authorised dealers will not be able to sell the product in question. The main risk is therefore a reduction in "intra-brand competition". In many cases there may be no adverse effect on inter-brand competition which may even be enhanced. Paragraph 185 of the Guidelines identifies as competition risks:

"a reduction in intra-brand competition and, especially in case of cumulative effect, foreclosure of certain type(s) of distributor and facilitation of collusion between suppliers or buyers."

Cumulative effect here means a number of similar systems operating in parallel in the market and is discussed below.

QUALITATIVE SYSTEMS OUTSIDE ARTICLE 81(1)

The general principle that a qualitative system can fall outside Article 81(1) was recognised by the European Court in the Metro cases[5]. The Metro cases concerned the distribution system operated by a German company, SABA, for the sale of television, radio and music equipment in Germany and certain other Member States. SABA notified its system to the Commission and received exemption under Article 81(3) in 1976 and this exemption was renewed in 1983. Both Commission decisions were challenged by Metro which was a distribution warehouse which had been refused supplies by SABA.

SABA was prepared to supply wholesalers who firstly fulfilled certain qualitative criteria: ie that they were technically qualified, employed specialised staff, operated a specialist shop or department, provided adequate servicing facilities etc. and secondly fulfilled certain conditional criteria (ie were willing to enter into six months supply contracts to achieve certain levels of turnover, to maintain certain stock levels etc.). The Commission held that the first set of qualitative criteria fell outside Article 85(1) and that the second set fell within Article 85(1) but could be granted exemption under Article 85(3).

In reviewing the Commission's decision, the Court held that:

"the Commission was justified in recognising that selective distribution systems [constitute], together with others, an aspect of competition which accords with

5 Case 26/76 *Metro v. Commission* (No.1) [1977] ECR 1875 and Case 75/84 *Metro v. Commission* (No.2) [1986] ECR 3021.

Article 85(1), provided that resellers are chosen on the basis of objective criteria of a qualitative nature relating to the technical qualification of the reseller and his staff and suitability of his trading premises and that such conditions are laid down uniformly for all potential resellers and are not applied in a discriminatory fashion"[6]

In summary, selective distribution agreements will not infringe Article 81(1) provided that three conditions are satisfied. These are identified in page 185 of the Guidelines, as follows:

"First, the nature of the product in question must necessitate a selective distribution system, in the sense that such a system must constitute a legitimate requirement, having regard to the nature of the product concerned, to preserve its quality and ensure its proper use. Secondly, resellers must be chosen on the basis of objective criteria of a qualitative nature which are laid down uniformly for all potential resellers and are not applied in a discriminatory manner. Thirdly, the criteria laid down must not go beyond what is necessary."

NATURE OF GOODS

Not all products require selective distribution system to protect quality. The types of products which have in the past been held to be worthy of selective distribution tend to be either technically complex products such as cars, televisions, hi-fi, cameras, computers, etc. or prestige or branded products such as perfumes, high quality watches, jewellery, glass crystal etc.

Of course, there will be border line cases. For example, in *Yves St Laurent* and *Givenchy*[7] the Commission exempted selective distribution in relation to fine fragrances, noting in particular prestige brand image. Whereas in an earlier case, *Givenchy*[8], the Commission had objected to a selective system for retail sale of "para-pharmaceutical" cosmetic products in France. In the latter case the Commission found no justification for selective distribution and noted that Givenchy sold the same products to a wider group of outlets in countries outside France.

6 [1977] ECR 1975, 1904.

7 Cases T-19 88/92 [1996] ECR II 1851 and 1961.

8 OJ 1991 L75/57.

CRITERIA OBJECTIVELY APPLIED

All dealers meeting the required criteria must be admitted to the network. Suppliers must not operate admissions criteria in a discriminatory way. Suppliers are also expected to generate standard procedures for admission. For example, in Yves St Laurent[9], the Commission required the supplier to amend its procedures to specify, in particular, time limits for inspection of the applicant's outlet and decision for admission and also to provide written and reasoned responses to the dealers who are refused, identifying if possible what work is needed to bring the premises up to the necessary standard.

CRITERIA MUST BE NECESSARY

The following obligations and restrictions have been found in previous cases to be necessary for the purposes of ensuring proper distribution:

- requirement for technically qualified staff;
- requirement for suitable premises or maintenance of a specialist department;
- prohibition on sale of "down-market" goods in proximity to the contract goods;
- ability to display the products appropriately;
- requirement that the dealer provide after sales service;[10]
- ban on mail order;[11]
- obligation on dealers not to supply retailers who do not fulfil the qualitative criteria and to maintain checks on the system;
- prohibition on a wholesaler supplying private customers and on certain specialised traders reselling to the general trade.

---

9 OJ 1992 L12/24.

10 A requirement on the dealer not to advertise at cash and carry, self service or take away prices was justified on the basis that the dealer was impliedly waiving after sales service: Grundig OJ 1985 L233/1[1998] 4CMLR 865.

11 A ban on mail order has been justified as being subsumed under the dealer's obligation to display the goods and provide advice but see comments on internal sales below.

Other restrictions are likely to be viewed as quantitative restrictions which would, subject to de minimis, infringe Article 81(1).

For example, the following restrictions have been found to infringe Article 81(1):

- sales promotional obligations aimed at efficient planning, manufacturing, marketing of goods have been held to infringe Article 81(1) but qualify for individual exemption under Article 81(3) provided they do not result in undue rigidity in prices or exclude certain types of dealer[12].

- territorial limitation of outlets will infringe Article 81(1) and have been granted exemption only in the most exceptional circumstances where the nature of the product is such that the necessary close cooperation between manufacturer and dealer could not be secured by any other means. For example in Omega[13], BMW[14] and Ivoclar[15], the Commission has granted exemption to agreements involving territorial limitation on the grounds that the dealers were thereby encouraged to undertake the substantial investment necessary to sell the product.

- obligation to hold minimum quantities of stocks or the agreed range of products has been held in some cases to infringe Article 81(1) but capable of exemption. Although in some circumstances such an obligation will be purely qualitative and so outside Article 81(1).

- limit of dealers in an area: in Chanel[16], the Commission stated its intention to clear a requirement that concession area for luxury watches should be established only in terms of a minimum population or high level of tourist trade.

- restrictions on customers to whom the dealer can sell will be likely to infringe Article 81(1) but in some circumstances will be capable of exemption.

---

12 Metro, *ibid.*

13 OJ 1970 L242-2.

14 OJ1975 L29-1.

15 OJ 1975 L69-1.

16 OJ 1974 see 334-11.

The Guidelines (paragraphs 53 and 54) describe the operation of Article 4(c) in the following terms:

> *"The hardcore restriction set out in Article 4(c) of the Block Exemption Regulation concerns the restriction of active or passive sales to end users, whether professional end users or final consumers, by members of a selective distribution network. This means that dealers in a selective distribution system, as defined in Article 1(d) of the Block Exemption Regulation, cannot be restricted in the users or purchasing agents acting on behalf of these users to whom they may sell. For instance, also in a selective distribution system the dealer should be free to advertise and sell with the help of the Internet. Selective distribution may be combined with exclusive distribution provided that active and passive selling is not restricted anywhere. The supplier may therefore commit itself to supplying only one dealer or a limited number of dealers in a given territory.*
>
> *In addition, in the case of selective distribution, restrictions can be imposed on the dealer's ability to determine the location of his business premises. Selected dealers may be prevented from running their business from different premises or from opening a new outlet in a different location. If the dealer's outlet is mobile ('shop on wheels'), an area may be defined outside which the mobile outlet cannot be operated."*

One of the most important implications of the clause is in relation to internet and mail order sales. Previously, the Commission had taken the view that a ban on mail order sales in the context of a selective distribution system would not infringe competition since it reflected the need for personal advice and appropriate display at the dealer's premises.[17]

However, the text of para. 53 of the Guidelines suggests that the Commission is taking a different view in relation to internet sales. This appears to be borne out by Commission press releases in relation to two cases: Yves Saint Laurent Parfums[18] and B&W loudspeakers.[19] In announcing its decision to extend the exemption to the Yves Saint Laurent Parfums system, the Commission noted "*Yves Saint Laurent Parfums has applied selection criteria authorising approved retailers already operating a physical sales point to sell via the internet as well.*" In B&W loud-

---

17 Grundig *ibid.*

18 IP/01/713.

19 IP/00/1418.

speakers the Commission opened proceedings, inter alia, against a prohibition on distant selling internet sales.

It would appear that the Commission takes the view that even in the context of a selective system, an outright ban on internet selling will be permitted only in the most exceptional circumstances. As noted in para. 51, *"an outright ban on internet or catalogue selling is only possible if there is objective justification"*. There must be considerable doubt whether justification such as the need for personal advice and demonstration of the product will be sufficient to prohibit internet selling if the dealer in question operates a qualifying outlet as well as selling over the internet. Paragraph 51 does, however, permit suppliers to require quality standards for the use of the internet site to resell his goods in the same way as they would require standards for a shop or for advertising and promotion in general.

Article 4(d) prohibits the restriction of cross-supplies between distributors within a selective distribution system including between distributors at a different level of trade. The purpose of this restriction appears to be to ensure that dealers can source products from within the system in order to prevent the manufacturer operating different price levels in different territories. Paragraph 55 of the Guidelines describes it thus:

> *"The hardcore restriction set out in Article 4(d) of the Block Exemption Regulation concerns the restriction of cross-supplies between appointed distributors within a selective distribution system. This means that an agreement or concerted practice may not have as its direct or indirect object to prevent or restrict the active or passive selling of the contract products between the selected distributors. Selected distributors must remain free to purchase the contract products from other appointed distributors within the network, operating either at the same or at a different level of trade. This means that selective distribution cannot be combined with vertical restraints aimed at forcing distributors to purchase the contract products exclusively from a given source, for instance exclusive purchasing. It also means that within a selective distribution network no restrictions can be imposed on appointed wholesalers as regards their sales of the product to appointed retailers."*

In addition, the exemption of the Regulation will not benefit from any of the clauses listed in Article 5 (although the inclusion of such non-exempted clauses will not remove the benefit of the exemption from the rest of the agreement). All of the restrictions identified in Article 5 are likely to be relevant in the context of an selective distribution system and these are considered in more detail in Chapter 4.

Article 5(c) is specific to selective distribution. It provides that exemption will not apply to *"any direct or indirect obligation causing the members of a selective distribution system not to sell the brands of particular competing suppliers"*.

The purpose of this clause is apparently to avoid the specific situation whereby one or more suppliers using the same selective distribution outlet prevent one or more specific competitors from using the outlet to distribute their products (see paragraph 61 of the Guidelines). The clause is not intended to prohibit a general non-compete covenant not to supply competing brands which will be exempted subject to Articles 5(a) and 5(b). (See paragraph 192 of the Guidelines.)

WITHDRAWAL OF THE REGULATION

The possibility of withdrawal of the Regulation remains a concern especially for selective distribution systems which do not meet the three criteria for being a qualitative system.

Paragraph 186 of the Guidelines specifically states that:

> *"However, where the nature of the product does not require selective distribution, such a distribution system does not generally bring about sufficient efficiency enhancing effects to counterbalance a significant reduction in intra-brand competition. If appreciable anti-competitive effects occur, the benefit of the Block Exemption Regulation is likely to be withdrawn."*

SUMMARY OF THE CHANGES FOR SELECTIVE DISTRIBUTION

In summary, the Regulation makes important changes for selective distribution in conferring a block exemption for the first time.

- Simple qualitative systems will continue to fall outside Article 81(1).
- Selective distribution systems which impose additional non-qualitative restrictions may benefit from the Regulation and this gives suppliers greater flexibility in imposing additional restrictions such as promotional stocking obligations or minimum sales obligations on their dealers.
- The Regulation may however be withdrawn if the nature of the product does not justify selective distribution and anti-competitive effects flow from the system. Disapplication of the Regulation under Article 6 might occur as a result of the cumulative effect of parallel networks if they cover 50% of the market.

- Outright bans on internet or mail order sales are only likely to be permitted in exceptional circumstances where objective justification exists.
- Quantitative restrictions are treated in exactly the same way as qualitative restrictions under the Regulation.
- A supplier can combine an exclusive territory with selective distribution but cannot in any way restrict active or passive sales by the dealer. In practice this probably means that suppliers wishing to operate an exclusive sales area will draft their agreements outside the definition of selective distribution system in Article 1 of the Block Exemption Regulation.

SELECTIVE DISTRIBUTION OUTSIDE THE REGULATION

Paragraphs 187-198 of the Guidelines discuss the applicability of Article 81 to agreements outside the Block Exemption Regulation or where parallel networks of selective distribution agreements have a cumulative anti-competitive effect. These paragraphs principally cover the situation where the supplier will have a market share greater than 30% but does not impose a blacklisted clause.

The approach adopted by the Commission is to analyse the key factors identified at para. 121 and to apply each in turn:

- Market position of the supplier is obviously of major importance. The stronger the position of the supplier, the more problematic is the loss of intra-brand competition. In the case of selective distribution networks it is also important to assess the number of similar selective systems operating in the market as in many cases it is likely that selective distribution will be applied by all, or a significant number, of suppliers in a given market (para. 187).
- The position of competitors is therefore very important. Whilst strong competitors suggests that the reduction in intra-brand competition will be outweighed by inter-brand competition, the presence of a number of other selective distribution networks may result in foreclosure of certain types of distributors making it impossible for non-authorised distributors to obtain supplies of products (para. 188). In extreme cases the risk of cumulative effective may result in the withdrawal of the Block Exemption Regulation. Paragraph 189 suggests that cumulative effect is unlikely to arise when the share of the market covered by selective distribution is below 50% or, even if it is above 50%, if the five largest suppliers between them account for less than 50%. Exemption will not be available if the structure of the market is

such that new distributors, particular price discounters, cannot get access to the market.

- Paragraph 189 suggests that the combination of purely qualitative selection criteria with the requirement to achieve minimum annual purchases is less likely to present a problem if such demand does not represent a significant proportion of the dealer's total turnover in respect of this type of product. Presumably the same applies to a minimum stocking obligation. Paragraph 189 also suggests that a supplier with a market share of less than 5% is in general not considered to contribute significantly to any cumulative effect.
- Entry barriers are relevant in so far as they foreclose the market to non-authorised dealers. Paragraph 190 recognises that in the case of branded products, barriers may be significant.
- Paragraph 191 identifies buyer power as being a risk if it results in collusion between dealers. Foreclosure of suppliers is not normally a problem (see para. 193). However, problems may occur when a selective distribution system includes a non-compete obligation if, as a result other suppliers are prevented from gaining access to distributors. Generally, foreclosure of suppliers, for example as a result of obligations imposed by other suppliers requiring a dealer to devote a certain amount of shelf space or percentage of turnover, will only be a problem where the market share of the five largest suppliers is above the 50%.
- Maturity of the market is important as a loss of intra-brand competition is more likely to be a problem in a mature market.
- Above the 30% market share threshold the combination of selective and exclusive distribution is unlikely to be exempted, even where active sales between territories remain free. Exemption will be available only if such a combination is indispensable to protect substantial and relationship specific investments made by the authorised dealers (para. 195).
- Paragraphs 197 and 198 include examples of how quantitative selective distribution systems might be treated outside of the Block Exemption Regulation.

MOTOR VEHICLES

The broad principles outlined above are reflected in the Commission's approach to distribution of motor vehicles. The important difference is that for the motor vehicle sector, the Commission has issued specific block exemption regulations. The first regulation (Regulation 123/85) expired and was replaced by Regulation 1475/95 which was accompanied by explanatory brochure entitled "Distribution of Motor Vehicles" (IV/950/95-EN). Regulation 1475/95 can be contrasted with the Block Exemption Regulation in that it is highly prescriptive and is sector specific. Regulation 1475/95 is itself due to expire 30 September 2002 and the Commission initiated a consultation on the future regulation of the motor vehicle sector after 2002. One option for the Commission would be to bring motor vehicles within the umbrella of the Block Exemption Regulation and the Guidelines.

CHAPTER 9

CHECKLIST

1. **Is the agreement a vertical agreement?**
A vertical agreement is one "entered into between two or more undertakings each of which operates, for the purposes of the agreement, at a different level of the production or distribution chain, and relating to the conditions under which the parties may purchase, sell or resell certain goods or services" (Regulation Article 2(1)).

- If the answer is no, the Regulation will not apply (go to Question 8).
- If the answer is yes, the Regulation may apply (go to Question 2).

2. **If the agreement is made between actual or potential competitors does it meet the conditions in Article 2(4)?**

- If the answer is no, the Regulation will not apply (go to Question 8).
- If the answer is yes, the Regulation may apply (go to Question 3).

3. **If the agreement is made between a trade association and its members or suppliers to the association, does it meet the conditions in Article 2(2)?** (Regulation Article 2(2).)

- If the answer is no, the Regulation will not apply (go to Question 8).
- If the answer is yes, the Regulation may apply (go to Question 4).

4. **If the agreement contains provisions relating to assignment to or use by the buyer of intellectual property rights, are these provisions ancillary to the sale or resale of goods or services?** (Regulation Article 2(3).)

- If the answer is no, the Regulation will not apply (go to Question 8).
- If the answer is yes, the Regulation may apply (go to Question 5).

5. **Does the supplier have less than 30% of the relevant market on which it sells the contract goods or services?** (Article 3(1).)

- What are the contract goods or services?
- How is the market share calculated?

  "The market share of 30% provided for in Article 3(1) shall be calculated on the basis of the market sales value of the contract goods or services sold by the supplier, which are regarded as inter-changeable or substitutable by the buyer by reason of the products' characteristics, their prices and intended use". (Article 9)

- If the payment contains an exclusive supply obligation accepted by the supplier, does the buyer have less than 30% of the relevant market on which it buys the contract goods or services? (Article 3(2))
- If the answer is no, the Regulation will not apply (go to Question 8).
- If the answer is yes, the Regulation may apply (go to Question 6).

6. **Do any of the hardcore provisions apply?** (See Article 4.)

(a) Is there any direct or indirect restriction on the buyers ability to determine its sale price?

- if the answer is yes the Regulation will not apply, unless the restriction is either a maximum price or a recommended resale price which do not amount to a fixed minimum sale price as a result of pressure from incentives offered by any of the parties.

(b) Is there a restriction of the territory into which or of the customer to whom the buyer may sell the contract goods or services.

If the answer is yes, the Regulation will not apply unless:

- the restriction applies to the exclusive territory or to an exclusive customer group reserved to the supplier or allocated by the supplier to another buyer where the restriction does not limit sales by the customer of the buyer
- there is a restriction of sales to end users by a buyer operating at the wholesale level of trade
- there is a restriction of sales to unauthorised distributors by the members of a selective distribution system, and

  - there is a restriction of the buyer's ability to sell components, supplied for the purposes of incorporation, to customers who would use them to manufacture the same type of goods as those produced by the supplier.

(c) Is there a restriction of active or passive sales to end users by members of a selective distribution system operating at the retail level of trade without prejudice to the possibility of prohibiting a member of the system from operating out of an unauthorised place of establishment.

  - If the answer is yes, the Regulation will not apply.

(d) Is there a restriction of cross-supplies between distributors within a selective distribution system, including between distributors operating at different level of trade.

  - If the answer is yes, the Regulation will not apply.

(e) Is there a restriction agreed between a supplier of components and a buyer who incorporates those components, which limits the supplier to selling the components as spare parts to end-users or to repairers or other service providers not entrusted by the buyer with the repair of servicing of its goods.

  - If the answer is yes, the Regulation will not apply.

If the answer is no to all of the above the Regulation will apply to exempt the agreement but not any non-exempted clauses under Article 5 (Go to Question 7 below).
If the answer is yes, the Regulation will not apply. (Go to Question 8 below).

7. **Do any of the conditions apply?** (See Article 5.) If the answer is yes, the conditions need to be assessed individually for compatibility with Article 81. (Go to Question 8.)

NOTE: If the agreement contains a condition then, by contrast within Article 4 (hard core provisions), the exemption will still be available for the rest of the agreement but the offending condition will not benefit.

8. **If the agreement falls outside the Regulation, a full analysis of the agreement under Article 81 is required.**

- Does the agreement fall within Article 81(1)?
- What restrictions are there in the agreement?

- Is there an appreciable effect on trade between Member States? (See De Minimis Notice and Guidelines, paragraphs 8-11.)
- Is there an appreciable effect on competition? (See De Minimis Notice and Guidelines, paragraphs 8-20.)
- If the agreement is likely to fall within Article 81(1), will it benefit from exemption under Article 81(3)?
- If the agreement contains hardcore restrictions, exemption unlikely (see Guidelines, paragraphs 46-56).
- Does the agreement benefit from another block exemption regulation (e.g. Regulation 240/96 (technology transfer)) meet the criteria for individual exemption under Article 81(3)? (See Guidelines, paragraphs 134-136.)
- If so, is it appropriate to make an individual notification? (See Guidelines, paragraphs 63-65.)

APPENDIX A

ARTICLE 81 OF THE EC TREATY (EX ARTICLE 85)

1. The following shall be prohibited as incompatible with the common market: all agreements between undertakings, decisions by associations of undertakings and concerted practices which may affect trade between Member States and which have as their object or effect the prevention, restriction or distortion of competition within the common market, and in particular those which:
   (a) directly or indirectly fix purchase or selling prices or any other trading conditions;
   (b) limit or control production, markets, technical development, or investment;
   (c) share markets or sources of supply;
   (d) apply dissimilar conditions to equivalent transactions with other trading parties, thereby placing them at a competitive disadvantage;
   (e) make the conclusion of contracts subject to acceptance by the other parties of supplementary obligations which, by their nature or according to commercial usage, have no connection with the subject of such contracts.
2. Any agreements or decisions prohibited pursuant to this Article shall be automatically void.
3. The provisions of paragraph 1 may, however, be declared inapplicable in the case of:
   - any agreement or category of agreements between undertakings;
   - any decision or category of decisions by associations of undertakings;
   - any concerted practice or category of concerted practices,

   which contributes to improving the production or distribution of goods or to promoting technical or economic progress, while allowing consumers a fair share of the resulting benefit, and which does not:
   (a) impose on the undertakings concerned restrictions which are not indispensable to the attainment of these objectives;

(b) afford such undertakings the possibility of eliminating competition in respect of a substantial part of the products in question.

APPENDIX B

COMMISSION REGULATION (EC) NO 2790/1999

of 22 December 1999

on the application of Article 81(3) of the Treaty to categories of vertical agreements and concerted practices

(Text with EEA relevance)

THE COMMISSION OF THE EUROPEAN COMMUNITIES,

Having regard to the Treaty establishing the European Community,
Having regard to Council Regulation No 19/65/EEC of 2 March 1965 on the application of Article 85(3) of the Treaty to certain categories of agreements and concerted practices[1], as last amended by Regulation (EC) No 1215/1999[2], and in particular Article 1 thereof,
Having published a draft of this Regulation[3],
Having consulted the Advisory Committee on Restrictive Practices and Dominant Positions,

Whereas:

(1) Regulation No 19/65/EEC empowers the Commission to apply Article 81(3) of the Treaty (formerly Article 85(3)) by regulation to certain categories of vertical agreements and corresponding concerted practices falling within Article 81(1).

(2) Experience acquired to date makes it possible to define a category of vertical agreements which can be regarded as normally satisfying the conditions laid down in Article 81(3).

---

1 OJ 36, 6.3.1965, p. 533/65.

2 OJ L 148, 15.6.1999, p. 1.

3 OJ C 270, 24.9.1999, p. 7.

(3) This category includes vertical agreements for the purchase or sale of goods or services where these agreements are concluded between non-competing undertakings, between certain competitors or by certain associations of retailers of goods; it also includes vertical agreements containing ancillary provisions on the assignment or use of intellectual property rights; for the purposes of this Regulation, the term "vertical agreements" includes the corresponding concerted practices.

(4) For the application of Article 81(3) by regulation, it is not necessary to define those vertical agreements which are capable of falling within Article 81(1); in the individual assessment of agreements under Article 81(1), account has to be taken of several factors, and in particular the market structure on the supply and purchase side.

(5) The benefit of the block exemption should be limited to vertical agreements for which it can be assumed with sufficient certainty that they satisfy the conditions of Article 81(3).

(6) Vertical agreements of the category defined in this Regulation can improve economic efficiency within a chain of production or distribution by facilitating better coordination between the participating undertakings; in particular, they can lead to a reduction in the transaction and distribution costs of the parties and to an optimisation of their sales and investment levels.

(7) The likelihood that such efficiency-enhancing effects will outweigh any anti-competitive effects due to restrictions contained in vertical agreements depends on the degree of market power of the undertakings concerned and, therefore, on the extent to which those undertakings face competition from other suppliers of goods or services regarded by the buyer as interchangeable or substitutable for one another, by reason of the products' characteristics, their prices and their intended use.

(8) It can be presumed that, where the share of the relevant market accounted for by the supplier does not exceed 30 %, vertical agreements which do not contain certain types of severely anti-competitive restraints generally lead to an improvement in production or distribution and allow consumers a fair share of the resulting benefits; in the case of vertical agreements containing exclusive supply obligations, it is the market share of the buyer which is relevant in determining the overall effects of such vertical agreements on the market.

(9) Above the market share threshold of 30 %, there can be no presumption that

vertical agreements falling within the scope of Article 81(1) will usually give rise to objective advantages of such a character and size as to compensate for the disadvantages which they create for competition.

(10) This Regulation should not exempt vertical agreements containing restrictions which are not indispensable to the attainment of the positive effects mentioned above; in particular, vertical agreements containing certain types of severely anti-competitive restraints such as minimum and fixed resale-prices, as well as certain types of territorial protection, should be excluded from the benefit of the block exemption established by this Regulation irrespective of the market share of the undertakings concerned.

(11) In order to ensure access to or to prevent collusion on the relevant market, certain conditions are to be attached to the block exemption; to this end, the exemption of non-compete obligations should be limited to obligations which do not exceed a definite duration; for the same reasons, any direct or indirect obligation causing the members of a selective distribution system not to sell the brands of particular competing suppliers should be excluded from the benefit of this Regulation.

(12) The market-share limitation, the non-exemption of certain vertical agreements and the conditions provided for in this Regulation normally ensure that the agreements to which the block exemption applies do not enable the participating undertakings to eliminate competition in respect of a substantial part of the products in question.

(13) In particular cases in which the agreements falling under this Regulation nevertheless have effects incompatible with Article 81(3), the Commission may withdraw the benefit of the block exemption; this may occur in particular where the buyer has significant market power in the relevant market in which it resells the goods or provides the services or where parallel networks of vertical agreements have similar effects which significantly restrict access to a relevant market or competition therein; such cumulative effects may for example arise in the case of selective distribution or non-compete obligations.

(14) Regulation No 19/65/EEC empowers the competent authorities of Member States to withdraw the benefit of the block exemption in respect of vertical agreements having effects incompatible with the conditions laid down in Article 81(3), where such effects are felt in their respective territory, or in a part thereof,

and where such territory has the characteristics of a distinct geographic market; Member States should ensure that the exercise of this power of withdrawal does not prejudice the uniform application throughout the common market of the Community competition rules or the full effect of the measures adopted in implementation of those rules.

(15) In order to strengthen supervision of parallel networks of vertical agreements which have similar restrictive effects and which cover more than 50 % of a given market, the Commission may declare this Regulation inapplicable to vertical agreements containing specific restraints relating to the market concerned, thereby restoring the full application of Article 81 to such agreements.

(16) This Regulation is without prejudice to the application of Article 82.

(17) In accordance with the principle of the primacy of Community law, no measure taken pursuant to national laws on competition should prejudice the uniform application throughout the common market of the Community competition rules or the full effect of any measures adopted in implementation of those rules, including this Regulation,

HAS ADOPTED THIS REGULATION:

Article 1

For the purposes of this Regulation:

(a) "competing undertakings" means actual or potential suppliers in the same product market; the product market includes goods or services which are regarded by the buyer as interchangeable with or substitutable for the contract goods or services, by reason of the products' characteristics, their prices and their intended use;

(b) "non-compete obligation" means any direct or indirect obligation causing the buyer not to manufacture, purchase, sell or resell goods or services which compete with the contract goods or services, or any direct or indirect obligation on the buyer to purchase from the supplier or from another undertaking designated by the supplier more than 80 % of the buyer's total purchases of the contract goods or services and their substitutes on the relevant market, calculated on the basis of the value of its purchases in the preceding calendar year;

(c) "exclusive supply obligation" means any direct or indirect obligation causing the supplier to sell the goods or services specified in the agreement only to one buyer inside the Community for the purposes of a specific use or for resale;

(d) "Selective distribution system" means a distribution system where the supplier undertakes to sell the contract goods or services, either directly or indirectly, only to distributors selected on the basis of specified criteria and where these distributors undertake not to sell such goods or services to unauthorised distributors;

(e) "intellectual property rights" includes industrial property rights, copyright and neighbouring rights;

(f) "know-how" means a package of non-patented practical information, resulting from experience and testing by the supplier, which is secret, substantial and identified: in this context, "secret" means that the know-how, as a body or in the precise configuration and assembly of its components, is not generally known or easily accessible; "substantial" means that the know-how includes information which is indispensable to the buyer for the use, sale or resale of the contract goods or services; "identified" means that the know-how must be described in a sufficiently comprehensive manner so as to make it possible to verify that it fulfils the criteria of secrecy and substantiality;

(g) "buyer" includes an undertaking which, under an agreement falling within Article 81(1) of the Treaty, sells goods or services on behalf of another undertaking.

Article 2

1. Pursuant to Article 81(3) of the Treaty and subject to the provisions of this Regulation, it is hereby declared that Article 81(1) shall not apply to agreements or concerted practices entered into between two or more undertakings each of which operates, for the purposes of the agreement, at a different level of the production or distribution chain, and relating to the conditions under which the parties may purchase, sell or resell certain goods or services ("vertical agreements").

This exemption shall apply to the extent that such agreements contain restrictions of competition falling within the scope of Article 81(1) ("vertical restraints").

2. The exemption provided for in paragraph 1 shall apply to vertical agreements entered into between an association of undertakings and its members, or between such an association and its suppliers, only if all its members are retailers of goods and if no individual member of the association, together with its connected undertakings, has a total annual turnover exceeding EUR 50 million; vertical agreements entered into by such associations shall be covered by this Regulation without prejudice to the application of Article 81 to horizontal agreements concluded between the members of the association or decisions adopted by the association.

3. The exemption provided for in paragraph 1 shall apply to vertical agreements containing provisions which relate to the assignment to the buyer or use by the buyer of intellectual property rights, provided that those provisions do not constitute the primary object of such agreements and are directly related to the use, sale or resale of goods or services by the buyer or its customers. The exemption applies on condition that, in relation to the contract goods or services, those provisions do not contain restrictions of competition having the same object or effect as vertical restraints which are not exempted under this Regulation.

4. The exemption provided for in paragraph 1 shall not apply to vertical agreements entered into between competing undertakings; however, it shall apply where competing undertakings enter into a non-reciprocal vertical agreement and:

(a) the buyer has a total annual turnover not exceeding EUR 100 million, or

(b) the supplier is a manufacturer and a distributor of goods, while the buyer is a distributor not manufacturing goods competing with the contract goods, or

(c) the supplier is a provider of services at several levels of trade, while the buyer does not provide competing services at the level of trade where it purchases the contract services.

5. This Regulation shall not apply to vertical agreements the subject matter of which falls within the scope of any other block exemption regulation.

Article 3

1. Subject to paragraph 2 of this Article, the exemption provided for in Article 2 shall apply on condition that the market share held by the supplier does not exceed 30 % of the relevant market on which it sells the contract goods or services.

2. In the case of vertical agreements containing exclusive supply obligations, the exemption provided for in Article 2 shall apply on condition that the market share held by the buyer does not exceed 30 % of the relevant market on which it purchases the contract goods or services.

Article 4

The exemption provided for in Article 2 shall not apply to vertical agreements which, directly or indirectly, in isolation or in combination with other factors under the control of the parties, have as their object:

(a) the restriction of the buyer's ability to determine its sale price, without prejudice to the possibility of the supplier's imposing a maximum sale price or recommending a sale price, provided that they do not amount to a fixed or minimum sale price as a result of pressure from, or incentives offered by, any of the parties;

(b) the restriction of the territory into which, or of the customers to whom, the buyer may sell the contract goods or services, except:

- the restriction of active sales into the exclusive territory or to an exclusive customer group reserved to the supplier or allocated by the supplier to another buyer, where such a restriction does not limit sales by the customers of the buyer,
- the restriction of sales to end users by a buyer operating at the wholesale level of trade,
- the restriction of sales to unauthorised distributors by the members of a selective distribution system, and
- the restriction of the buyer's ability to sell components, supplied for the purposes of incorporation, to customers who would use them to manufacture the same type of goods as those produced by the supplier;

(c) the restriction of active or passive sales to end users by members of a selective distribution system operating at the retail level of trade, without prejudice to the possibility of prohibiting a member of the system from operating out of an unauthorised place of establishment;

(d) the restriction of cross-supplies between distributors within a selective distribution system, including between distributors operating at different level of trade;

(e) the restriction agreed between a supplier of components and a buyer who incorporates those components, which limits the supplier to selling the components as spare parts to end-users or to repairers or other service providers not entrusted by the buyer with the repair or servicing of its goods.

Article 5

The exemption provided for in Article 2 shall not apply to any of the following obligations contained in vertical agreements:

(a) any direct or indirect non-compete obligation, the duration of which is indefinite or exceeds five years. A non-compete obligation which is tacitly renewable beyond a period of five years is to be deemed to have been concluded for an indefinite duration. However, the time limitation of five years shall not apply where the contract goods or services are sold by the buyer from premises and land owned by the supplier or leased by the supplier from third parties not connected with the buyer, provided that the duration of the non-compete obligation does not exceed the period of occupancy of the premises and land by the buyer;

(b) any direct or indirect obligation causing the buyer, after termination of the agreement, not to manufacture, purchase, sell or resell goods or services, unless such obligation:

- relates to goods or services which compete with the contract goods or services, and
- is limited to the premises and land from which the buyer has operated during the contract period, and
- is indispensable to protect know-how transferred by the supplier to the buyer,

and provided that the duration of such non-compete obligation is limited to a period of one year after termination of the agreement; this obligation is without prejudice to the possibility of imposing a restriction which is unlimited in time on the use and disclosure of know-how which has not entered the public domain;

(c) any direct or indirect obligation causing the members of a selective distribution system not to sell the brands of particular competing suppliers.

Article 6

The Commission may withdraw the benefit of this Regulation, pursuant to Article 7(1) of Regulation No 19/65/EEC, where it finds in any particular case that vertical agreements to which this Regulation applies nevertheless have effects which are incompatible with the conditions laid down in Article 81(3) of the Treaty, and in particular where access to the relevant market or competition therein is significantly restricted by the cumulative effect of parallel networks of similar vertical restraints implemented by competing suppliers or buyers.

Article 7

Where in any particular case vertical agreements to which the exemption provided for in Article 2 applies have effects incompatible with the conditions laid down in Article 81(3) of the Treaty in the territory of a Member State, or in a part thereof, which has all the characteristics of a distinct geographic market, the competent authority of that Member State may withdraw the benefit of application of this Regulation in respect of that territory, under the same conditions as provided in Article 6.

Article 8

1. Pursuant to Article 1 a of Regulation No 19/65/EEC, the Commission may by regulation declare that, where parallel networks of similar vertical restraints cover more than 50 % of a relevant market, this Regulation shall not apply to vertical agreements containing specific restraints relating to that market.

2. A regulation pursuant to paragraph 1 shall not become applicable earlier than six months following its adoption.

Article 9

1. The market share of 30 % provided for in Article 3(1) shall be calculated on the basis of the market sales value of the contract goods or services and other goods or services sold by the supplier, which are regarded as interchangeable or substitutable by the buyer, by reason of the products' characteristics, their prices and their intended use; if market sales value data are not available, estimates based on other reliable market information, including market sales volumes, may be used to establish the market share of the undertaking concerned. For the purposes of Article 3(2), it is

either the market purchase value or estimates thereof which shall be used to calculate the market share.

2. For the purposes of applying the market share, threshold provided for in Article 3 the following rules shall apply:

(a) the market share shall be calculated on the basis of data relating to the preceding calendar year;

(b) the market share shall include any goods or services supplied to integrated distributors for the purposes of sale;

(c) if the market share is initially not more than 30 % but subsequently rises above that level without exceeding 35 %, the exemption provided for in Article 2 shall continue to apply for a period of two consecutive calendar years following the year in which the 30 % market share threshold was first exceeded;

(d) if the market share is initially not more than 30 % but subsequently rises above 35 %, the exemption provided for in Article 2 shall continue to apply for one calendar year following the year in which the level of 35 % was first exceeded;

(e) the benefit of points (c) and (d) may not be combined so as to exceed a period of two calendar years.

Article 10

1. For the purpose of calculating total annual turnover within the meaning of Article 2(2) and (4), the turnover achieved during the previous financial year by the relevant party to the vertical agreement and the turnover achieved by its connected undertakings in respect of all goods and services, excluding all taxes and other duties, shall be added together. For this purpose, no account shall be taken of dealings between the party to the vertical agreement and its connected undertakings or between its connected undertakings.

2. The exemption provided for in Article 2 shall remain applicable where, for any period of two consecutive financial years, the total annual turnover threshold is exceeded by no more than 10 %.

Article 11

1. For the purposes of this Regulation, the terms "undertaking", "supplier" and "buyer" shall include their respective connected undertakings.

2. "Connected undertakings" are:

(a) undertakings in which a party to the agreement, directly or indirectly:
  - has the power to exercise more than half the voting rights, or
  - has the power to appoint more than half the members of the supervisory board, board of management or bodies legally representing the undertaking, or
  - has the right to manage the undertaking's affairs;

(b) undertakings which directly or indirectly have, over a party to the agreement, the rights or powers listed in (a);

(c) undertakings in which an undertaking referred to in (b) has, directly or indirectly, the rights or powers listed in (a);

(d) undertakings in which a party to the agreement together with one or more of the undertakings referred to in (a), (b) or (c), or in which two or more of the latter undertakings, jointly have the rights or powers listed in (a);

(e) undertakings in which the rights or the powers listed in (a) are jointly held by:
  - parties to the agreement or their respective connected undertakings referred to in (a) to (d), or
  - one or more of the parties to the agreement or one or more of their connected undertakings referred to in (a) to (d) and one or more third parties.

3. For the purposes of Article 3, the market share held by the undertakings referred to in paragraph 2(e) of this Article shall be apportioned equally to each undertaking having the rights or the powers listed in paragraph 2(a).

APPENDIX C

COMMISSION NOTICE – GUIDELINES ON VERTICAL RESTRAINTS (2000/C 291/01)

(Text with EEA relevance)

I. INTRODUCTION

1. Purpose of the Guidelines

(1) These Guidelines set out the principles for the assessment of vertical agreements under Article 81 of the EC Treaty. What are considered vertical agreements is defined in Article 2(1) of Commission Regulation (EC) No 2790/1999 of 22 December 1999 on the application of Article 81(3) of the Treaty to categories of vertical agreements and concerted practices[1] (Block Exemption Regulation) (see paragraphs 23 to 45). These Guidelines are without prejudice to the possible parallel application of Article 82 of the Treaty to vertical agreements. The Guidelines are structured in the following way:

- Section II (paragraphs 8 to 20) describes vertical agreements which generally fall outside Article 81(1);
- Section III (paragraphs 21 to 70) comments on the application of the Block Exemption Regulation;
- Section IV (paragraphs 71 to 87) describes the principles concerning the withdrawal of the block exemption and the disapplication of the Block Exemption Regulation;
- Section V (paragraphs 88 to 99) addresses market definition and market share calculation issues;
- Section VI (paragraphs 100 to 229) describes the general framework of analysis and the enforcement policy of the Commission in individual cases concerning vertical agreements.

---

1 OJ L 336, 29.12.1999, p. 21.

(2) Throughout these Guidelines the analysis applies to both goods and services, although certain vertical restraints are mainly used in the distribution of goods. Similarly, vertical agreements can be concluded for intermediate and final goods and services. Unless otherwise stated, the analysis and arguments in the text apply to all types of goods and services and to all levels of trade. The term "products" includes both goods and services. The terms "supplier" and "buyer" are used for all levels of trade.

(3) By issuing these Guidelines the Commission aims to help companies to make their own assessment of vertical agreements under the EC competition rules. The standards set forth in these Guidelines must be applied in circumstances specific to each case. This rules out a mechanical application. Each case must be evaluated in the light of its own facts. The Commission will apply the Guidelines reasonably and flexibly.

(4) These Guidelines are without prejudice to the interpretation that may be given by the Court of First Instance and the Court of Justice of the European Communities in relation to the application of Article 81 to vertical agreements.

2. Applicability of Article 81 to vertical agreements

(5) Article 81 of the EC Treaty applies to vertical agreements that may affect trade between Member States and that prevent, restrict or distort competition (hereinafter referred to as "vertical restraints").[2] For vertical restraints, Article 81 provides an appropriate legal framework for assessment, recognising the distinction between anti-competitive and pro-competitive effects: Article 81(1) prohibits those agreements which appreciably restrict or distort competition, while Article 81(3) allows for exemption of those agreements which confer sufficient benefits to outweigh the anti-competitive effects.

(6) For most vertical restraints, competition concerns can only arise if there is insufficient inter-brand competition, i.e. if there is some degree of market power at the level of the supplier or the buyer or at both levels. If there is insufficient inter-

2 See *inter alia* judgment of the Court of Justice of the European Communities in Joined Cases 56/64 and 58/64 *Grundig-Consten v Commission* [1966] ECR 299; Case 56/65 *Technique Minière v Machinenbau Ulm* [1966] ECR 235; and of the Court of First Instance of the European Communities in Case T-77/92 *Parker Pen v Commission* [1994] ECR II 549.

brand competition, the protection of inter- and intra-brand competition becomes important.

(7) The protection of competition is the primary objective of EC competition policy, as this enhances consumer welfare and creates an efficient allocation of resources. In applying the EC competition rules, the Commission will adopt an economic approach which is based on the effects on the market; vertical agreements have to be analysed in their legal and economic context. However, in the case of restrictions by object as listed in Article 4 of the Block Exemption Regulation, the Commission is not required to assess the actual effects on the market. Market integration is an additional goal of EC competition policy. Market integration enhances competition in the Community. Companies should not be allowed to recreate private barriers between Member States where State barriers have been successfully abolished.

II. VERTICAL AGREEMENTS WHICH GENERALLY FALL OUTSIDE ARTICLE 81(1)

1. Agreements of minor importance and SMEs

(8) Agreements which are not capable of appreciably affecting trade between Member States or capable of appreciably restricting competition by object or effect are not caught by Article 81(1). The Block Exemption Regulation applies only to agreements falling within the scope of application of Article 81(1). These Guidelines are without prejudice to the application of the present or any future "de minimis" notice.[3]

(9) Subject to the conditions set out in points 11, 18 and 20 of the "de minimis" notice concerning hardcore restrictions and cumulative effect issues, vertical agreements entered into by undertakings whose market share on the relevant market does not exceed 10% are generally considered to fall outside the scope of Article 81(1). There is no presumption that vertical agreements concluded by undertakings having more than 10% market share automatically infringe Article 81(1). Agreements between undertakings whose market share exceeds the 10% threshold may still not have an appreciable effect on trade between Member States or may not

3 See Notice on agreements of minor importance of 9 December 1997, OJ C 372, 9.12.1997, p. 13.

constitute an appreciable restriction of competition.[4] Such agreements need to be assessed in their legal and economic context. The criteria for the assessment of individual agreements are set out in paragraphs 100 to 229.

(10) As regards hardcore restrictions defined in the "de minimis" notice, Article 81(1) may apply below the 10% threshold, provided that there is an appreciable effect on trade between Member States and on competition. The applicable case-law of the Court of Justice and the Court of First Instance is relevant in this respect.[5] Reference is also made to the particular situation of launching a new product or entering a new market which is dealt with in these Guidelines (paragraph 119, point 10).

(11) In addition, the Commission considers that, subject to cumulative effect and hardcore restrictions, agreements between small and medium-sized undertakings as defined in the Annex to Commission Recommendation 96/280/EC[6] are rarely capable of appreciably affecting trade between Member States or of appreciably restricting competition within the meaning of Article 81(1), and therefore generally fall outside the scope of Article 81(1). In cases where such agreements nonetheless meet the conditions for the application of Article 81(1), the Commission will normally refrain from opening proceedings for lack of sufficient Community interest unless those undertakings collectively or individually hold a dominant position in a substantial part of the common market.

2. *Agency agreements*

(12) Paragraphs 12 to 20 replace the Notice on exclusive dealing contracts with commercial agents of 1962.[7] They must be read in conjunction with Council Directive 86/653/EEC.[8]

---

4 See judgment of the Court of First Instance in Case T-7/93 *Langnese-Iglo v Commission* [1995] ECR II-1533, paragraph 98.

5 See judgment of the Court of Justice in Case 5/69 *Völk v Vervaecke* [1969] ECR 295; Case 1/71 *Cadillon v Höss* [1971] ECR 351 and Case C-306/96 *Javico v Yves Saint Laurent* [1998] ECR I-1983, paragraphs 16 and 17.

6 OJ L 107, 30.4.1996, p. 4.

7 OJ 139, 24.12.1962, p. 2921/62.

8 OJ L 382, 31.12.1986, p. 17.

Agency agreements cover the situation in which a legal or physical person (the agent) is vested with the power to negotiate and/or conclude contracts on behalf of another person (the principal), either in the agent's own name or in the name of the principal, for the:

- purchase of goods or services by the principal, or
- sale of goods or services supplied by the principal.

(13) In the case of genuine agency agreements, the obligations imposed on the agent as to the contracts negotiated and/or concluded on behalf of the principal do not fall within the scope of application of Article 81(1). The determining factor in assessing whether Article 81(1) is applicable is the financial or commercial risk borne by the agent in relation to the activities for which he has been appointed as an agent by the principal. In this respect it is not material for the assessment whether the agent acts for one or several principals. Non-genuine agency agreements may be caught by Article 81(1), in which case the Block Exemption Regulation and the other sections of these Guidelines will apply.

(14) There are two types of financial or commercial risk that are material to the assessment of the genuine nature of an agency agreement under Article 81(1). First there are the risks which are directly related to the contracts concluded and/or negotiated by the agent on behalf of the principal, such as financing of stocks. Secondly, there are the risks related to market-specific investments. These are investments specifically required for the type of activity for which the agent has been appointed by the principal, i.e. which are required to enable the agent to conclude and/or negotiate this type of contract. Such investments are usually sunk, if upon leaving that particular field of activity the investment cannot be used for other activities or sold other than at a significant loss.

(15) The agency agreement is considered a genuine agency agreement and consequently falls outside Article 81(1) if the agent does not bear any, or bears only insignificant, risks in relation to the contracts concluded and/or negotiated on behalf of the principal and in relation to market-specific investments for that field of activity. In such a situation, the selling or purchasing function forms part of the principal's activities, despite the fact that the agent is a separate undertaking. The principal thus bears the related financial and commercial risks and the agent does not exercise an independent economic activity in relation to the activities for which he has been appointed as an agent by the principal. In the opposite situation the agency agreement is considered a non-genuine agency agreement and may fall under Article 81(1).

In that case the agent does bear such risks and will be treated as an independent dealer who must remain free in determining his marketing strategy in order to be able to recover his contract- or market-specific investments. Risks that are related to the activity of providing agency services in general, such as the risk of the agent's income being dependent upon his success as an agent or general investments in for instance premises or personnel, are not material to this assessment.

(16) The question of risk must be assessed on a case-by-case basis, and with regard to the economic reality of the situation rather than the legal form. Nonetheless, the Commission considers that Article 81(1) will generally not be applicable to the obligations imposed on the agent as to the contracts negotiated and/or concluded on behalf of the principal where property in the contract goods bought or sold does not vest in the agent, or the agent does not himself supply the contract services and where the agent:

- does not contribute to the costs relating to the supply/purchase of the contract goods or services, including the costs of transporting the goods. This does not preclude the agent from carrying out the transport service, provided that the costs are covered by the principal;
- is not, directly or indirectly, obliged to invest in sales promotion, such as contributions to the advertising budgets of the principal;
- does not maintain at his own cost or risk stocks of the contract goods, including the costs of financing the stocks and the costs of loss of stocks and can return unsold goods to the principal without charge, unless the agent is liable for fault (for example, by failing to comply with reasonable security measures to avoid loss of stocks);
- does not create and/or operate an after-sales service, repair service or a warranty service unless it is fully reimbursed by the principal;
- does not make market-specific investments in equipment, premises or training of personnel, such as for example the petrol storage tank in the case of petrol retailing or specific software to sell insurance policies in case of insurance agents;
- does not undertake responsibility towards third parties for damage caused by the product sold (product liability), unless, as agent, he is liable for fault in this respect;
- does not take responsibility for customers' non-performance of the contract, with the exception of the loss of the agent's commission, unless the agent is

liable for fault (for example, by failing to comply with reasonable security or anti-theft measures or failing to comply with reasonable measures to report theft to the principal or police or to communicate to the principal all necessary information available to him on the customer's financial reliability).

(17) This list is not exhaustive. However, where the agent incurs one or more of the above risks or costs, then Article 81(1) may apply as with any other vertical agreement.

(18) If an agency agreement does not fall within the scope of application of Article 81(1), then all obligations imposed on the agent in relation to the contracts concluded and/or negotiated on behalf of the principal fall outside Article 81(1). The following obligations on the agent's part will generally be considered to form an inherent part of an agency agreement, as each of them relates to the ability of the principal to fix the scope of activity of the agent in relation to the contract goods or services, which is essential if the principal is to take the risks and therefore to be in a position to determine the commercial strategy:

- limitations on the territory in which the agent may sell these goods or services;
- limitations on the customers to whom the agent may sell these goods or services;
- the prices and conditions at which the agent must sell or purchase these goods or services.

(19) In addition to governing the conditions of sale or purchase of the contract goods or services by the agent on behalf of the principal, agency agreements often contain provisions which concern the relationship between the agent and the principal. In particular, they may contain a provision preventing the principal from appointing other agents in respect of a given type of transaction, customer or territory (exclusive agency provisions) and/or a provision preventing the agent from acting as an agent or distributor of undertakings which compete with the principal (non-compete provisions). Exclusive agency provisions concern only intra-brand competition and will in general not lead to anti-competitive effects. Non-compete provisions, including post-term non-compete provisions, concern inter-brand competition and may infringe Article 81(1) if they lead to foreclosure on the relevant market where the contract goods or services are sold or purchased (see Section VI.2.1).

(20) An agency agreement may also fall within the scope of Article 81(1), even if the principal bears all the relevant financial and commercial risks, where it facilitates collusion. This could for instance be the case when a number of principals use the same agents while collectively excluding others from using these agents, or when they use the agents to collude on marketing strategy or to exchange sensitive market information between the principals.

III. APPLICATION OF THE BLOCK EXEMPTION REGULATION

1. Safe harbour created by the Block Exemption Regulation

(21) The Block Exemption Regulation creates a presumption of legality for vertical agreements depending on the market share of the supplier or the buyer. Pursuant to Article 3 of the Block Exemption Regulation, it is in general the market share of the supplier on the market where it sells the contract goods or services which determines the applicability of the block exemption. This market share may not exceed the threshold of 30% in order for the block exemption to apply. Only where the agreement contains an exclusive supply obligation, as defined in Article 1(c) of the Block Exemption Regulation, is it the buyer's market share on the market where it purchases the contract goods or services which may not exceed the threshold of 30% in order for the block exemption to apply. For market share issues see Section V (paragraphs 88 to 99).

(22) From an economic point of view, a vertical agreement may have effects not only on the market between supplier and buyer but also on markets downstream of the buyer. The simplified approach of the Block Exemption Regulation, which only takes into account the market share of the supplier or the buyer (as the case may be) on the market between these two parties, is justified by the fact that below the threshold of 30% the effects on downstream markets will in general be limited. In addition, only having to consider the market between supplier and buyer makes the application of the Block Exemption Regulation easier and enhances the level of legal certainty, while the instrument of withdrawal (see paragraphs 71 to 87) remains available to remedy possible problems on other related markets.

2. Scope of the Block Exemption Regulation

(i) Definition of vertical agreements

(23) Vertical agreements are defined in Article 2(1) of the Block Exemption Regulation as "agreements or concerted practices entered into between two or

more undertakings each of which operates, for the purposes of the agreement, at a different level of the production or distribution chain, and relating to the conditions under which the parties may purchase, sell or resell certain goods or services".

(24) There are three main elements in this definition:

- the agreement or concerted practice is between two or more undertakings. Vertical agreements with final consumers not operating as an undertaking are not covered; More generally, agreements with final consumers do not fall under Article 81(1), as that article applies only to agreements between undertakings, decisions by associations of undertakings and concerted practices. This is without prejudice to the possible application of Article 82 of the Treaty;
- the agreement or concerted practice is between undertakings each operating, for the purposes of the agreement, at a different level of the production or distribution chain. This means for instance that one undertaking produces a raw material which the other undertaking uses as an input, or that the first is a manufacturer, the second a wholesaler and the third a retailer. This does not preclude an undertaking from being active at more than one level of the production or distribution chain;
- the agreements or concerted practices relate to the conditions under which the parties to the agreement, the supplier and the buyer, "may purchase, sell or resell certain goods or services". This reflects the purpose of the Block Exemption Regulation to cover purchase and distribution agreements. These are agreements which concern the conditions for the purchase, sale or resale of the goods or services supplied by the supplier and/or which concern the conditions for the sale by the buyer of the goods or services which incorporate these goods or services. For the application of the Block Exemption Regulation both the goods or services supplied by the supplier and the resulting goods or services are considered to be contract goods or services. Vertical agreements relating to all final and intermediate goods and services are covered.The only exception is the automobile sector, as long as this sector remains covered by a specific block exemption such as that granted by Commission Regulation (EC) No 1475/95.[9] The goods or services provided by the supplier may be resold by the buyer or may be used as an input by the buyer to produce his own goods or services.

---

9 OJ L 145, 29.6.1995, p. 25.

(25) The Block Exemption Regulation also applies to goods sold and purchased for renting to third parties. However, rent and lease agreements as such are not covered, as no good or service is being sold by the supplier to the buyer. More generally, the Block Exemption Regulation does not cover restrictions or obligations that do not relate to the conditions of purchase, sale and resale, such as an obligation preventing parties from carrying out independent research and development which the parties may have included in an otherwise vertical agreement. In addition, Articles 2(2) to (5) directly or indirectly exclude certain vertical agreements from the application of the Block Exemption Regulation.

(ii) Vertical agreements between competitors

(26) Article 2(4) of the Block Exemption Regulation explicitly excludes from its application "vertical agreements entered into between competing undertakings". Vertical agreements between competitors will be dealt with, as regards possible collusion effects, in the forthcoming Guidelines on the applicability of Article 81 to horizontal cooperation.[10] However, the vertical aspects of such agreements need to be assessed under these Guidelines. Article 1(a) of the Block Exemption Regulation defines competing undertakings as "actual or potential suppliers in the same product market", irrespective of whether or not they are competitors on the same geographic market. Competing undertakings are undertakings that are actual or potential suppliers of the contract goods or services or goods or services that are substitutes for the contract goods or services. A potential supplier is an undertaking that does not actually produce a competing product but could and would be likely to do so in the absence of the agreement in response to a small and permanent increase in relative prices. This means that the undertaking would be able and likely to undertake the necessary additional investments and supply the market within 1 year. This assessment has to be based on realistic grounds; the mere theoretical possibility of entering a market is not sufficient.[11]

(27) There are three exceptions to the general exclusion of vertical agreements between competitors, all three being set out in Article 2(4) and relating to non-reciprocal agreements. Non-reciprocal means, for instance, that while one

---

10 Draft text published in OJ C 118, 27.4.2000, p. 14.

11 See Commission Notice on the definition of the relevant market for the purposes of Community competition law, OJ C 372, 9.12.1997, p. 5, at paras. 20-24, the Commission's Thirteenth Report on Competition Policy, point 55, and Commission Decision 90/410/EEC in Case No IV/32.009 – Elopak/Metal Box-Odin, OJ L 209, 8.8.1990, p. 15.

manufacturer becomes the distributor of the products of another manufacturer, the latter does not become the distributor of the products of the first manufacturer. Non-reciprocal agreements between competitors are covered by the Block Exemption Regulation where (1) the buyer has a turnover not exceeding EUR 100 million, or (2) the supplier is a manufacturer and distributor of goods, while the buyer is only a distributor and not also a manufacturer of competing goods, or (3) the supplier is a provider of services operating at several levels of trade, while the buyer does not provide competing services at the level of trade where it purchases the contract services. The second exception covers situations of dual distribution, i.e. the manufacturer of particular goods also acts as a distributor of the goods in competition with independent distributors of his goods. A distributor who provides specifications to a manufacturer to produce particular goods under the distributor's brand name is not to be considered a manufacturer of such own-brand goods. The third exception covers similar situations of dual distribution, but in this case for services, when the supplier is also a provider of services at the level of the buyer.

(iii) Associations of retailers

(28) Article 2(2) of the Block Exemption Regulation includes in its application vertical agreements entered into by an association of undertakings which fulfils certain conditions and thereby excludes from the Block Exemption Regulation vertical agreements entered into by all other associations. Vertical agreements entered into between an association and its members, or between an association and its suppliers, are covered by the Block Exemption Regulation only if all the members are retailers of goods (not services) and if each individual member of the association has a turnover not exceeding EUR 50 million. Retailers are distributors reselling goods to final consumers. Where only a limited number of the members of the association have a turnover not significantly exceeding the EUR 50 million threshold, this will normally not change the assessment under Article 81.

(29) An association of undertakings may involve both horizontal and vertical agreements. The horizontal agreements have to be assessed according to the principles set out in the forthcoming Guidelines on the applicability of Article 81 to horizontal cooperation. If this assessment leads to the conclusion that a cooperation between undertakings in the area of purchasing or selling is acceptable, a further assessment will be necessary to examine the vertical agreements concluded by the association with its suppliers or its individual members. The latter assessment will follow the rules of the Block Exemption Regulation and these Guidelines. For instance, horizontal agreements concluded between the members of the association or decisions adopted by the association, such as the decision to require the members

to purchase from the association or the decision to allocate exclusive territories to the members have to be assessed first as a horizontal agreement. Only if this assessment is positive does it become relevant to assess the vertical agreements between the association and individual members or between the association and suppliers.

(iv) Vertical agreements containing provisions on intellectual property rights (IPRs)

(30) Article 2(3) of the Block Exemption Regulation includes in its application vertical agreements containing certain provisions relating to the assignment of IPRs to or use of IPRs by the buyer and thereby excludes from the Block Exemption Regulation all other vertical agreements containing IPR provisions. The Block Exemption Regulation applies to vertical agreements containing IPR provisions when five conditions are fulfilled:

- The IPR provisions must be part of a vertical agreement, i.e. an agreement with conditions under which the parties may purchase, sell or resell certain goods or services;
- The IPRs must be assigned to, or for use by, the buyer;
- The IPR provisions must not constitute the primary object of the agreement;
- The IPR provisions must be directly related to the use, sale or resale of goods or services by the buyer or his customers. In the case of franchising where marketing forms the object of the exploitation of the IPRs, the goods or services are distributed by the master franchisee or the franchisees;
- The IPR provisions, in relation to the contract goods or services, must not contain restrictions of competition having the same object or effect as vertical restraints which are not exempted under the Block Exemption Regulation.

(31) These conditions ensure that the Block Exemption Regulation applies to vertical agreements where the use, sale or resale of goods or services can be performed more effectively because IPRs are assigned to or transferred for use by the buyer. In other words, restrictions concerning the assignment or use of IPRs can be covered when the main object of the agreement is the purchase or distribution of goods or services.

(32) The first condition makes clear that the context in which the IPRs are provided is an agreement to purchase or distribute goods or an agreement to purchase or

provide services and not an agreement concerning the assignment or licensing of IPRs for the manufacture of goods, nor a pure licensing agreement. The Block Exemption Regulation does not cover for instance:

- agreements where a party provides another party with a recipe and licenses the other party to produce a drink with this recipe;
- agreements under which one party provides another party with a mould or master copy and licenses the other party to produce and distribute copies;
- the pure licence of a trade mark or sign for the purposes of merchandising;
- sponsorship contracts concerning the right to advertise oneself as being an official sponsor of an event;
- copyright licensing such as broadcasting contracts concerning the right to record and/or the right to broadcast an event.

(33) The second condition makes clear that the Block Exemption Regulation does not apply when the IPRs are provided by the buyer to the supplier, no matter whether the IPRs concern the manner of manufacture or of distribution. An agreement relating to the transfer of IPRs to the supplier and containing possible restrictions on the sales made by the supplier is not covered by the Block Exemption Regulation. This means in particular that subcontracting involving the transfer of know-how to a subcontractor[12] does not fall within the scope of application of the Block Exemption Regulation. However, vertical agreements under which the buyer provides only specifications to the supplier which describe the goods or services to be supplied are covered by the Block Exemption Regulation.

(34) The third condition makes clear that in order to be covered by the Block Exemption Regulation the primary object of the agreement must not be the assignment or licensing of IPRs. The primary object must be the purchase or distribution of goods or services and the IPR provisions must serve the implementation of the vertical agreement.

(35) The fourth condition requires that the IPR provisions facilitate the use, sale or resale of goods or services by the buyer or his customers. The goods or services for use or resale are usually supplied by the licensor but may also be purchased by the

12 See Notice on subcontracting, OJ C 1, 3.1.1979, p. 2.

licensee from a third supplier. The IPR provisions will normally concern the marketing of goods or services. This is for instance the case in a franchise agreement where the franchisor sells to the franchisee goods for resale and in addition licenses the franchisee to use his trade mark and know-how to market the goods. Also covered is the case where the supplier of a concentrated extract licenses the buyer to dilute and bottle the extract before selling it as a drink.

(36) The fifth condition signifies in particular that the IPR provisions should not have the same object or effect as any of the hardcore restrictions listed in Article 4 of the Block Exemption Regulation or any of the restrictions excluded from the coverage of the Block Exemption Regulation by Article 5 (see paragraphs 46 to 61).

(37) Intellectual property rights which may be considered to serve the implementation of vertical agreements within the meaning of Article 2(3) of the Block Exemption Regulation generally concern three main areas: trade marks, copyright and know-how.

Trade mark

(38) A trade mark licence to a distributor may be related to the distribution of the licensor's products in a particular territory. If it is an exclusive licence, the agreement amounts to exclusive distribution.

Copyright

(39) Resellers of goods covered by copyright (books, software, etc.) may be obliged by the copyright holder only to resell under the condition that the buyer, whether another reseller or the end user, shall not infringe the copyright. Such obligations on the reseller, to the extent that they fall under Article 81(1) at all, are covered by the Block Exemption Regulation.

(40) Agreements under which hard copies of software are supplied for resale and where the reseller does not acquire a licence to any rights over the software but only has the right to resell the hard copies, are to be regarded as agreements for the supply of goods for resale for the purpose of the Block Exemption Regulation. Under this form of distribution the licence of the software only takes place between the copyright owner and the user of the software. This may take the form of a "shrink wrap" licence, i.e. a set of conditions included in the package of the hard copy which the end user is deemed to accept by opening the package.

(41) Buyers of hardware incorporating software protected by copyright may be obliged by the copyright holder not to infringe the copyright, for example not to make copies and resell the software or not to make copies and use the software in combination with other hardware. Such use-restrictions, to the extent that they fall within Article 81(1) at all, are covered by the Block Exemption Regulation.

Know-how

(42) Franchise agreements, with the exception of industrial franchise agreements, are the most obvious example where know-how for marketing purposes is communicated to the buyer. Franchise agreements contain licences of intellectual property rights relating to trade marks or signs and know-how for the use and distribution of goods or the provision of services. In addition to the licence of IPR, the franchisor usually provides the franchisee during the life of the agreement with commercial or technical assistance, such as procurement services, training, advice on real estate, financial planning etc. The licence and the assistance are integral components of the business method being franchised.

(43) Licensing contained in franchise agreements is covered by the Block Exemption Regulation if all five conditions listed in point 30 are fulfilled. This is usually the case, as under most franchise agreements, including master franchise agreements, the franchisor provides goods and/or services, in particular commercial or technical assistance services, to the franchisee. The IPRs help the franchisee to resell the products supplied by the franchisor or by a supplier designated by the franchisor or to use those products and sell the resulting goods or services. Where the franchise agreement only or primarily concerns licensing of IPRs, such an agreement is not covered by the Block Exemption Regulation, but it will be treated in a way similar to those franchise agreements which are covered by the Block Exemption Regulation.

(44) The following IPR-related obligations are generally considered to be necessary to protect the franchisor's intellectual property rights and are, if these obligations fall under Article 81(1), also covered by the Block Exemption Regulation:

(a) an obligation on the franchisee not to engage, directly or indirectly, in any similar business;

(b) an obligation on the franchisee not to acquire financial interests in the capital of a competing undertaking such as would give the franchisee the power to influence the economic conduct of such undertaking;

(c) an obligation on the franchisee not to disclose to third parties the know-how provided by the franchisor as long as this know-how is not in the public domain;

(d) an obligation on the franchisee to communicate to the franchisor any experience gained in exploiting the franchise and to grant it, and other franchisees, a non-exclusive licence for the know-how resulting from that experience;

(e) an obligation on the franchisee to inform the franchisor of infringements of licensed intellectual property rights, to take legal action against infringers or to assist the franchisor in any legal actions against infringers;

(f) an obligation on the franchisee not to use know-how licensed by the franchisor for purposes other than the exploitation of the franchise;

(g) an obligation on the franchisee not to assign the rights and obligations under the franchise agreement without the franchisor's consent.

(v) Relationship to other block exemption regulations

(45) Article 2(5) states that the Block Exemption Regulation does "not apply to vertical agreements the subject matter of which falls within the scope of any other block exemption regulation." This means that the Block Exemption Regulation does not apply to vertical agreements covered by Commission Regulation (EC) No 240/96[13] on technology transfer, Commission Regulation (EC) No 1475/1995[14] for car distribution or Regulations (EEC) No 417/85[15] and (EEC) No 418/85[16] exempting vertical agreements concluded in connection with horizontal agreements, as last amended by Regulation (EC) No 2236/97[17] or any future regulations of that kind.

---

13 OJ L 31, 9.2.1996, p. 2.

14 OJ L 145, 29.6.1995, p. 25.

15 OJ L 53, 22.2.1985, p. 1.

16 OJ L 53, 22.2.1985, p. 5.

17 OJ L 306, 11.11.1997, p. 12.

3. Hardcore restrictions under the Block Exemption Regulation

(46) The Block Exemption Regulation contains in Article 4 a list of hardcore restrictions which lead to the exclusion of the whole vertical agreement from the scope of application of the Block Exemption Regulation. This list of hardcore restrictions applies to vertical agreements concerning trade within the Community. In so far as vertical agreements concern exports outside the Community or imports/ re-imports from outside the Community see the judgment in Javico v Yves Saint Laurent. Individual exemption of vertical agreements containing such hardcore restrictions is also unlikely.

(47) The hardcore restriction set out in Article 4(a) of the Block Exemption Regulation concerns resale price maintenance (RPM), that is agreements or concerted practices having as their direct or indirect object the establishment of a fixed or minimum resale price or a fixed or minimum price level to be observed by the buyer. In the case of contractual provisions or concerted practices that directly establish the resale price, the restriction is clear cut. However, RPM can also be achieved through indirect means. Examples of the latter are an agreement fixing the distribution margin, fixing the maximum level of discount the distributor can grant from a prescribed price level, making the grant of rebates or reimbursement of promotional costs by the supplier subject to the observance of a given price level, linking the prescribed resale price to the resale prices of competitors, threats, intimidation, warnings, penalties, delay or suspension of deliveries or contract terminations in relation to observance of a given price level. Direct or indirect means of achieving price fixing can be made more effective when combined with measures to identify price-cutting distributors, such as the implementation of a price monitoring system, or the obligation on retailers to report other members of the distribution network who deviate from the standard price level. Similarly, direct or indirect price fixing can be made more effective when combined with measures which may reduce the buyer's incentive to lower the resale price, such as the supplier printing a recommended resale price on the product or the supplier obliging the buyer to apply a most-favoured-customer clause. The same indirect means and the same "supportive" measures can be used to make maximum or recommended prices work as RPM. However, the provision of a list of recommended prices or maximum prices by the supplier to the buyer is not considered in itself as leading to RPM.

(48) In the case of agency agreements, the principal normally establishes the sales price, as the agent does not become the owner of the goods. However, where an agency agreement falls within Article 81(1) (see paragraphs 12 to 20), an obligation

preventing or restricting the agent from sharing his commission, fixed or variable, with the customer would be a hardcore restriction under Article 4(a) of the Block Exemption Regulation. The agent should thus be left free to lower the effective price paid by the customer without reducing the income for the principal.[18]

(49) The hardcore restriction set out in Article 4(b) of the Block Exemption Regulation concerns agreements or concerted practices that have as their direct or indirect object the restriction of sales by the buyer, in as far as those restrictions relate to the territory into which or the customers to whom the buyer may sell the contract goods or services. That hardcore restriction relates to market partitioning by territory or by customer. That may be the result of direct obligations, such as the obligation not to sell to certain customers or to customers in certain territories or the obligation to refer orders from these customers to other distributors. It may also result from indirect measures aimed at inducing the distributor not to sell to such customers, such as refusal or reduction of bonuses or discounts, refusal to supply, reduction of supplied volumes or limitation of supplied volumes to the demand within the allocated territory or customer group, threat of contract termination or profit pass-over obligations. It may further result from the supplier not providing a Community-wide guarantee service, whereby all distributors are obliged to provide the guarantee service and are reimbursed for this service by the supplier, even in relation to products sold by other distributors into their territory. These practices are even more likely to be viewed as a restriction of the buyer's sales when used in conjunction with the implementation by the supplier of a monitoring system aimed at verifying the effective destination of the supplied goods, e.g. the use of differentiated labels or serial numbers. However, a prohibition imposed on all distributors to sell to certain end users is not classified as a hardcore restriction if there is an objective justification related to the product, such as a general ban on selling dangerous substances to certain customers for reasons of safety or health. It implies that also the supplier himself does not sell to these customers. Nor are obligations on the reseller relating to the display of the supplier's brand name classified as hardcore.

(50) There are four exceptions to the hardcore restriction in Article 4(b) of the Block Exemption Regulation. The first exception allows a supplier to restrict active sales by his direct buyers to a territory or a customer group which has been allocated

---

[18] See, for instance, Commission Decision 91/562/EEC in Case No IV/32.737 – Eirpage, OJ L 306, 7.11.1991, p. 22, in particular point (6).

exclusively to another buyer or which the supplier has reserved to itself. A territory or customer group is exclusively allocated when the supplier agrees to sell his product only to one distributor for distribution in a particular territory or to a particular customer group and the exclusive distributor is protected against active selling into his territory or to his customer group by the supplier and all the other buyers of the supplier inside the Community. The supplier is allowed to combine the allocation of an exclusive territory and an exclusive customer group by for instance appointing an exclusive distributor for a particular customer group in a certain territory. This protection of exclusively allocated territories or customer groups must, however, permit passive sales to such territories or customer groups. For the application of Article 4(b) of the Block Exemption Regulation, the Commission interprets "active" and "passive" sales as follows:

- "Active" sales mean actively approaching individual customers inside another distributor's exclusive territory or exclusive customer group by for instance direct mail or visits; or actively approaching a specific customer group or customers in a specific territory allocated exclusively to another distributor through advertisement in media or other promotions specifically targeted at that customer group or targeted at customers in that territory; or establishing a warehouse or distribution outlet in another distributor's exclusive territory.
- "Passive" sales mean responding to unsolicited requests from individual customers including delivery of goods or services to such customers. General advertising or promotion in media or on the Internet that reaches customers in other distributors' exclusive territories or customer groups but which is a reasonable way to reach customers outside those territories or customer groups, for instance to reach customers in non-exclusive territories or in one's own territory, are passive sales.

(51) Every distributor must be free to use the Internet to advertise or to sell products. A restriction on the use of the Internet by distributors could only be compatible with the Block Exemption Regulation to the extent that promotion on the Internet or sales over the Internet would lead to active selling into other distributors' exclusive territories or customer groups. In general, the use of the Internet is not considered a form of active sales into such territories or customer groups, since it is a reasonable way to reach every customer. The fact that it may have effects outside one's own territory or customer group results from the technology, i.e. the easy access from everywhere. If a customer visits the web site of a distributor and contacts the distributor and if such contact leads to a sale, including delivery, then that is

considered passive selling. The language used on the website or in the communication plays normally no role in that respect. Insofar as a web site is not specifically targeted at customers primarily inside the territory or customer group exclusively allocated to another distributor, for instance with the use of banners or links in pages of providers specifically available to these exclusively allocated customers, the website is not considered a form of active selling. However, unsolicited e-mails sent to individual customers or specific customer groups are considered active selling. The same considerations apply to selling by catalogue. Notwithstanding what has been said before, the supplier may require quality standards for the use of the Internet site to resell his goods, just as the supplier may require quality standards for a shop or for advertising and promotion in general. The latter may be relevant in particular for selective distribution. An outright ban on Internet or catalogue selling is only possible if there is an objective justification. In any case, the supplier cannot reserve to itself sales and/or advertising over the Internet.

(52) There are three other exceptions to the second hardcore restriction set out in Article 4(b) of the Block Exemption Regulation. All three exceptions allow for the restriction of both active and passive sales. Thus, it is permissible to restrict a wholesaler from selling to end users, to restrict an appointed distributor in a selective distribution system from selling, at any level of trade, to unauthorised distributors in markets where such a system is operated, and to restrict a buyer of components supplied for incorporation from reselling them to competitors of the supplier. The term "component" includes any intermediate goods and the term "incorporation" refers to the use of any input to produce goods.

(53) The hardcore restriction set out in Article 4(c) of the Block Exemption Regulation concerns the restriction of active or passive sales to end users, whether professional end users or final consumers, by members of a selective distribution network. This means that dealers in a selective distribution system, as defined in Article 1(d) of the Block Exemption Regulation, cannot be restricted in the users or purchasing agents acting on behalf of these users to whom they may sell. For instance, also in a selective distribution system the dealer should be free to advertise and sell with the help of the Internet. Selective distribution may be combined with exclusive distribution provided that active and passive selling is not restricted anywhere. The supplier may therefore commit itself to supplying only one dealer or a limited number of dealers in a given territory.

(54) In addition, in the case of selective distribution, restrictions can be imposed on the dealer's ability to determine the location of his business premises. Selected

dealers may be prevented from running their business from different premises or from opening a new outlet in a different location. If the dealer's outlet is mobile ("shop on wheels"), an area may be defined outside which the mobile outlet cannot be operated.

(55) The hardcore restriction set out in Article 4(d) of the Block Exemption Regulation concerns the restriction of cross-supplies between appointed distributors within a selective distribution system. This means that an agreement or concerted practice may not have as its direct or indirect object to prevent or restrict the active or passive selling of the contract products between the selected distributors. Selected distributors must remain free to purchase the contract products from other appointed distributors within the network, operating either at the same or at a different level of trade. This means that selective distribution cannot be combined with vertical restraints aimed at forcing distributors to purchase the contract products exclusively from a given source, for instance exclusive purchasing. It also means that within a selective distribution network no restrictions can be imposed on appointed wholesalers as regards their sales of the product to appointed retailers.

(56) The hardcore restriction set out in Article 4(e) of the Block Exemption Regulation concerns agreements that prevent or restrict end-users, independent repairers and service providers from obtaining spare parts directly from the manufacturer of these spare parts. An agreement between a manufacturer of spare parts and a buyer who incorporates these parts into his own products (original equipment manufacturer (OEM)), may not, either directly or indirectly, prevent or restrict sales by the manufacturer of these spare parts to end users, independent repairers or service providers. Indirect restrictions may arise in particular when the supplier of the spare parts is restricted in supplying technical information and special equipment which are necessary for the use of spare parts by users, independent repairers or service providers. However, the agreement may place restrictions on the supply of the spare parts to the repairers or service providers entrusted by the original equipment manufacturer with the repair or servicing of his own goods. In other words, the original equipment manufacturer may require his own repair and service network to buy the spare parts from it.

4. Conditions under the Block Exemption Regulation

(57) Article 5 of the Block Exemption Regulation excludes certain obligations from the coverage of the Block Exemption Regulation even though the market share threshold is not exceeded. However, the Block Exemption Regulation

continues to apply to the remaining part of the vertical agreement if that part is severable from the non-exempted obligations.

(58) The first exclusion is provided in Article 5(a) of the Block Exemption Regulation and concerns non-compete obligations. Non-compete obligations are obligations that require the buyer to purchase from the supplier or from another undertaking designated by the supplier more than 80% of the buyer's total purchases during the previous year of the contract goods and services and their substitutes (see the definition in Article 1(b) of the Block Exemption Regulation), thereby preventing the buyer from purchasing competing goods or services or limiting such purchases to less than 20% of total purchases. Where for the year preceding the conclusion of the contract no relevant purchasing data for the buyer are available, the buyer's best estimate of his annual total requirements may be used. Such non-compete obligations are not covered by the Block Exemption Regulation when their duration is indefinite or exceeds five years. Non-compete obligations that are tacitly renewable beyond a period of five years are also not covered by the Block Exemption Regulation. However, non-compete obligations are covered when their duration is limited to five years or less, or when renewal beyond five years requires explicit consent of both parties and no obstacles exist that hinder the buyer from effectively terminating the non-compete obligation at the end of the five year period. If for instance the agreement provides for a five-year non-compete obligation and the supplier provides a loan to the buyer, the repayment of that loan should not hinder the buyer from effectively terminating the non-compete obligation at the end of the five-year period; the repayment needs to be structured in equal or decreasing instalments and should not increase over time. This is without prejudice to the possibility, in the case for instance of a new distribution outlet, to delay repayment for the first one or two years until sales have reached a certain level. The buyer must have the possibility to repay the remaining debt where there is still an outstanding debt at the end of the non-compete obligation. Similarly, when the supplier provides the buyer with equipment which is not relationship-specific, the buyer should have the possibility to take over the equipment at its market asset value at the end of the non-compete obligation.

(59) The five-year duration limit does not apply when the goods or services are resold by the buyer "from premises and land owned by the supplier or leased by the supplier from third parties not connected with the buyer." In such cases the non-compete obligation may be of the same duration as the period of occupancy of the point of sale by the buyer (Article 5(a) of the Block Exemption Regulation). The reason for this exception is that it is normally unreasonable to expect a supplier

to allow competing products to be sold from premises and land owned by the supplier without his permission. Artificial ownership constructions intended to avoid the five-year limit cannot benefit from this exception.

(60) The second exclusion from the block exemption is provided for in Article 5(b) of the Block Exemption Regulation and concerns post term non-compete obligations. Such obligations are normally not covered by the Block Exemption Regulation, unless the obligation is indispensable to protect know-how transferred by the supplier to the buyer, is limited to the point of sale from which the buyer has operated during the contract period, and is limited to a maximum period of one year. According to the definition in Article 1(f) of the Block Exemption Regulation the know-how needs to be "substantial", meaning "that the know-how includes information which is indispensable to the buyer for the use, sale or resale of the contract goods or services".

(61) The third exclusion from the block exemption is provided for in Article 5(c) of the Block Exemption Regulation and concerns the sale of competing goods in a selective distribution system. The Block Exemption Regulation covers the combination of selective distribution with a non-compete obligation, obliging the dealers not to resell competing brands in general. However, if the supplier prevents his appointed dealers, either directly or indirectly, from buying products for resale from specific competing suppliers, such an obligation cannot enjoy the benefit of the Block Exemption Regulation. The objective of the exclusion of this obligation is to avoid a situation whereby a number of suppliers using the same selective distribution outlets prevent one specific competitor or certain specific competitors from using these outlets to distribute their products (foreclosure of a competing supplier which would be a form of collective boycott).[19]

5. No presumption of illegality outside the Block Exemption Regulation

(62) Vertical agreements falling outside the Block Exemption Regulation will not be presumed to be illegal but may need individual examination. Companies are encouraged to do their own assessment without notification. In the case of an individual examination by the Commission, the latter will bear the burden of proof

[19] An example of indirect measures having such exclusionary effects can be found in Commission Decision 92/428/EEC in Case No IV/33.542 – Parfum Givenchy (OJ L 236, 19.8.1992, p. 11).

that the agreement in question infringes Article 81(1). When appreciable anti-competitive effects are demonstrated, undertakings may substantiate efficiency claims and explain why a certain distribution system is likely to bring about benefits which are relevant to the conditions for exemption under Article 81(3).

6. No need for precautionary notification

(63) Pursuant to Article 4(2) of Council Regulation No 17 of 6 February 1962, First Regulation implementing Articles 85 and 86 of the Treaty,[20] as last amended by Regulation (EC) No 1216/1999,[21] vertical agreements can benefit from an exemption under Article 81(3) from their date of entry into force, even if notification occurs after that date. This means in practice that no precautionary notification needs to be made. If a dispute arises, an undertaking can still notify, in which case the Commission can exempt the vertical agreement with retroactive effect from the date of entry into force of the agreement if all four conditions of Article 81(3) are fulfilled. A notifying party does not have to explain why the agreement was not notified earlier and will not be denied retroactive exemption simply because it did not notify earlier. Any notification will be reviewed on its merits. This amendment to Article 4(2) of Regulation No 17 should eliminate artificial litigation before national courts and thus strengthen the civil enforceability of contracts. It also takes account of the situation where undertakings have not notified because they assumed the agreement was covered by the Block Exemption Regulation.

(64) Since the date of notification no longer limits the possibility of exemption by the Commission, national courts have to assess the likelihood that Article 81(3) will apply in respect of vertical agreements falling within Article 81(1). If such likelihood exists, they should suspend proceedings pending adoption of a position by the Commission. However, national courts may adopt interim measures pending the assessment by the Commission of the applicability of Article 81(3), in the same way as they do when they refer a preliminary question to the Court of Justice under Article 234 of the EC Treaty. No suspension is necessary in respect of injunction proceedings, where national courts themselves are empowered to assess the likelihood of application of Article 81(3).[22]

---

20 OJ 13, 21.2.1962, p. 204/62.

21 OJ L 148, 15.6.1999, p. 5.

22 Case C-234/89 *Delimitis v Henninger Bräu* [1991] ECR I-935, at paragraph 52.

(65) Unless there is litigation in national courts or complaints, notifications of vertical agreements will not be given priority in the Commission's enforcement policy. Notifications as such do not provide provisional validity for the execution of agreements. Where undertakings have not notified an agreement because they assumed in good faith that the market share threshold under the Block Exemption Regulation was not exceeded, the Commission will not impose fines.

7. Severability

(66) The Block Exemption Regulation exempts vertical agreements on condition that no hardcore restriction, as set out in Article 4, is contained in or practised with the vertical agreement. If there are one or more hardcore restrictions, the benefit of the Block Exemption Regulation is lost for the entire vertical agreement. There is no severability for hardcore restrictions.

(67) The rule of severability does apply, however, to the conditions set out in Article 5 of the Block Exemption Regulation. Therefore, the benefit of the block exemption is only lost in relation to that part of the vertical agreement which does not comply with the conditions set out in Article 5.

8. Portfolio of products distributed through the same distribution system

(68) Where a supplier uses the same distribution agreement to distribute several goods/services some of these may, in view of the market share threshold, be covered by the Block Exemption Regulation while others may not. In that case, the Block Exemption Regulation applies to those goods and services for which the conditions of application are fulfilled.

(69) In respect of the goods or services which are not covered by the Block Exemption Regulation, the ordinary rules of competition apply, which means:

- there is no block exemption but also no presumption of illegality;
- if there is an infringement of Article 81(1) which is not exemptable, consideration may be given to whether there are appropriate remedies to solve the competition problem within the existing distribution system;
- if there are no such appropriate remedies, the supplier concerned will have to make other distribution arrangements.

This situation can also arise where Article 82 applies in respect of some products but not in respect of others.

9. Transitional period

(70) The Block Exemption Regulation applies from 1 June 2000. Article 12 of the Block Exemption Regulation provides for a transitional period for vertical agreements already in force before 1 June 2000 which do not satisfy the conditions for exemption provided in the Block Exemption Regulation, but which do satisfy the conditions for exemption under the Block Exemption Regulations which expired on 31 May 2000 (Commissions Regulations (EEC) No 1983/83, (EEC) No 1984/83 and (EEC) No 4087/88). The Commission Notice concerning Regulations (EEC) Nos 1983/83 and 1984/83 also ceases to apply on 31 May 2000. The latter agreements may continue to benefit from these outgoing Regulations until 31 December 2001. Agreements of suppliers with a market share not exceeding 30% who signed with their buyers non-compete agreements with a duration exceeding five years are covered by the Block Exemption Regulation if on 1 January 2002 the non-compete agreements have no more than five years to run.

IV. WITHDRAWAL OF THE BLOCK EXEMPTION AND DISAPPLICATION OF THE BLOCK EXEMPTION REGULATION

1. Withdrawal procedure

(71) The presumption of legality conferred by the Block Exemption Regulation may be withdrawn if a vertical agreement, considered either in isolation or in conjunction with similar agreements enforced by competing suppliers or buyers, comes within the scope of Article 81(1) and does not fulfil all the conditions of Article 81(3). This may occur when a supplier, or a buyer in the case of exclusive supply agreements, holding a market share not exceeding 30%, enters into a vertical agreement which does not give rise to objective advantages such as to compensate for the damage which it causes to competition. This may particularly be the case with respect to the distribution of goods to final consumers, who are often in a much weaker position than professional buyers of intermediate goods. In the case of sales to final consumers, the disadvantages caused by a vertical agreement may have a stronger impact than in a case concerning the sale and purchase of intermediate goods. When the conditions of Article 81(3) are not fulfilled, the Commission may withdraw the benefit of the Block Exemption Regulation under

Article 6 and establish an infringement of Article 81(1).

(72) Where the withdrawal procedure is applied, the Commission bears the burden of proof that the agreement falls within the scope of Article 81(1) and that the agreement does not fulfil all four conditions of Article 81(3).

(73) The conditions for an exemption under Article 81(3) may in particular not be fulfilled when access to the relevant market or competition therein is significantly restricted by the cumulative effect of parallel networks of similar vertical agreements practised by competing suppliers or buyers. Parallel networks of vertical agreements are to be regarded as similar if they contain restraints producing similar effects on the market. Similar effects will normally occur when vertical restraints practised by competing suppliers or buyers come within one of the four groups listed in paragraphs 104 to 114. Such a situation may arise for example when, on a given market, certain suppliers practise purely qualitative selective distribution while other suppliers practise quantitative selective distribution. In such circumstances, the assessment must take account of the anti-competitive effects attributable to each individual network of agreements. Where appropriate, withdrawal may concern only the quantitative limitations imposed on the number of authorised distributors. Other cases in which a withdrawal decision may be taken include situations where the buyer, for example in the context of exclusive supply or exclusive distribution, has significant market power in the relevant downstream market where he resells the goods or provides the services.

(74) Responsibility for an anti-competitive cumulative effect can only be attributed to those undertakings which make an appreciable contribution to it. Agreements entered into by undertakings whose contribution to the cumulative effect is insignificant do not fall under the prohibition provided for in Article 81(1)[23] and are therefore not subject to the withdrawal mechanism. The assessment of such a contribution will be made in accordance with the criteria set out in paragraphs 137 to 229.

(75) A withdrawal decision can only have ex nunc effect, which means that the exempted status of the agreements concerned will not be affected until the date at which the withdrawal becomes effective.

---

23 Judgment in the Delimitis Case.

(76) Under Article 7 of the Block Exemption Regulation, the competent authority of a Member State may withdraw the benefit of the Block Exemption Regulation in respect of vertical agreements whose anti-competitive effects are felt in the territory of the Member State concerned or a part thereof, which has all the characteristics of a distinct geographic market. Where a Member State has not enacted legislation enabling the national competition authority to apply Community competition law or at least to withdraw the benefit of the Block Exemption Regulation, the Member State may ask the Commission to initiate proceedings to this effect.

(77) The Commission has the exclusive power to withdraw the benefit of the Block Exemption Regulation in respect of vertical agreements restricting competition on a relevant geographic market which is wider than the territory of a single Member State. When the territory of a single Member State, or a part thereof, constitutes the relevant geographic market, the Commission and the Member State concerned have concurrent competence for withdrawal. Often, such cases lend themselves to decentralised enforcement by national competition authorities. However, the Commission reserves the right to take on certain cases displaying a particular Community interest, such as cases raising a new point of law.

(78) National decisions of withdrawal must be taken in accordance with the procedures laid down under national law and will only have effect within the territory of the Member State concerned. Such national decisions must not prejudice the uniform application of the Community competition rules and the full effect of the measures adopted in implementation of those rules.[24] Compliance with this principle implies that national competition authorities must carry out their assessment under Article 81 in the light of the relevant criteria developed by the Court of Justice and the Court of First Instance and in the light of notices and previous decisions adopted by the Commission.

(79) The Commission considers that the consultation mechanisms provided for in the Notice on cooperation between national competition authorities and the Commission[25] should be used to avert the risk of conflicting decisions and duplication of procedures.

---

24 Judgment of the Court of Justice in Case 14/68 *Walt Wilhelm and Others v Bundeskartellamt* [1969] ECR 1, paragraph 4, and judgment in Delimitis.

25 OJ C 313, 15.10.1997, p. 3, points 49 to 53.

2. Disapplication of the Block Exemption Regulation

(80) Article 8 of the Block Exemption Regulation enables the Commission to exclude from the scope of the Block Exemption Regulation, by means of regulation, parallel networks of similar vertical restraints where these cover more than 50% of a relevant market. Such a measure is not addressed to individual undertakings but concerns all undertakings whose agreements are defined in the regulation disapplying the Block Exemption Regulation.

(81) Whereas the withdrawal of the benefit of the Block Exemption Regulation under Article 6 implies the adoption of a decision establishing an infringement of Article 81 by an individual company, the effect of a regulation under Article 8 is merely to remove, in respect of the restraints and the markets concerned, the benefit of the application of the Block Exemption Regulation and to restore the full application of Article 81(1) and (3). Following the adoption of a regulation declaring the Block Exemption inapplicable in respect of certain vertical restraints on a particular market, the criteria developed by the relevant case-law of the Court of Justice and the Court of First Instance and by notices and previous decisions adopted by the Commission will guide the application of Article 81 to individual agreements. Where appropriate, the Commission will take a decision in an individual case, which can provide guidance to all the undertakings operating on the market concerned.

(82) For the purpose of calculating the 50% market coverage ratio, account must be taken of each individual network of vertical agreements containing restraints, or combinations of restraints, producing similar effects on the market. Similar effects normally result when the restraints come within one of the four groups listed in paragraphs 104 to 114.

(83) Article 8 does not entail an obligation on the part of the Commission to act where the 50% market-coverage ratio is exceeded. In general, disapplication is appropriate when it is likely that access to the relevant market or competition therein is appreciably restricted. This may occur in particular when parallel networks of selective distribution covering more than 50% of a market make use of selection criteria which are not required by the nature of the relevant goods or discriminate against certain forms of distribution capable of selling such goods.

(84) In assessing the need to apply Article 8, the Commission will consider whether individual withdrawal would be a more appropriate remedy. This may depend, in

particular, on the number of competing undertakings contributing to a cumulative effect on a market or the number of affected geographic markets within the Community.

(85) Any regulation adopted under Article 8 must clearly set out its scope. This means, first, that the Commission must define the relevant product and geographic market(s) and, secondly, that it must identify the type of vertical restraint in respect of which the Block Exemption Regulation will no longer apply. As regards the latter aspect, the Commission may modulate the scope of its regulation according to the competition concern which it intends to address. For instance, while all parallel networks of single-branding type arrangements shall be taken into account in view of establishing the 50% market coverage ratio, the Commission may nevertheless restrict the scope of the disapplication regulation only to non-compete obligations exceeding a certain duration. Thus, agreements of a shorter duration or of a less restrictive nature might be left unaffected, in consideration of the lesser degree of foreclosure attributable to such restraints. Similarly, when on a particular market selective distribution is practised in combination with additional restraints such as non-compete or quantity-forcing on the buyer, the disapplication regulation may concern only such additional restraints. Where appropriate, the Commission may also provide guidance by specifying the market share level which, in the specific market context, may be regarded as insufficient to bring about a significant contribution by an individual undertaking to the cumulative effect.

(86) The transitional period of not less than six months that the Commission will have to set under Article 8(2) should allow the undertakings concerned to adapt their agreements to take account of the regulation disapplying the Block Exemption Regulation.

(87) A regulation disapplying the Block Exemption Regulation will not affect the exempted status of the agreements concerned for the period preceding its entry into force.

V. Market Definition and Market Share Calculation Issues

1. Commission Notice on definition of the relevant market

(88) The Commission Notice on definition of the relevant market for the purposes of Community competition law[26] provides guidance on the rules, criteria and evidence which the Commission uses when considering market definition issues. That Notice will not be further explained in these Guidelines and should serve as the basis for market definition issues. These Guidelines will only deal with specific issues that arise in the context of vertical restraints and that are not dealt with in the general notice on market definition.

2. The relevant market for calculating the 30% market share threshold under the Block Exemption Regulation

(89) Under Article 3 of the Block Exemption Regulation, it is in general the market share of the supplier that is decisive for the application of the block exemption. In the case of vertical agreements concluded between an association of retailers and individual members, the association is the supplier and needs to take into account its market share as a supplier. Only in the case of exclusive supply as defined in Article 1(c) of the Block Exemption Regulation is it the market share of the buyer, and only that market share, which is decisive for the application of the Block Exemption Regulation.

(90) In order to calculate the market share, it is necessary to determine the relevant market. For this, the relevant product market and the relevant geographic market must be defined. The relevant product market comprises any goods or services which are regarded by the buyer as interchangeable, by reason of their characteristics, prices and intended use. The relevant geographic market comprises the area in which the undertakings concerned are involved in the supply and demand of relevant goods or services, in which the conditions of competition are sufficiently homogeneous, and which can be distinguished from neighbouring geographic areas because, in particular, conditions of competition are appreciably different in those areas.

---

26 OJ C 372, 9.12.1997, p. 5.

(93) Where a vertical agreement involves three parties, each operating at a different level of trade, their market shares will have to be below the market share threshold of 30% at both levels in order to benefit from the block exemption. If for instance, in an agreement between a manufacturer, a wholesaler (or association of retailers) and a retailer, a non-compete obligation is agreed, then the market share of both the manufacturer and the wholesaler (or association of retailers) must not exceed 30% in order to benefit from the block exemption.

(94) Where a supplier produces both original equipment and the repair or replacement parts for this equipment, the supplier will often be the only or the major supplier on the after-market for the repair and replacement parts. This may also arise where the supplier (OEM supplier) subcontracts the manufacturing of the repair or replacement parts. The relevant market for application of the Block Exemption Regulation may be the original equipment market including the spare parts or a separate original equipment market and after-market depending on the circumstances of the case, such as the effects of the restrictions involved, the lifetime of the equipment and importance of the repair or replacement costs.[29]

(95) Where the vertical agreement, in addition to the supply of the contract goods, also contains IPR provisions – such as a provision concerning the use of the supplier's trademark – which help the buyer to market the contract goods, the supplier's market share on the market where he sells the contract goods is decisive for the application of the Block Exemption Regulation. Where a franchisor does not supply goods to be resold but provides a bundle of services combined with IPR provisions which together form the business method being franchised, the franchisor needs to take account of his market share as a provider of a business method. For that purpose, the franchisor needs to calculate his market share on the market where the business method is exploited, which is the market where the franchisees exploit the business method to provide goods or services to end users. The franchisor must base his market share on the value of the goods or services supplied by his

---

29 See for example Pelikan/Kyocera in XXV Report on Competition Policy, point 87, and Commission Decision 91/595/EEC in Case No IV/M.12 – Varta/Bosch, OJ L 320, 22.11.1991, p. 26, Commission Decision in Case No IV/M.1094 – Caterpillar/Perkins Engines, OJ C 94, 28.3.1998, p. 23, and Commission Decision in Case No IV/M.768 – Lucas/Varity, OJ C 266, 13.9.1996, p. 6. See also *Eastman Kodak Co v Image Technical Services, Inc et al*, Supreme Court of the United States, No 90 1029. See also point 56 of the Commission Notice on the definition of relevant market for the purposes of Community competition law.

franchisees on this market. On such a market the competitors may be providers of other franchised business methods but also suppliers of substitutable goods or services not applying franchising. For instance, without prejudice to the definition of such market, if there was a market for fast-food services, a franchisor operating on such a market would need to calculate his market share on the basis of the relevant sales figures of his franchisees on this market. If the franchisor, in addition to the business method, also supplies certain inputs, such as meat and spices, then the franchisor also needs to calculate his market share on the market where these goods are sold.

3. The relevant market for individual assessment

(96) For individual assessment of vertical agreements not covered by the Block Exemption Regulation, additional markets may need to be investigated besides the relevant market defined for the application of the Block Exemption Regulation. A vertical agreement may not only have effects on the market between supplier and buyer but may also have effects on downstream markets. For an individual assessment of a vertical agreement the relevant markets at each level of trade affected by restraints contained in the agreement will be examined:

(i) For "intermediate goods or services" that are incorporated by the buyer into his own goods or services, vertical restraints generally have effects only on the market between supplier and buyer. A non-compete obligation imposed on the buyer for instance may foreclose other suppliers but will not lead to reduced in-store competition downstream. However, in cases of exclusive supply the position of the buyer on his downstream market is also relevant because the buyer's foreclosing behaviour may only have appreciable negative effects if he has market power on the downstream market.

(ii) For "final products" an analysis limited to the market between supplier and buyer is less likely to be sufficient since vertical restraints may have negative effects of reduced inter-brand and/or intra-brand competition on the resale market, that is on the market downstream of the buyer. For instance, exclusive distribution may not only lead to foreclosure effects on the market between the supplier and the buyer, but may above all lead to less intra-brand competition in the resale territories of the distributors. The resale market is in particular important if the buyer is a retailer selling to final consumers. A non-compete obligation agreed between a manufacturer and a wholesaler may foreclose this wholesaler to other manufacturers but a loss of in-store competition is not very likely at the wholesale level. The same agreement concluded with a retailer may however cause this added loss of in-store inter-brand competition on the resale market.

(iii) In cases of individual assessment of an "after-market", the relevant market may be the original equipment market or the after-market depending on the circumstances of the case. In any event, the situation on a separate after-market will be evaluated taking account of the situation on the original equipment market. A less significant position on the original equipment market will normally reduce possible anti-competitive effects on the after-market.

4. Calculation of the market share under the Block Exemption Regulation

(97) The calculation of the market share needs to be based in principle on value figures. Where value figures are not available substantiated estimates can be made. Such estimates may be based on other reliable market information such as volume figures (see Article 9(1) of the Block Exemption Regulation).

(98) In-house production, that is production of an intermediate product for own use, may be very important in a competition analysis as one of the competitive constraints or to accentuate the market position of a company. However, for the purpose of market definition and the calculation of market share for intermediate goods and services, in-house production will not be taken into account.

(99) However, in the case of dual distribution of final goods, i.e. where a producer of final goods also acts as a distributor on the market, the market definition and market share calculation need to include the goods sold by the producer and competing producers through their integrated distributors and agents (see Article 9(2)(b) of the Block Exemption Regulation). "Integrated distributors" are connected undertakings within the meaning of Article 11 of the Block Exemption Regulation.

VI. ENFORCEMENT POLICY IN INDIVIDUAL CASES

(100) Vertical restraints are generally less harmful than horizontal restraints. The main reason for treating a vertical restraint more leniently than a horizontal restraint lies in the fact that the latter may concern an agreement between competitors producing identical or substitutable goods or services. In such horizontal relationships the exercise of market power by one company (higher price of its product) may benefit its competitors. This may provide an incentive to competitors to induce

each other to behave anti-competitively. In vertical relationships the product of the one is the input for the other. This means that the exercise of market power by either the upstream or downstream company would normally hurt the demand for the product of the other. The companies involved in the agreement therefore usually have an incentive to prevent the exercise of market power by the other.

(101) However, this self-restraining character should not be over-estimated. When a company has no market power it can only try to increase its profits by optimising its manufacturing and distribution processes, with or without the help of vertical restraints. However, when it does have market power it can also try to increase its profits at the expense of its direct competitors by raising their costs and at the expense of its buyers and ultimately consumers by trying to appropriate some of their surplus. This can happen when the upstream and downstream company share the extra profits or when one of the two uses vertical restraints to appropriate all the extra profits.

(102) In the assessment of individual cases, the Commission will adopt an economic approach in the application of Article 81 to vertical restraints. This will limit the scope of application of Article 81 to undertakings holding a certain degree of market power where inter-brand competition may be insufficient. In those cases, the protection of inter-brand and intra-brand competition is important to ensure efficiencies and benefits for consumers.

1. The framework of analysis

1.1. Negative effects of vertical restraints

(103) The negative effects on the market that may result from vertical restraints which EC competition law aims at preventing are the following:

(i) foreclosure of other suppliers or other buyers by raising barriers to entry;

(ii) reduction of inter-brand competition between the companies operating on a market, including facilitation of collusion amongst suppliers or buyers; by collusion is meant both explicit collusion and tacit collusion (conscious parallel behaviour);

(iii) reduction of intra-brand competition between distributors of the same brand;

(iv) the creation of obstacles to market integration, including, above all, limitations on the freedom of consumers to purchase goods or services in any Member State they may choose.

(104) Such negative effects may result from various vertical restraints. Agreements which are different in form may have the same substantive impact on competition. To analyse these possible negative effects, it is appropriate to divide vertical restraints into four groups: a single branding group, a limited distribution group, a resale price maintenance group and a market partitioning group. The vertical restraints within each group have largely similar negative effects on competition.

(105) The classification into four groups is based upon what can be described as the basic components of vertical restraints. In paragraphs 103 to 136, the four different groups are analysed. In 137 to 229, vertical agreements are analysed as they are used in practice because many vertical agreements make use of more than one of these components.

Single branding group

(106) Under the heading of "single branding" come those agreements which have as their main element that the buyer is induced to concentrate his orders for a particular type of product with one supplier. This component can be found amongst others in non-compete and quantity-forcing on the buyer, where an obligation or incentive scheme agreed between the supplier and the buyer makes the latter purchase his requirements for a particular product and its substitutes only, or mainly, from one supplier. The same component can be found in tying, where the obligation or incentive scheme relates to a product that the buyer is required to purchase as a condition of purchasing another distinct product. The first product is referred to as the "tied" product and the second is referred to as the "tying" product.

(107) There are four main negative effects on competition: (1) other suppliers in that market cannot sell to the particular buyers and this may lead to foreclosure of the market or, in the case of tying, to foreclosure of the market for the tied product; (2) it makes market shares more rigid and this may help collusion when applied by several suppliers; (3) as far as the distribution of final goods is concerned, the particular retailers will only sell one brand and there will therefore be no inter-brand competition in their shops (no in-store competition); and (4) in the case of tying, the buyer may pay a higher price for the tied product than he would otherwise do. All these effects may lead to a reduction in inter-brand competition.

(108) The reduction in inter-brand competition may be mitigated by strong initial competition between suppliers to obtain the single branding contracts, but the longer the duration of the non-compete obligation, the more likely it will be that this

(112) There are two main negative effects of RPM on competition: (1) a reduction in intra-brand price competition, and (2) increased transparency on prices. In the case of fixed or minimum RPM, distributors can no longer compete on price for that brand, leading to a total elimination of intra-brand price competition. A maximum or recommended price may work as a focal point for resellers, leading to a more or less uniform application of that price level. Increased transparency on price and responsibility for price changes makes horizontal collusion between manufacturers or distributors easier, at least in concentrated markets. The reduction in intra-brand competition may, as it leads to less downward pressure on the price for the particular goods, have as an indirect effect a reduction of inter-brand competition.

Market partitioning group

(113) Under the heading of "market partitioning" come agreements whose main element is that the buyer is restricted in where he either sources or resells a particular product. This component can be found in exclusive purchasing, where an obligation or incentive scheme agreed between the supplier and the buyer makes the latter purchase his requirements for a particular product, for instance beer of brand X, exclusively from the designated supplier, but leaving the buyer free to buy and sell competing products, for instance competing brands of beer. It also includes territorial resale restrictions, the allocation of an area of primary responsibility, restrictions on the location of a distributor and customer resale restrictions.

(114) The main negative effect on competition is a reduction of intra-brand competition that may help the supplier to partition the market and thus hinder market integration. This may facilitate price discrimination. When most or all of the competing suppliers limit the sourcing or resale possibilities of their buyers this may facilitate collusion, either at the distributors' level or at the suppliers' level.

1.2. Positive effects of vertical restraints

(115) It is important to recognise that vertical restraints often have positive effects by, in particular, promoting non-price competition and improved quality of services. When a company has no market power, it can only try to increase its profits by optimising its manufacturing or distribution processes. In a number of situations vertical restraints may be helpful in this respect since the usual arm's length dealings between supplier and buyer, determining only price and quantity of a certain transaction, can lead to a sub-optimal level of investments and sales.

(116) While trying to give a fair overview of the various justifications for vertical restraints, these Guidelines do not claim to be complete or exhaustive. The following reasons may justify the application of certain vertical restraints:

(1) To "solve a 'free-rider' problem". One distributor may free-ride on the promotion efforts of another distributor. This type of problem is most common at the wholesale and retail level. Exclusive distribution or similar restrictions may be helpful in avoiding such free-riding. Free-riding can also occur between suppliers, for instance where one invests in promotion at the buyer's premises, in general at the retail level, that may also attract customers for its competitors. Non-compete type restraints can help to overcome this situation of free-riding.

For there to be a problem, there needs to be a real free-rider issue. Free-riding between buyers can only occur on pre-sales services and not on after-sales services. The product will usually need to be relatively new or technically complex as the customer may otherwise very well know what he or she wants, based on past purchases. And the product must be of a reasonably high value as it is otherwise not attractive for a customer to go to one shop for information and to another to buy. Lastly, it must not be practical for the supplier to impose on all buyers, by contract, effective service requirements concerning pre-sales services.

Free-riding between suppliers is also restricted to specific situations, namely in cases where the promotion takes place at the buyer's premises and is generic, not brand specific.

(2) To "open up or enter new markets". Where a manufacturer wants to enter a new geographic market, for instance by exporting to another country for the first time, this may involve special "first time investments" by the distributor to establish the brand in the market. In order to persuade a local distributor to make these investments it may be necessary to provide territorial protection to the distributor so that he can recoup these investments by temporarily charging a higher price. Distributors based in other markets should then be restrained for a limited period from selling in the new market. This is a special case of the free-rider problem described under point (1).

(3) The "certification free-rider issue". In some sectors, certain retailers have a reputation for stocking only "quality" products. In such a case, selling through these retailers may be vital for the introduction of a new product. If the manufacturer cannot initially limit his sales to the premium stores, he runs the risk of being de-listed and the product introduction may fail. This means that there may be a reason for allowing for a limited duration a restriction

such as exclusive distribution or selective distribution. It must be enough to guarantee introduction of the new product but not so long as to hinder large-scale dissemination. Such benefits are more likely with "experience" goods or complex goods that represent a relatively large purchase for the final consumer.

(4) The so-called "hold-up problem". Sometimes there are client-specific investments to be made by either the supplier or the buyer, such as in special equipment or training. For instance, a component manufacturer that has to build new machines and tools in order to satisfy a particular requirement of one of his customers. The investor may not commit the necessary investments before particular supply arrangements are fixed.

However, as in the other free-riding examples, there are a number of conditions that have to be met before the risk of under-investment is real or significant. Firstly, the investment must be relationship-specific. An investment made by the supplier is considered to be relationship-specific when, after termination of the contract, it cannot be used by the supplier to supply other customers and can only be sold at a significant loss. An investment made by the buyer is considered to be relationship-specific when, after termination of the contract, it cannot be used by the buyer to purchase and/or use products supplied by other suppliers and can only be sold at a significant loss. An investment is thus relationship-specific because for instance it can only be used to produce a brand-specific component or to store a particular brand and thus cannot be used profitably to produce or resell alternatives. Secondly, it must be a long-term investment that is not recouped in the short run. And thirdly, the investment must be asymmetric; i.e. one party to the contract invests more than the other party. When these conditions are met, there is usually a good reason to have a vertical restraint for the duration it takes to depreciate the investment. The appropriate vertical restraint will be of the non-compete type or quantity-forcing type when the investment is made by the supplier and of the exclusive distribution, exclusive customer allocation or exclusive supply type when the investment is made by the buyer.

(5) The "specific hold-up problem that may arise in the case of transfer of substantial know-how". The know-how, once provided, cannot be taken back and the provider of the know-how may not want it to be used for or by his competitors. In as far as the know-how was not readily available to the buyer, is substantial and indispensable for the operation of the agreement, such a transfer may justify a non-compete type of restriction. This would

normally fall outside Article 81(1).

(6) "Economies of scale in distribution". In order to have scale economies exploited and thereby see a lower retail price for his product, the manufacturer may want to concentrate the resale of his products on a limited number of distributors. For this he could use exclusive distribution, quantity forcing in the form of a minimum purchasing requirement, selective distribution containing such a requirement or exclusive purchasing.

(7) "Capital market imperfections". The usual providers of capital (banks, equity markets) may provide capital sub-optimally when they have imperfect information on the quality of the borrower or there is an inadequate basis to secure the loan. The buyer or supplier may have better information and be able, through an exclusive relationship, to obtain extra security for his investment. Where the supplier provides the loan to the buyer this may lead to non-compete or quantity forcing on the buyer. Where the buyer provides the loan to the supplier this may be the reason for having exclusive supply or quantity forcing on the supplier.

(8) "Uniformity and quality standardisation". A vertical restraint may help to increase sales by creating a brand image and thereby increasing the attractiveness of a product to the final consumer by imposing a certain measure of uniformity and quality standardisation on the distributors. This can for instance be found in selective distribution and franchising.

(117) The eight situations mentioned in paragraph 116 make clear that under certain conditions vertical agreements are likely to help realise efficiencies and the development of new markets and that this may offset possible negative effects. The case is in general strongest for vertical restraints of a limited duration which help the introduction of new complex products or protect relationship-specific investments. A vertical restraint is sometimes necessary for as long as the supplier sells his product to the buyer (see in particular the situations described in paragraph 116, points (1), (5), (6) and (8).

(118) There is a large measure of substitutability between the different vertical restraints. This means that the same inefficiency problem can be solved by different vertical restraints. For instance, economies of scale in distribution may possibly be achieved by using exclusive distribution, selective distribution, quantity forcing or exclusive purchasing. This is important as the negative effects on competition may differ between the various vertical restraints. This plays a role when

indispensability is discussed under Article 81(3).

1.3. General rules for the evaluation of vertical restraints

(119) In evaluating vertical restraints from a competition policy perspective, some general rules can be formulated:

(1) For most vertical restraints competition concerns can only arise if there is insufficient inter-brand competition, i.e. if there exists a certain degree of market power at the level of the supplier or the buyer or both. Conceptually, market power is the power to raise price above the competitive level and, at least in the short term, to obtain supra-normal profits. Companies may have market power below the level of market dominance, which is the threshold for the application of Article 82. Where there are many firms competing in an unconcentrated market, it can be assumed that non-hardcore vertical restraints will not have appreciable negative effects. A market is deemed unconcentrated when the HHI index, i.e. the sum of the squares of the individual market shares of all companies in the relevant market, is below 1000.

(2) Vertical restraints which reduce inter-brand competition are generally more harmful than vertical restraints that reduce intra-brand competition. For instance, non-compete obligations are likely to have more net negative effects than exclusive distribution. The former, by possibly foreclosing the market to other brands, may prevent those brands from reaching the market. The latter, while limiting intra-brand competition, does not prevent goods from reaching the final consumer.

(3) Vertical restraints from the limited distribution group, in the absence of sufficient inter-brand competition, may significantly restrict the choices available to consumers. They are particularly harmful when more efficient distributors or distributors with a different distribution format are foreclosed. This can reduce innovation in distribution and denies consumers the particular service or price-service combination of these distributors.

(4) Exclusive dealing arrangements are generally worse for competition than non-exclusive arrangements. Exclusive dealing makes, by the express language of the contract or its practical effects, one party fulfil all or practically all its requirements from another party. For instance, under a non-compete obligation the buyer purchases only one brand. Quantity forcing, on the other hand, leaves the buyer some scope to purchase competing goods. The degree of foreclosure may therefore be less with quantity forcing.

(5) Vertical restraints agreed for non-branded goods and services are in general less harmful than restraints affecting the distribution of branded goods and services. Branding tends to increase product differentiation and reduce substitutability of the product, leading to a reduced elasticity of demand and an increased possibility to raise price. The distinction between branded and non-branded goods or services will often coincide with the distinction between intermediate goods and services and final goods and services.

Intermediate goods and services are sold to undertakings for use as an input to produce other goods or services and are generally not recognisable in the final goods or services. The buyers of intermediate products are usually well-informed customers, able to assess quality and therefore less reliant on brand and image. Final goods are, directly or indirectly, sold to final consumers who often rely more on brand and image. As distributors (retailers, wholesalers) have to respond to the demand of final consumers, competition may suffer more when distributors are foreclosed from selling one or a number of brands than when buyers of intermediate products are prevented from buying competing products from certain sources of supply.

The undertakings buying intermediate goods or services normally have specialist departments or advisers who monitor developments in the supply market. Because they effect sizeable transactions, search costs are in general not prohibitive. A loss of intra-brand competition is therefore less important at the intermediate level.

(6) In general, a combination of vertical restraints aggravates their negative effects. However, certain combinations of vertical restraints are better for competition than their use in isolation from each other. For instance, in an exclusive distribution system, the distributor may be tempted to increase the price of the products as intra-brand competition has been reduced. The use of quantity forcing or the setting of a maximum resale price may limit such price increases.

(7) Possible negative effects of vertical restraints are reinforced when several suppliers and their buyers organise their trade in a similar way. These so-called cumulative effects may be a problem in a number of sectors.

(8) The more the vertical restraint is linked to the transfer of know-how, the more reason there may be to expect efficiencies to arise and the more a vertical restraint may be necessary to protect the know-how transferred or the investment costs incurred.

(9) The more the vertical restraint is linked to investments which are relationship-

specific, the more justification there is for certain vertical restraints. The justified duration will depend on the time necessary to depreciate the investment.

(10) In the case of a new product, or where an existing product is sold for the first time on a different geographic market, it may be difficult for the company to define the market or its market share may be very high. However, this should not be considered a major problem, as vertical restraints linked to opening up new product or geographic markets in general do not restrict competition. This rule holds, irrespective of the market share of the company, for two years after the first putting on the market of the product. It applies to all non-hardcore vertical restraints and, in the case of a new geographic market, to restrictions on active and passive sales imposed on the direct buyers of the supplier located in other markets to intermediaries in the new market. In the case of genuine testing of a new product in a limited territory or with a limited customer group, the distributors appointed to sell the new product on the test market can be restricted in their active selling outside the test market for a maximum period of 1 year without being caught by Article 81(1).

1.4. Methodology of analysis

(120) The assessment of a vertical restraint involves in general the following four steps:

(1) First, the undertakings involved need to define the relevant market in order to establish the market share of the supplier or the buyer, depending on the vertical restraint involved (see paragraphs 88 to 99, in particular 89 to 95).

(2) If the relevant market share does not exceed the 30% threshold, the vertical agreement is covered by the Block Exemption Regulation, subject to the hardcore restrictions and conditions set out in that regulation.

(3) If the relevant market share is above the 30% threshold, it is necessary to assess whether the vertical agreement falls within Article 81(1).

(4) If the vertical agreement falls within Article 81(1), it is necessary to examine whether it fulfils the conditions for exemption under Article 81(3).

1.4.1. Relevant factors for the assessment under Article 81(1)

(121) In assessing cases above the market share threshold of 30%, the Commission will make a full competition analysis. The following factors are the most important

to establish whether a vertical agreement brings about an appreciable restriction of competition under Article 81(1):

(a) market position of the supplier;

(b) market position of competitors;

(c) market position of the buyer;

(d) entry barriers;

(e) maturity of the market;

(f) level of trade;

(g) nature of the product;

(h) other factors.

(122) The importance of individual factors may vary from case to case and depends on all other factors. For instance, a high market share of the supplier is usually a good indicator of market power, but in the case of low entry barriers it may not indicate market power. It is therefore not possible to provide strict rules on the importance of the individual factors. However the following can be said:

Market position of the supplier

(123) The market position of the supplier is established first and foremost by his market share on the relevant product and geographic market. The higher his market share, the greater his market power is likely to be. The market position of the supplier is further strengthened if he has certain cost advantages over his competitors. These competitive advantages may result from a first mover advantage (having the best site, etc.), holding essential patents, having superior technology, being the brand leader or having a superior portfolio.

Market position of competitors

(124) The same indicators, that is market share and possible competitive advantages, are used to describe the market position of competitors. The stronger the established competitors are and the greater their number, the less risk there is that the supplier or buyer in question will be able to foreclose the market individually and the less there is a risk of a reduction of inter-brand competition. However, if the number of competitors becomes rather small and their market position (size, costs, R& D potential, etc.) is rather similar, this market structure may increase the risk of collusion. Fluctuating or rapidly changing market shares are in general an indication

of intense competition.

Market position of the buyer
(125) Buying power derives from the market position of the buyer. The first indicator of buying power is the market share of the buyer on the purchase market. This share reflects the importance of his demand for his possible suppliers. Other indicators focus on the market position of the buyer on his resale market including characteristics such as a wide geographic spread of his outlets, own brands of the buyer/distributor and his image amongst final consumers. The effect of buying power on the likelihood of anti-competitive effects is not the same for the different vertical restraints. Buying power may in particular increase the negative effects in case of restraints from the limited distribution and market partitioning groups such as exclusive supply, exclusive distribution and quantitative selective distribution.

Entry barriers
(126) Entry barriers are measured by the extent to which incumbent companies can increase their price above the competitive level, usually above minimum average total cost, and make supra-normal profits without attracting entry. Without any entry barriers, easy and quick entry would eliminate such profits. In as far as effective entry, which would prevent or erode the supra-normal profits, is likely to occur within one or two years, entry barriers can be said to be low.

(127) Entry barriers may result from a wide variety of factors such as economies of scale and scope, government regulations, especially where they establish exclusive rights, state aid, import tariffs, intellectual property rights, ownership of resources where the supply is limited due to for instance natural limitations,[30] essential facilities, a first mover advantage and brand loyalty of consumers created by strong advertising. Vertical restraints and vertical integration may also work as an entry barrier by making access more difficult and foreclosing (potential) competitors. Entry barriers may be present at only the supplier or buyer level or at both levels.

(128) The question whether certain of these factors should be described as entry barriers depends on whether they are related to sunk costs. Sunk costs are those costs that have to be incurred to enter or be active on a market but that are lost

---

30 See Commission Decision 97/26/EC (Case No IV/M.619 – Gencor/Lonrho), (OJ L 11, 14.1.1997, p. 30).

when the market is exited. Advertising costs to build consumer loyalty are normally sunk costs, unless an exiting firm could either sell its brand name or use it somewhere else without a loss. The more costs are sunk, the more potential entrants have to weigh the risks of entering the market and the more credibly incumbents can threaten that they will match new competition, as sunk costs make it costly for incumbents to leave the market. If, for instance, distributors are tied to a manufacturer via a non-compete obligation, the foreclosing effect will be more significant if setting up its own distributors will impose sunk costs on the potential entrant.

(129) In general, entry requires sunk costs, sometimes minor and sometimes major. Therefore, actual competition is in general more effective and will weigh more in the assessment of a case than potential competition.

Maturity of the market
(130) A mature market is a market that has existed for some time, where the technology used is well known and widespread and not changing very much, where there are no major brand innovations and in which demand is relatively stable or declining. In such a market negative effects are more likely than in more dynamic markets.

Level of trade
(131) The level of trade is linked to the distinction between intermediate and final goods and services. As indicated earlier, negative effects are in general less likely at the level of intermediate goods and services.

Nature of the product
(132) The nature of the product plays a role in particular for final products in assessing both the likely negative and the likely positive effects. When assessing the likely negative effects, it is important whether the products on the market are more homogeneous or heterogeneous, whether the product is expensive, taking up a large part of the consumer's budget, or is inexpensive and whether the product is a one-off purchase or repeatedly purchased. In general, when the product is more heterogeneous, less expensive and resembles more a one-off purchase, vertical restraints are more likely to have negative effects.

Other factors
(133) In the assessment of particular restraints other factors may have to be taken into account. Among these factors can be the cumulative effect, i.e. the coverage of the market by similar agreements, the duration of the agreements, whether the

agreement is "imposed" (mainly one party is subject to the restrictions or obligations) or "agreed" (both parties accept restrictions or obligations), the regulatory environment and behaviour that may indicate or facilitate collusion like price leadership, pre-announced price changes and discussions on the "right" price, price rigidity in response to excess capacity, price discrimination and past collusive behaviour.

1.4.2. Relevant factors for the assessment under Article 81(3)

(134) There are four cumulative conditions for the application of Article 81(3):

- the vertical agreement must contribute to improving production or distribution or to promoting technical or economic progress;
- the vertical agreement must allow consumers a fair share of these benefits;
- the vertical agreement must not impose on the undertakings concerned vertical restraints which are not indispensable to the attainment of these benefits;
- the vertical agreement must not afford such undertakings the possibility of eliminating competition in respect of a substantial part of the products in question.

(135) The last criterion of elimination of competition for a substantial part of the products in question is related to the question of dominance. Where an undertaking is dominant or becoming dominant as a consequence of the vertical agreement, a vertical restraint that has appreciable anti-competitive effects can in principle not be exempted. The vertical agreement may however fall outside Article 81(1) if there is an objective justification, for instance if it is necessary for the protection of relationship-specific investments or for the transfer of substantial know-how without which the supply or purchase of certain goods or services would not take place.

(136) Where the supplier and the buyer are not dominant, the other three criteria become important. The first, concerning the improvement of production or distribution and the promotion of technical or economic progress, refers to the type of efficiencies described inparagraphs 115 to 118. These efficiencies have to be substantiated and must produce a net positive effect. Speculative claims on avoidance of free-riding or general statements on cost savings will not be accepted. Cost savings that arise from the mere exercise of market power or from anti-competitive conduct cannot be accepted. Secondly, economic benefits have to favour not only the parties to the agreement, but also the consumer. Generally the

transmission of the benefits to consumers will depend on the intensity of competition on the relevant market. Competitive pressures will normally ensure that cost-savings are passed on by way of lower prices or that companies have an incentive to bring new products to the market as quickly as possible. Therefore, if sufficient competition which effectively constrains the parties to the agreement is maintained on the market, the competitive process will normally ensure that consumers receive a fair share of the economic benefits. The third criterion will play a role in ensuring that the least anti-competitive restraint is chosen to obtain certain positive effects.

2. Analysis of specific vertical restraints

(137) Vertical agreements may contain a combination of two or more of the components of vertical restraints described in paragraphs 103 to 114. The most common vertical restraints and combinations of vertical restraints are analysed below following the methodology of analysis developed in paragraphs 120 to 136.

2.1. Single branding

(138) A non-compete arrangement is based on an obligation or incentive scheme which makes the buyer purchase practically all his requirements on a particular market from only one supplier. It does not mean that the buyer can only buy directly from the supplier, but that the buyer will not buy and resell or incorporate competing goods or services. The possible competition risks are foreclosure of the market to competing suppliers and potential suppliers, facilitation of collusion between suppliers in case of cumulative use and, where the buyer is a retailer selling to final consumers, a loss of in-store inter-brand competition. All three restrictive effects have a direct impact on inter-brand competition.

(139) Single branding is exempted by the Block Exemption Regulation when the supplier's market share does not exceed 30% and subject to a limitation in time of five years for the non-compete obligation. Above the market share threshold or beyond the time limit of five years, the following guidance is provided for the assessment of individual cases.

(140) The "market position of the supplier" is of main importance to assess possible anti-competitive effects of non-compete obligations. In general, this type of obligation is imposed by the supplier and the supplier has similar agreements with other buyers.

(141) It is not only the market position of the supplier that is of importance but also

the extent to and the duration for which he applies a non-compete obligation. The higher his tied market share, i.e. the part of his market share sold under a single branding obligation, the more significant foreclosure is likely to be. Similarly, the longer the duration of the non-compete obligations, the more significant foreclosure is likely to be. Non-compete obligations shorter than one year entered into by non-dominant companies are in general not considered to give rise to appreciable anti-competitive effects or net negative effects. Non-compete obligations between one and five years entered into by non-dominant companies usually require a proper balancing of pro- and anti-competitive effects, while non-compete obligations exceeding five years are for most types of investments not considered necessary to achieve the claimed efficiencies or the efficiencies are not sufficient to outweigh their foreclosure effect. Dominant companies may not impose non-compete obligations on their buyers unless they can objectively justify such commercial practice within the context of Article 82.

(142) In assessing the supplier's market power, the "market position of his competitors" is important. As long as the competitors are sufficiently numerous and strong, no appreciable anti-competitive effects can be expected. It is only likely that competing suppliers will be foreclosed if they are significantly smaller than the supplier applying the non-compete obligation. Foreclosure of competitors is not very likely where they have similar market positions and can offer similarly attractive products. In such a case foreclosure may however occur for potential entrants when a number of major suppliers enter into non-compete contracts with a significant number of buyers on the relevant market (cumulative effect situation). This is also a situation where non-compete agreements may facilitate collusion between competing suppliers. If individually these suppliers are covered by the Block Exemption Regulation, a withdrawal of the block exemption may be necessary to deal with such a negative cumulative effect. A tied market share of less than 5% is not considered in general to contribute significantly to a cumulative foreclosure effect.

(143) In cases where the market share of the largest supplier is below 30% and the market share of the five largest suppliers (concentration rate (CR) 5) is below 50%, there is unlikely to be a single or a cumulative anti-competitive effect situation. If a potential entrant cannot penetrate the market profitably, this is likely to be due to factors other than non-compete obligations, such as consumer preferences. A competition problem is unlikely to arise when, for instance, 50 companies, of which none has an important market share, compete fiercely on a particular market.

(144) "Entry barriers" are important to establish whether there is real foreclosure. Wherever it is relatively easy for competing suppliers to create new buyers or find alternative buyers for the product, foreclosure is unlikely to be a real problem. However, there are often entry barriers, both at the manufacturing and at the distribution level.

(145) "Countervailing power" is relevant, as powerful buyers will not easily allow themselves to be cut off from the supply of competing goods or services. Foreclosure which is not based on efficiency and which has harmful effects on ultimate consumers is therefore mainly a risk in the case of dispersed buyers. However, where non-compete agreements are concluded with major buyers this may have a strong foreclosure effect.

(146) Lastly, "the level of trade" is relevant for foreclosure. Foreclosure is less likely in case of an intermediate product. When the supplier of an intermediate product is not dominant, the competing suppliers still have a substantial part of demand that is "free". Below the level of dominance a serious foreclosure effect may however arise for actual or potential competitors where there is a cumulative effect. A serious cumulative effect is unlikely to arise as long as less than 50% of the market is tied. When the supplier is dominant, any obligation to buy the products only or mainly from the dominant supplier may easily lead to significant foreclosure effects on the market. The stronger his dominance, the higher the risk of foreclosure of other competitors.

(147) Where the agreement concerns supply of a final product at the wholesale level, the question whether a competition problem is likely to arise below the level of dominance depends in large part on the type of wholesaling and the entry barriers at the wholesale level. There is no real risk of foreclosure if competing manufacturers can easily establish their own wholesaling operation. Whether entry barriers are low depends in part on the type of wholesaling, i.e. whether or not wholesalers can operate efficiently with only the product concerned by the agreement (for example ice cream) or whether it is more efficient to trade in a whole range of products (for example frozen foodstuffs). In the latter case, it is not efficient for a manufacturer selling only one product to set up his own wholesaling operation. In that case anti-competitive effects may arise below the level of dominance. In addition, cumulative effect problems may arise if several suppliers tie most of the available wholesalers.

(148) For final products, foreclosure is in general more likely to occur at the retail level, given the significant entry barriers for most manufacturers to start retail

outlets just for their own products. In addition, it is at the retail level that non-compete agreements may lead to reduced in-store inter-brand competition. It is for these reasons that for final products at the retail level, significant anti-competitive effects may start to arise, taking into account all other relevant factors, if a non-dominant supplier ties 30% or more of the relevant market. For a dominant company, even a modest tied market share may already lead to significant anti-competitive effects. The stronger its dominance, the higher the risk of foreclosure of other competitors.

(149) At the retail level a cumulative foreclosure effect may also arise. When all companies have market shares below 30% a cumulative foreclosure effect is unlikely if the total tied market share is less than 40% and withdrawal of the block exemption is therefore unlikely. This figure may be higher when other factors like the number of competitors, entry barriers etc. are taken into account. When not all companies have market shares below the threshold of the Block Exemption Regulation but none is dominant, a cumulative foreclosure effect is unlikely if the total tied market share is below 30%.

(150) Where the buyer operates from premises and land owned by the supplier or leased by the supplier from a third party not connected with the buyer, the possibility of imposing effective remedies for a possible foreclosure effect will be limited. In that case intervention by the Commission below the level of dominance is unlikely.

(151) In certain sectors the selling of more than one brand from a single site may be difficult, in which case a foreclosure problem can better be remedied by limiting the effective duration of contracts.

(152) A so-called "English clause", requiring the buyer to report any better offer and allowing him only to accept such an offer when the supplier does not match it, can be expected to have the same effect as a non-compete obligation, especially when the buyer has to reveal who makes the better offer. In addition, by increasing the transparency of the market it may facilitate collusion between the suppliers. An English clause may also work as quantity-forcing. Quantity-forcing on the buyer is a weaker form of non-compete, where incentives or obligations agreed between the supplier and the buyer make the latter concentrate his purchases to a large extent with one supplier. Quantity-forcing may for example take the form of minimum purchase requirements or non-linear pricing, such as quantity rebate schemes, loyalty rebate schemes or a two-part tariff (fixed fee plus a price per unit). Quantity-forcing on the buyer will have similar but weaker foreclosure effects

part of the loan at any point in time and without payment of any penalty. This means that the repayment of the loan should be structured in equal or decreasing instalments and should not increase over time and that the buyer should have the possibility to take over the equipment provided by the supplier at its market asset value.This is without prejudice to the possibility, in case for example of a new point of distribution, to delay repayment for the first one or two years until sales have reached a certain level.

(157) The transfer of substantial know-how (efficiency 5 in paragraph 116) usually justifies a non-compete obligation for the whole duration of the supply agreement, as for example in the context of franchising.

(158) Below the level of dominance the combination of non-compete with exclusive distribution may also justify the non-compete obligation lasting the full length of the agreement. In the latter case, the non-compete obligation is likely to improve the distribution efforts of the exclusive distributor in his territory (see paragraphs 161 to 177).

(159) Example of non-compete

The market leader in a national market for an impulse consumer product, with a market share of 40%, sells most of its products (90%) through tied retailers (tied market share 36%). The agreements oblige the retailers to purchase only from the market leader for at least four years. The market leader is especially strongly represented in the more densely populated areas like the capital. Its competitors, 10 in number, of which some are only locally available, all have much smaller market shares, the biggest having 12%. These 10 competitors together supply another 10% of the market via tied outlets. There is strong brand and product differentiation in the market. The market leader has the strongest brands. It is the only one with regular national advertising campaigns. It provides its tied retailers with special stocking cabinets for its product.

The result on the market is that in total 46% (36% + 10%) of the market is foreclosed to potential entrants and to incumbents not having tied outlets. Potential entrants find entry even more difficult in the densely populated areas where foreclosure is even higher, although it is there that they would prefer to enter the market. In addition, owing to the strong brand and product differentiation and the high search costs relative to the price of the product, the absence of in-store inter-brand competition leads to an extra welfare loss for consumers. The possible efficiencies of the outlet exclusivity, which the market leader claims result from reduced transport costs and a possible hold-up problem concerning the stocking cabinets, are limited and do not outweigh the negative effects on competition. The efficiencies are limited, as the transport costs are linked to quantity and not exclusivity and the stocking cabinets do not contain special know-how and are not brand specific. Accordingly, it is unlikely that the conditions for exemption are fulfilled.

(160) Example of quantity forcing

A producer X with a 40% market share sells 80% of its products through contracts which specify that the reseller is required to purchase at least 75% of its requirements for that type of product from X. In return X is offering financing and equipment at favourable rates. The contracts have a duration of five years in which repayment of the loan is foreseen in equal instalments. However, after the first two years buyers have the possibility to terminate the contract with a six-month notice period if they repay the outstanding loan and take over the equipment at its market asset value. At the end of the five-year period the equipment becomes the property of the buyer. Most of the competing producers are small, twelve in total with the biggest having a market share of 20%, and engage in similar contracts with different durations. The producers with market shares below 10% often have contracts with longer durations and with less generous termination clauses. The contracts of producer X leave 25% of requirements free to be supplied by competitors. In the last three years, two new producers have entered the market and gained a combined market share of around 8%, partly by taking over the loans of a number of resellers in return for contracts with these resellers.

Producer X's tied market share is 24% (0,75 x 0,80 x 40%). The other producers' tied market share is around 25%. Therefore, in total around 49% of the market is foreclosed to potential entrants and to incumbents not having tied outlets for at least the first two years of the supply contracts. The market shows that the resellers often have difficulty in obtaining loans from banks and are too small in general to obtain capital through other means like the issuing of shares. In addition, producer X is able to demonstrate that concentrating his sales on a limited number of resellers allows him to plan his sales better and to save transport costs. In the light of the 25% non-tied part in the contracts of producer X, the real possibility for early termination of the contract, the recent entry of new producers and the fact that around half the resellers are not tied, the quantity forcing of 75% applied by producer X is likely to fulfil the conditions for exemption.

2.2. Exclusive distribution

(161) In an exclusive distribution agreement the supplier agrees to sell his products only to one distributor for resale in a particular territory. At the same time the

distributor is usually limited in his active selling into other exclusively allocated territories. The possible competition risks are mainly reduced intra-brand competition and market partitioning, which may in particular facilitate price discrimination. When most or all of the suppliers apply exclusive distribution this may facilitate collusion, both at the suppliers' and distributors' level.

(162) Exclusive distribution is exempted by the Block Exemption Regulation when the supplier's market share does not exceed 30%, even if combined with other non-hardcore vertical restraints, such as a non-compete obligation limited to five years, quantity forcing or exclusive purchasing. A combination of exclusive distribution and selective distribution is only exempted by the Block Exemption Regulation if active selling in other territories is not restricted. Above the 30% market share threshold, the following guidance is provided for the assessment of exclusive distribution in individual cases.

(163) The market position of the supplier and his competitors is of major importance, as the loss of intra-brand competition can only be problematic if inter-brand competition is limited. The stronger the "position of the supplier", the more serious is the loss of intra-brand competition. Above the 30% market share threshold there may be a risk of a significant reduction of intra-brand competition. In order to be exemptable, the loss of intra-brand competition needs to be balanced with real efficiencies.

(164) The "position of the competitors" can have a dual significance. Strong competitors will generally mean that the reduction in intra-brand competition is outweighed by sufficient inter-brand competition. However, if the number of competitors becomes rather small and their market position is rather similar in terms of market share, capacity and distribution network, there is a risk of collusion. The loss of intra-brand competition can increase this risk, especially when several suppliers operate similar distribution systems. Multiple exclusive dealerships, i.e. when different suppliers appoint the same exclusive distributor in a given territory, may further increase the risk of collusion. If a dealer is granted the exclusive right to distribute two or more important competing products in the same territory, inter-brand competition is likely to be substantially restricted for those brands. The higher the cumulative market share of the brands distributed by the multiple dealer, the higher the risk of collusion and the more inter-brand competition will be reduced. Such cumulative effect situations may be a reason to withdraw the benefit of the Block Exemption Regulation when the market shares of the suppliers are below the threshold of the Block Exemption Regulation.

(165) "Entry barriers" that may hinder suppliers from creating new distributors or finding alternative distributors are less important in assessing the possible anti-competitive effects of exclusive distribution. Foreclosure of other suppliers does not arise as long as exclusive distribution is not combined with single branding.

(166) Foreclosure of other distributors is not a problem if the supplier which operates the exclusive distribution system appoints a high number of exclusive distributors in the same market and these exclusive distributors are not restricted in selling to other non-appointed distributors. Foreclosure of other distributors may however become a problem where there is "buying power" and market power downstream, in particular in the case of very large territories where the exclusive distributor becomes the exclusive buyer for a whole market. An example would be a supermarket chain which becomes the only distributor of a leading brand on a national food retail market. The foreclosure of other distributors may be aggravated in the case of multiple exclusive dealership. Such a case, covered by the Block Exemption Regulation when the market share of each supplier is below 30%, may give reason for withdrawal of the block exemption.

(167) "Buying power" may also increase the risk of collusion on the buyers' side when the exclusive distribution arrangements are imposed by important buyers, possibly located in different territories, on one or several suppliers.

(168) "Maturity of the market" is important, as loss of intra-brand competition and price discrimination may be a serious problem in a mature market but may be less relevant in a market with growing demand, changing technologies and changing market positions.

(169) "The level of trade" is important as the possible negative effects may differ between the wholesale and retail level. Exclusive distribution is mainly applied in the distribution of final goods and services. A loss of intra-brand competition is especially likely at the retail level if coupled with large territories, since final consumers may be confronted with little possibility of choosing between a high price/high service and a low price/low service distributor for an important brand.

(170) A manufacturer which chooses a wholesaler to be his exclusive distributor will normally do so for a larger territory, such as a whole Member State. As long as the wholesaler can sell the products without limitation to downstream retailers there are not likely to be appreciable anti-competitive effects if the manufacturer is not dominant. A possible loss of intra-brand competition at the wholesale level

may be easily outweighed by efficiencies obtained in logistics, promotion etc, especially when the manufacturer is based in a different country. Foreclosure of other wholesalers within that territory is not likely as a supplier with a market share above 30% usually has enough bargaining power not to choose a less efficient wholesaler. The possible risks for inter-brand competition of multiple exclusive dealerships are however higher at the wholesale than at the retail level.

(171) The combination of exclusive distribution with single branding may add the problem of foreclosure of the market to other suppliers, especially in case of a dense network of exclusive distributors with small territories or in case of a cumulative effect. This may necessitate application of the principles set out above on single branding. However, when the combination does not lead to significant foreclosure, the combination of exclusive distribution and single branding may be pro-competitive by increasing the incentive for the exclusive distributor to focus his efforts on the particular brand. Therefore, in the absence of such a foreclosure effect, the combination of exclusive distribution with non-compete is exemptable for the whole duration of the agreement, particularly at the wholesale level.

(172) The combination of exclusive distribution with exclusive purchasing increases the possible competition risks of reduced intra-brand competition and market partitioning which may in particular facilitate price discrimination. Exclusive distribution already limits arbitrage by customers, as it limits the number of distributors and usually also restricts the distributors in their freedom of active selling. Exclusive purchasing, requiring the exclusive distributors to buy their supplies for the particular brand directly from the manufacturer, eliminates in addition possible arbitrage by the exclusive distributors, who are prevented from buying from other distributors in the system. This enhances the possibilities for the supplier to limit intra-brand competition while applying dissimilar conditions of sale. The combination of exclusive distribution and exclusive purchasing is therefore unlikely to be exempted for suppliers with a market share above 30% unless there are very clear and substantial efficiencies leading to lower prices to all final consumers. Lack of such efficiencies may also lead to withdrawal of the block exemption where the market share of the supplier is below 30%.

(173) The "nature of the product" is not very relevant to assessing the possible anti-competitive effects of exclusive distribution. It is, however, relevant when the issue of possible efficiencies is discussed, that is after an appreciable anti-competitive effect is established.

(174) Exclusive distribution may lead to efficiencies, especially where investments by the distributors are required to protect or build up the brand image. In general, the case for efficiencies is strongest for new products, for complex products, for products whose qualities are difficult to judge before consumption (so-called experience products) or of which the qualities are difficult to judge even after consumption (so-called credence products). In addition, exclusive distribution may lead to savings in logistic costs due to economies of scale in transport and distribution.

(175) Example of exclusive distribution at the wholesale level

In the market for a consumer durable, A is the market leader. A sells its product through exclusive wholesalers. Territories for the wholesalers correspond to the entire Member State for small Member States, and to a region for larger Member States. These exclusive distributors take care of sales to all the retailers in their territories. They do not sell to final consumers. The wholesalers are in charge of promotion in their markets. This includes sponsoring of local events, but also explaining and promoting the new products to the retailers in their territories. Technology and product innovation are evolving fairly quickly on this market, and pre-sale service to retailers and to final consumers plays an important role. The wholesalers are not required to purchase all their requirements of the brand of supplier A from the producer himself, and arbitrage by wholesalers or retailers is practicable because the transport costs are relatively low compared to the value of the product. The wholesalers are not under a non-compete obligation. Retailers also sell a number of brands of competing suppliers, and there are no exclusive or selective distribution agreements at the retail level. On the European market of sales to wholesalers A has around 50% market share. Its market share on the various national retail markets varies between 40% and 60%. A has between 6 and 10 competitors on every national market: B, C and D are its biggest competitors and are also present on each national market, with market shares varying between 20% and 5%. The remaining producers are national producers, with smaller market shares. B, C and D have similar distribution networks, whereas the local producers tend to sell their products directly to retailers.

On the wholesale market described above, the risk of reduced intra-brand competition and price discrimination is low. Arbitrage is not hindered, and the absence of intra-brand competition is not very relevant at the wholesale level. At the retail level neither intra- nor inter-brand competition are hindered. Moreover, inter-brand competition is largely unaffected by the exclusive arrangements at the wholesale level. This makes it likely, if anti-competitive effects exist, that the conditions for exemption are fulfilled.

(176) Example of multiple exclusive dealerships in an oligopolistic market

In a national market for a final product, there are four market leaders, who each have a market share of around 20%. These four market leaders sell their product through exclusive distributors at the retail level. Retailers are given an exclusive territory which corresponds to the town in which they are located or a district of the town for large towns. In most territories, the four market leaders happen to appoint the same exclusive retailer ("multiple dealership"), often centrally located and rather specialised in the product. The remaining 20% of the national market is composed of small local producers, the largest of these producers having a market share of 5% on the national market. These local producers sell their products in general through other retailers, in particular because the exclusive distributors of the four largest suppliers show in general little interest in selling less well-known and cheaper brands. There is strong brand and product differentiation on the market. The four market leaders have large national advertising campaigns and strong brand images, whereas the fringe producers do not advertise their products at the national level. The market is rather mature, with stable demand and no major product and technological innovation. The product is relatively simple.

In such an oligopolistic market, there is a risk of collusion between the four market leaders. This risk is increased through multiple dealerships. Intra-brand competition is limited by the territorial exclusivity. Competition between the four leading brands is reduced at the retail level, since one retailer fixes the price of all four brands in each territory. The multiple dealership implies that, if one producer cuts the price for its brand, the retailer will not be eager to transmit this price cut to the final consumer as it would reduce its sales and profits made with the other brands. Hence, producers have a reduced interest in entering into price competition with one another. Inter-brand price competition exists mainly with the low brand image goods of the fringe producers. The possible efficiency arguments for (joint) exclusive distributors are limited, as the product is relatively simple, the resale does not require any specific investments or training and advertising is mainly carried out at the level of the producers.

Even though each of the market leaders has a market share below the threshold, exemption under Article 81(3) may not be justified and withdrawal of the block exemption may be necessary.

(177) Example of exclusive distribution combined with exclusive purchasing

Manufacturer A is the European market leader for a bulky consumer durable, with a market share of between 40% and 60% in most national retail markets. In every Member State, it has about seven competitors with much smaller market shares, the largest of these competitors having a market share of 10%. These competitors are present on only one or two national markets. A sells its product through its national subsidiaries to exclusive distributors at the retail level, which are not allowed to sell actively into each other's territories. In addition, the retailers are obliged to purchase manufacturer A's products exclusively from the national subsidiary of manufacturer A in their own country. The retailers selling the brand of manufacturer A are the main resellers of that type of product in their territory. They handle competing brands, but with varying degrees of success and enthusiasm. A applies price differences of 10% to 15% between markets and smaller differences within markets. This is translated into smaller price differences at the retail level. The market is relatively stable on the demand and the supply side, and there are no significant technological changes.

In these markets, the loss of intra-brand competition results not only from the territorial exclusivity at the retail level but is aggravated by the exclusive purchasing obligation imposed on the retailers. The exclusive purchase obligation helps to keep markets and territories separate by making arbitrage between the exclusive retailers impossible. The exclusive retailers also cannot sell actively into each other's territory and in practice tend to avoid delivering outside their own territory. This renders price discrimination possible. Arbitrage by consumers or independent traders is limited due to the bulkiness of the product.

The possible efficiency arguments of this system, linked to economies of scale in transport and promotion efforts at the retailers' level, are unlikely to outweigh the negative effect of price discrimination and reduced intra-brand competition. Consequently, it is unlikely that the conditions for exemption are fulfilled.

2.3. Exclusive customer allocation

(178) In an exclusive customer allocation agreement, the supplier agrees to sell his products only to one distributor for resale to a particular class of customers. At the same time, the distributor is usually limited in his active selling to other exclusively allocated classes of customers. The possible competition risks are mainly reduced intra-brand competition and market partitioning, which may in particular facilitate price discrimination. When most or all of the suppliers apply exclusive customer allocation, this may facilitate collusion, both at the suppliers' and the distributors' level.

(179) Exclusive customer allocation is exempted by the Block Exemption Regulation when the supplier's market share does not exceed the 30% market share threshold, even if combined with other non-hardcore vertical restraints such as non-compete, quantity-forcing or exclusive purchasing. A combination of exclusive customer allocation and selective distribution is normally hardcore, as active selling

to end-users by the appointed distributors is usually not left free. Above the 30% market share threshold, the guidance provided in paragraphs 161 to 177 applies mutatis mutandis to the assessment of exclusive customer allocation, subject to the following specific remarks.

(180) The allocation of customers normally makes arbitrage by the customers more difficult. In addition, as each appointed distributor has his own class of customers, non-appointed distributors not falling within such a class may find it difficult to obtain the product. This will reduce possible arbitrage by non-appointed distributors. Therefore, above the 30% market share threshold of the Block Exemption Regulation exclusive customer allocation is unlikely to be exemptable unless there are clear and substantial efficiency effects.

(181) Exclusive customer allocation is mainly applied to intermediate products and at the wholesale level when it concerns final products, where customer groups with different specific requirements concerning the product can be distinguished.

(182) Exclusive customer allocation may lead to efficiencies, especially when the distributors are required to make investments in for instance specific equipment, skills or know-how to adapt to the requirements of their class of customers. The depreciation period of these investments indicates the justified duration of an exclusive customer allocation system. In general the case is strongest for new or complex products and for products requiring adaptation to the needs of the individual customer. Identifiable differentiated needs are more likely for intermediate products, that is products sold to different types of professional buyers. Allocation of final consumers is unlikely to lead to any efficiencies and is therefore unlikely to be exempted.

(183) Example of exclusive customer allocation

A company has developed a sophisticated sprinkler installation. The company has currently a market share of 40% on the market for sprinkler installations. When it started selling the sophisticated sprinkler it had a market share of 20% with an older product. The installation of the new type of sprinkler depends on the type of building that it is installed in and on the use of the building (office, chemical plant, hospital etc.). The company has appointed a number of distributors to sell and install the sprinkler installation. Each distributor needed to train its employees for the general and specific requirements of installing the sprinkler installation for a particular class of customers. To ensure that distributors would specialise the company assigned to each distributor an exclusive class of customers and prohibited

in question must necessitate a selective distribution system, in the sense that such a system must constitute a legitimate requirement, having regard to the nature of the product concerned, to preserve its quality and ensure its proper use. Secondly, resellers must be chosen on the basis of objective criteria of a qualitative nature which are laid down uniformly for all potential resellers and are not applied in a discriminatory manner. Thirdly, the criteria laid down must not go beyond what is necessary.[32] Quantitative selective distribution adds further criteria for selection that more directly limit the potential number of dealers by, for instance, requiring minimum or maximum sales, by fixing the number of dealers, etc.

(186) Qualitative and quantitative selective distribution is exempted by the Block Exemption Regulation up to 30% market share, even if combined with other non-hardcore vertical restraints, such as non-compete or exclusive distribution, provided active selling by the authorised distributors to each other and to end users is not restricted. The Block Exemption Regulation exempts selective distribution regardless of the nature of the product concerned. However, where the nature of the product does not require selective distribution, such a distribution system does not generally bring about sufficient efficiency enhancing effects to counterbalance a significant reduction in intra-brand competition. If appreciable anti-competitive effects occur, the benefit of the Block Exemption Regulation is likely to be withdrawn. In addition, the following guidance is provided for the assessment of selective distribution in individual cases which are not covered by the Block Exemption Regulation or in the case of cumulative effects resulting from parallel networks of selective distribution.

(187) The market position of the supplier and his competitors is of central importance in assessing possible anti-competitive effects, as the loss of intra-brand competition can only be problematic if inter-brand competition is limited. The stronger the position of the supplier, the more problematic is the loss of intra-brand competition. Another important factor is the number of selective distribution networks present in the same market. Where selective distribution is applied by only one supplier in the market which is not a dominant undertaking, quantitative selective distribution does not normally create net negative effects provided that the contract goods,

32 See judgments of the Court of Justice in Case 31/80 *L'Oréal v PVBA* [1980] ECR 3775, paragraphs 15 and 16; Case 26/76 Metro I [1977] ECR 1875, paragraphs 20 and 21; Case 107/82 AEG [1983] ECR 3151, paragraph 35; and of the Court of First Instance in Case T-19/91 *Vichy v Commission* [1992] ECR II-415, paragraph 65.

having regard to their nature, require the use of a selective distribution system and on condition that the selection criteria applied are necessary to ensure efficient distribution of the goods in question. The reality, however, seems to be that selective distribution is often applied by a number of the suppliers in a given market.

(188) The position of competitors can have a dual significance and plays in particular a role in case of a cumulative effect. Strong competitors will mean in general that the reduction in intra-brand competition is easily outweighed by sufficient inter-brand competition. However, when a majority of the main suppliers apply selective distribution there will be a significant loss of intra-brand competition and possible foreclosure of certain types of distributors as well as an increased risk of collusion between those major suppliers. The risk of foreclosure of more efficient distributors has always been greater with selective distribution than with exclusive distribution, given the restriction on sales to non-authorised dealers in selective distribution. This is designed to give selective distribution systems a closed character, making it impossible for non-authorised dealers to obtain supplies. This makes selective distribution particularly well suited to avoid pressure by price discounters on the margins of the manufacturer, as well as on the margins of the authorised dealers.

(189) Where the Block Exemption Regulation applies to individual networks of selective distribution, withdrawal of the block exemption or disapplication of the Block Exemption Regulation may be considered in case of cumulative effects. However, a cumulative effect problem is unlikely to arise when the share of the market covered by selective distribution is below 50%. Also, no problem is likely to arise where the market coverage ratio exceeds 50%, but the aggregate market share of the five largest suppliers (CR5) is below 50%. Where both the CR5 and the share of the market covered by selective distribution exceed 50%, the assessment may vary depending on whether or not all five largest suppliers apply selective distribution. The stronger the position of the competitors not applying selective distribution, the less likely the foreclosure of other distributors. If all five largest suppliers apply selective distribution, competition concerns may in particular arise with respect to those agreements that apply quantitative selection criteria by directly limiting the number of authorised dealers. The conditions of Article 81(3) are in general unlikely to be fulfilled if the selective distribution systems at issue prevent access to the market by new distributors capable of adequately selling the products in question, especially price discounters, thereby limiting distribution to the advantage of certain existing channels and to the detriment of final consumers. More indirect forms of quantitative selective distribution, resulting for instance from the combination of purely qualitative selection criteria with the requirement

imposed on the dealers to achieve a minimum amount of annual purchases, are less likely to produce net negative effects, if such an amount does not represent a significant proportion of the dealer's total turnover achieved with the type of products in question and it does not go beyond what is necessary for the supplier to recoup his relationship-specific investment and/or realise economies of scale in distribution. As regards individual contributions, a supplier with a market share of less than 5% is in general not considered to contribute significantly to a cumulative effect.

(190) "Entry barriers" are mainly of interest in the case of foreclosure of the market to non-authorised dealers. In general entry barriers will be considerable as selective distribution is usually applied by manufacturers of branded products. It will in general take time and considerable investment for excluded retailers to launch their own brands or obtain competitive supplies elsewhere.

(191) "Buying power" may increase the risk of collusion between dealers and thus appreciably change the analysis of possible anti-competitive effects of selective distribution. Foreclosure of the market to more efficient retailers may especially result where a strong dealer organisation imposes selection criteria on the supplier aimed at limiting distribution to the advantage of its members.

(192) Article 5(c) of the Block Exemption Regulation provides that the supplier may not impose an obligation causing the authorised dealers, either directly or indirectly, not to sell the brands of particular competing suppliers. This condition aims specifically at avoiding horizontal collusion to exclude particular brands through the creation of a selective club of brands by the leading suppliers. This kind of obligation is unlikely to be exemptable when the CR5 is equal to or above 50%, unless none of the suppliers imposing such an obligation belongs to the five largest suppliers in the market.

(193) Foreclosure of other suppliers is normally not a problem as long as other suppliers can use the same distributors, i.e. as long as the selective distribution system is not combined with single branding. In the case of a dense network of authorised distributors or in the case of a cumulative effect, the combination of selective distribution and a non-compete obligation may pose a risk of foreclosure to other suppliers. In that case the principles set out above on single branding apply. Where selective distribution is not combined with a non-compete obligation, foreclosure of the market to competing suppliers may still be a problem when the leading suppliers apply not only purely qualitative selection criteria, but impose

on their dealers certain additional obligations such as the obligation to reserve a minimum shelf-space for their products or to ensure that the sales of their products by the dealer achieve a minimum percentage of the dealer's total turnover. Such a problem is unlikely to arise if the share of the market covered by selective distribution is below 50% or, where this coverage ratio is exceeded, if the market share of the five largest suppliers is below 50%.

(194) Maturity of the market is important, as loss of intra-brand competition and possible foreclosure of suppliers or dealers may be a serious problem in a mature market but is less relevant in a market with growing demand, changing technologies and changing market positions.

(195) Selective distribution may be efficient when it leads to savings in logistical costs due to economies of scale in transport and this may happen irrespective of the nature of the product (efficiency 6 in paragraph 116). However, this is usually only a marginal efficiency in selective distribution systems. To help solve a free-rider problem between the distributors (efficiency 1 in paragraph 116) or to help create a brand image (efficiency 8 in paragraph 116), the nature of the product is very relevant. In general the case is strongest for new products, for complex products, for products of which the qualities are difficult to judge before consumption (so-called experience products) or of which the qualities are difficult to judge even after consumption (so-called credence products). The combination of selective and exclusive distribution is likely to infringe Article 81 if it is applied by a supplier whose market share exceeds 30% or in case of cumulative effects, even though active sales between the territories remain free. Such a combination may exceptionally fulfil the conditions of Article 81(3) if it is indispensable to protect substantial and relationship-specific investments made by the authorised dealers (efficiency 4 in paragraph 116).

(196) To ensure that the least anti-competitive restraint is chosen, it is relevant to see whether the same efficiencies can be obtained at a comparable cost by for instance service requirements alone.

(197) Example of quantitative selective distribution:

In a market for consumer durables, the market leader (brand A), with a market share of 35%, sells its product to final consumers through a selective distribution network. There are several criteria for admission to the network: the shop must employ trained staff and provide pre-sales services, there must be a specialised area in the shop devoted to the sales of the product and similar hi-tech products, and the shop is required to sell a wide range of models of the supplier and to display them in an attractive manner. Moreover, the number of admissible retailers in the network is directly limited through the establishment of a maximum number of retailers per number of inhabitants in each province or urban area. Manufacturer A has 6 competitors in this market. Its largest competitors, B, C and D, have market shares of respectively 25, 15 and 10%, whilst the other producers have smaller market shares. A is the only manufacturer to use selective distribution. The selective distributors of brand A always handle a few competing brands. However, competing brands are also widely sold in shops which are not member of A's selective distribution network. Channels of distribution are various: for instance, brands B and C are sold in most of A's selected shops, but also in other shops providing a high quality service and in hypermarkets. Brand D is mainly sold in high service shops. Technology is evolving quite rapidly in this market, and the main suppliers maintain a strong quality image for their products through advertising.

In this market, the coverage ratio of selective distribution is 35%. Inter-brand competition is not directly affected by the selective distribution system of A. Intra-brand competition for brand A may be reduced, but consumers have access to low service/low price retailers for brands B and C, which have a comparable quality image to brand A. Moreover, access to high service retailers for other brands is not foreclosed, since there is no limitation on the capacity of selected distributors to sell competing brands, and the quantitative limitation on the number of retailers for brand A leaves other high service retailers free to distribute competing brands. In this case, in view of the service requirements and the efficiencies these are likely to provide and the limited effect on intra-brand competition the conditions for exempting A's selective distribution network are likely to be fulfilled.

(198) Example of selective distribution with cumulative effects:

On a market for a particular sports article, there are seven manufacturers, whose respective market shares are: 25%, 20%, 15%, 15%, 10%, 8% and 7%. The five largest manufacturers distribute their products through quantitative selective distribution, whilst the two smallest use different types of distribution systems, which results in a coverage ratio of selective distribution of 85%. The criteria for access to the selective distribution networks are remarkably uniform amongst manufacturers: shops are required to have trained personnel and to provide pre-sale services, there must be a specialised area in the shop devoted to the sales of the article and a minimum size for this area is specified. The shop is required to sell a wide range of the brand in question and to display the article in an attractive manner, the shop must be located in a commercial street, and this type of article must represent at least 30% of the total turnover of the shop. In general, the same

concerning the products being distributed, in particular selective distribution and/ or non-compete and/or exclusive distribution or weaker forms thereof.

(200) The coverage by the Block Exemption Regulation of the licensing of IPRs contained in franchise agreements is dealt with in paragraphs 23 to 45. As for the vertical restraints on the purchase, sale and resale of goods and services within a franchising arrangement, such as selective distribution, non-compete or exclusive distribution, the Block Exemption Regulation applies up to the 30% market share threshold for the franchisor or the supplier designated by the franchisor.[33] The guidance provided earlier in respect of these types of restraints applies also to franchising, subject to the following specific remarks:

1) In line with general rule 8 (see paragraph 119), the more important the transfer of know-how, the more easily the vertical restraints fulfil the conditions for exemption.
2) A non-compete obligation on the goods or services purchased by the franchisee falls outside Article 81(1) when the obligation is necessary to maintain the common identity and reputation of the franchised network. In such cases, the duration of the non-compete obligation is also irrelevant under Article 81(1), as long as it does not exceed the duration of the franchise agreement itself.

(201) Example of franchising:

A manufacturer has developed a new format for selling sweets in so-called fun shops where the sweets can be coloured specially on demand from the consumer. The manufacturer of the sweets has also developed the machines to colour the sweets. The manufacturer also produces the colouring liquids. The quality and freshness of the liquid is of vital importance to producing good sweets. The manufacturer made a success of its sweets through a number of own retail outlets all operating under the same trade name and with the uniform fun image (style of lay-out of the shops, common advertising etc.). In order to expand sales the manufacturer started a franchising system. The franchisees are obliged to buy the sweets, liquid and colouring machine from the manufacturer, to have the same image and operate under the trade name, pay a franchise fee, contribute to common advertising and ensure the confidentiality of the operating manual prepared by the franchisor.

33 See also paragraphs AEG [1983] ECR 3151, paragraph 35; and of the Court of First Instance in Case T-19/91 *Vichy v Commission* [1992] ECR II-415, paragraph 65. See also paragraphs 89 to 95, in particular paragraph 95.

purposes of a specific use. For intermediate goods or services, exclusive supply is often referred to as industrial supply.

(203) Exclusive supply as defined in Article 1(c) of the Block Exemption Regulation is exempted by Article 2(1) read in conjunction with Article 3(2) of the Block Exemption Regulation up to 30% market share of the buyer, even if combined with other non-hardcore vertical restraints such as non-compete. Above the market share threshold the following guidance is provided for the assessment of exclusive supply in individual cases.

(204) The main competition risk of exclusive supply is foreclosure of other buyers. The market share of the buyer on the upstream purchase market is obviously important for assessing the ability of the buyer to "impose" exclusive supply which forecloses other buyers from access to supplies. The importance of the buyer on the downstream market is however the factor which determines whether a competition problem may arise. If the buyer has no market power downstream, then no appreciable negative effects for consumers can be expected. Negative effects can however be expected when the market share of the buyer on the downstream supply market as well as the upstream purchase market exceeds 30%. Where the market share of the buyer on the upstream market does not exceed 30%, significant foreclosure effects may still result, especially when the market share of the buyer on his downstream market exceeds 30%. In such cases withdrawal of the block exemption may be required. Where a company is dominant on the downstream market, any obligation to supply the products only or mainly to the dominant buyer may easily have significant anti-competitive effects.

(205) It is not only the market position of the buyer on the upstream and downstream market that is important but also the extent to and the duration for which he applies an exclusive supply obligation. The higher the tied supply share, and the longer the duration of the exclusive supply, the more significant the foreclosure is likely to be. Exclusive supply agreements shorter than five years entered into by non-dominant companies usually require a balancing of pro- and anti-competitive effects, while agreements lasting longer than five years are for most types of investments not considered necessary to achieve the claimed efficiencies or the efficiencies are not sufficient to outweigh the foreclosure effect of such long-term exclusive supply agreements.

(206) The market position of the competing buyers on the upstream market is important as it is only likely that competing buyers will be foreclosed for anti-

on the downstream market.

(211) Where appreciable anti-competitive effects are established, an exemption under Article 81(3) is possible as long as the company is not dominant. Efficiencies can be expected in the case of a hold-up problem (paragraph 116, points 4 and 5), and this is more likely for intermediate products than for final products. Other efficiencies are less likely. Possible economies of scale in distribution (paragraph 116, point 6) do not seem likely to justify exclusive supply.

(212) In the case of a hold-up problem and even more so in the case of scale economies in distribution, quantity forcing on the supplier, such as minimum supply requirements, could well be a less restrictive alternative.

(213) Example of exclusive supply:

On a market for a certain type of components (intermediate product market) supplier A agrees with buyer B to develop, with his own know-how and considerable investment in new machines and with the help of specifications supplied by buyer B, a different version of the component. B will have to make considerable investments to incorporate the new component. It is agreed that A will supply the new product only to buyer B for a period of five years from the date of first entry on the market. B is obliged to buy the new product only from A for the same period of five years. Both A and B can continue to sell and buy respectively other versions of the component elsewhere. The market share of buyer B on the upstream component market and on the downstream final goods market is 40%. The market share of the component supplier is 35%. There are two other component suppliers with around 20-25% market share and a number of small suppliers.

Given the considerable investments, the agreement is likely to fulfil the conditions for exemption in view of the efficiencies and the limited foreclosure effect. Other buyers are foreclosed from a particular version of a product of a supplier with 35% market share and there are other component suppliers that could develop similar new products. The foreclosure of part of buyer B's demand to other suppliers is limited to maximum 40% of the market.

(214) Exclusive supply is based on a direct or indirect obligation causing the supplier only to sell to one buyer. Quantity forcing on the supplier is based on incentives agreed between the supplier and the buyer that make the former concentrate his sales mainly with one buyer. Quantity forcing on the supplier may have similar but more mitigated effects than exclusive supply. The assessment of quantity forcing will depend on the degree of foreclosure of other buyers on the upstream market.

2.7. Tying

(215) Tying exists when the supplier makes the sale of one product conditional upon the purchase of another distinct product from the supplier or someone designated by the latter. The first product is referred to as the tying product and the second is referred to as the tied product. If the tying is not objectively justified by the nature of the products or commercial usage, such practice may constitute an abuse within the meaning of Article 82.[34] Article 81 may apply to horizontal agreements or concerted practices between competing suppliers which make the sale of one product conditional upon the purchase of another distinct product. Tying may also constitute a vertical restraint falling under Article 81 where it results in a single branding type of obligation (see paragraphs 138 to 160) for the tied product. Only the latter situation is dealt with in these Guidelines.

(216) What is to be considered as a distinct product is determined first of all by the demand of the buyers. Two products are distinct if, in the absence of tying, from the buyers' perspective, the products are purchased by them on two different markets. For instance, since customers want to buy shoes with laces, it has become commercial usage for shoe manufacturers to supply shoes with laces. Therefore, the sale of shoes with laces is not a tying practice. Often combinations have become accepted practice because the nature of the product makes it technically difficult to supply one product without the supply of another product.

(217) The main negative effect of tying on competition is possible foreclosure on the market of the tied product. Tying means that there is at least a form of quantity-forcing on the buyer in respect of the tied product. Where in addition a non-compete obligation is agreed in respect of the tied product, this increases the possible foreclosure effect on the market of the tied product. Tying may also lead to supra-competitive prices, especially in three situations. Firstly, when the tying and tied product are partly substitutable for the buyer. Secondly, when the tying allows price discrimination according to the use the customer makes of the tying product, for example the tying of ink cartridges to the sale of photocopying machines (metering). Thirdly, when in the case of long-term contracts or in the case of after-markets with original equipment with a long replacement time, it becomes difficult for the customers to calculate the consequences of the tying. Lastly, tying may also

[34] Judgment of the Court of Justice in Case C-333/94 P Tetrapak v Commission[1996] ECR I-5951, paragraph 37.

lead to higher entry barriers both on the market of the tying and on the market of the tied product.

(218) Tying is exempted by Article 2(1) read in conjunction with Article 3 of the Block Exemption Regulation when the market share of the supplier on both the market of the tied product and the market of the tying product does not exceed 30%. It may be combined with other non-hardcore vertical restraints such as non-compete or quantity forcing in respect of the tying product, or exclusive purchasing. Above the market share threshold the following guidance is provided for the assessment of tying in individual cases.

(219) The market position of the supplier on the market of the tying product is obviously of main importance to assess possible anti-competitive effects. In general this type of agreement is imposed by the supplier. The importance of the supplier on the market of the tying product is the main reason why a buyer may find it difficult to refuse a tying obligation.

(220) To assess the supplier's market power, the market position of his competitors on the market of the tying product is important. As long as his competitors are sufficiently numerous and strong, no anti-competitive effects can be expected, as buyers have sufficient alternatives to purchase the tying product without the tied product, unless other suppliers are applying similar tying. In addition, entry barriers on the market of the tying product are relevant to establish the market position of the supplier. When tying is combined with a non-compete obligation in respect of the tying product, this considerably strengthens the position of the supplier.

(221) Buying power is relevant, as important buyers will not easily be forced to accept tying without obtaining at least part of the possible efficiencies. Tying not based on efficiency is therefore mainly a risk where buyers do not have significant buying power.

(222) Where appreciable anti-competitive effects are established, the question of a possible exemption under Article 81(3) arises as long as the company is not dominant. Tying obligations may help to produce efficiencies arising from joint production or joint distribution. Where the tied product is not produced by the supplier, an efficiency may also arise from the supplier buying large quantities of the tied product. For tying to be exemptable, it must, however, be shown that at least part of these cost reductions are passed on to the consumer. Tying is therefore normally not exemptable when the retailer is able to obtain, on a regular basis,

supplies of the same or equivalent products on the same or better conditions than those offered by the supplier which applies the tying practice. Another efficiency may exist where tying helps to ensure a certain uniformity and quality standardisation (see efficiency 8 in paragraph 116). However, it needs to be demonstrated that the positive effects cannot be realised equally efficiently by requiring the buyer to use or resell products satisfying minimum quality standards, without requiring the buyer to purchase these from the supplier or someone designated by the latter. The requirements concerning minimum quality standards would not normally fall within Article 81(1). Where the supplier of the tying product imposes on the buyer the suppliers from which the buyer must purchase the tied product, for instance because the formulation of minimum quality standards is not possible, this may also fall outside Article 81(1), especially where the supplier of the tying product does not derive a direct (financial) benefit from designating the suppliers of the tied product.

(223) The effect of supra-competitive prices is considered anti-competitive in itself. The effect of foreclosure depends on the tied percentage of total sales on the market of the tied product. On the question of what can be considered appreciable foreclosure under Article 81(1), the analysis for single branding can be applied. Above the 30% market share threshold exemption of tying is unlikely, unless there are clear efficiencies that are transmitted, at least in part, to consumers. Exemption is even less likely when tying is combined with non-compete, either in respect of the tied or in respect of the tying product.

(224) Withdrawal of the block exemption is likely where no efficiencies result from tying or where such efficiencies are not passed on to the consumer (see paragraph 222). Withdrawal is also likely in the case of a cumulative effect where a majority of the suppliers apply similar tying arrangements without the possible efficiencies being transmitted at least in part to consumers.

2.8. Recommended and maximum resale prices

(225) The practice of recommending a resale price to a reseller or requiring the reseller to respect a maximum resale price is – subject to the comments in paragraphs 46 to 56 concerning RPM – covered by the Block Exemption Regulation when the market share of the supplier does not exceed the 30% threshold. For cases above the market share threshold and for cases of withdrawal of the block exemption the following guidance is provided.

(226) The possible competition risk of maximum and recommended prices is firstly

that the maximum or recommended price will work as a focal point for the resellers and might be followed by most or all of them. A second competition risk is that maximum or recommended prices may facilitate collusion between suppliers.

(227) The most important factor for assessing possible anti-competitive effects of maximum or recommended resale prices is the market position of the supplier. The stronger the market position of the supplier, the higher the risk that a maximum resale price or a recommended resale price leads to a more or less uniform application of that price level by the resellers, because they may use it as a focal point. They may find it difficult to deviate from what they perceive to be the preferred resale price proposed by such an important supplier on the market. Under such circumstances the practice of imposing a maximum resale price or recommending a resale price may infringe Article 81(1) if it leads to a uniform price level.

(228) The second most important factor for assessing possible anti-competitive effects of the practice of maximum and recommended prices is the market position of competitors. Especially in a narrow oligopoly, the practice of using or publishing maximum or recommended prices may facilitate collusion between the suppliers by exchanging information on the preferred price level and by reducing the likelihood of lower resale prices. The practice of imposing a maximum resale price or recommending resale prices leading to such effects may also infringe Article 81(1).

2.9. Other vertical restraints

(229) The vertical restraints and combinations described above are only a selection. There are other restraints and combinations for which no direct guidance is provided here. They will however be treated according to the same principles, with the help of the same general rules and with the same emphasis on the effect on the market.

Whereas there is consequently a need to make more flexible arrangements for the time being in respect of certain categories of agreement, decision and concerted practice without prejudging their validity under Article 85;

Whereas it may be in the interest of undertakings to know whether any agreements, decisions or practices to which they are party, or propose to become party, may lead to action on the part of the Commission pursuant to Article 85 (1) or Article 86;

Whereas, in order to secure uniform application of Articles 85 and 86 in the common market, rules must be made under which the Commission, acting in close and constant liaison with the competent authorities of the Member States, may take the requisite measures for applying those Articles;

Whereas for this purpose the Commission must have the co-operation of the competent authorities of the Member States and be empowered, throughout the common market, to require such information to be supplied and to undertake such investigations as are necessary to bring to light any agreement, decision or concerted practice prohibited by Article 85 (1) or any abuse of a dominant position prohibited by Article 86:

Whereas, in order to carry out its duty of ensuring that the provisions of the Treaty are applied, the Commission must be empowered to address to undertakings or associations of undertakings recommendations and decisions for the purpose of bringing to an end infringements of Articles 85 and 86;

Whereas compliance with Articles 85 and 86 and the fulfilment of obligations imposed on undertakings and associations of undertakings under this Regulation must be enforceable by means of fines and periodic penalty payments;

Whereas undertakings concerned must be accorded the right to be heard by the Commission, third parties whose interests may be affected by a decision must be given the opportunity of submitting their comments beforehand, and it must be ensured that wide publicity is given to decisions taken;

Whereas all decisions taken by the Commission under this Regulation are subject to review by the Court of Justice under the conditions specified in the Treaty; whereas it is moreover desirable to confer upon the Court of Justice, pursuant to Article 172, unlimited jurisdiction in respect of decisions under which the

Commission imposes fines or periodic penalty payments;

Whereas this Regulation may enter into force without prejudice to any other provisions that may hereafter be adopted pursuant to Article 87;

HAS ADOPTED THIS REGULATION:

ARTICLE 1

Basic provision

Without prejudice to Articles 6, 7 and 23 of this Regulation, agreements, decisions and concerted practices of the kind described in Article 85 (1) of the Treaty and the abuse of a dominant position in the market, within the meaning of Article 86 of the Treaty, shall be prohibited, no prior decision to that effect being required.

ARTICLE 2

Negative clearance

Upon application by the undertakings or associations of undertakings concerned, the Commission may certify that, on the basis of the facts in its possession, there are no grounds under Article 85 (1) or Article 86 of the Treaty for action on its part in respect of an agreement, decision or practice.

ARTICLE 3

Termination of infringements

1. Where the Commission, upon application or upon its own initiative, finds that there is infringement of Article 85 or Article 86 of the Treaty, it may by decision require the undertakings or associations of undertakings concerned to bring such infringement to an end.

2. Those entitled to make application are:

(a) Member States;

(b) natural or legal persons who claim a legitimate interest.

3. Without prejudice to the other provisions of this Regulation, the Commission may, before taking a decision under paragraph 1, address to the undertakings or associations of undertakings concerned recommendations for termination of the infringement.

ARTICLE 4

Notification of new agreements, decisions and practices

1. Agreements, decisions and concerted practices of the kind described in Article 85 (1) of the Treaty which come into existence after the entry into force of this Regulation and in respect of which the parties seek application of Article 85 (3) must be notified to the Commission. Until they have been notified, no decision in application of Article 85 (3) may be taken.

2. Paragraph 1 shall not apply to agreements, decisions and concerted practices where:

(1) the only parties thereto are undertakings from one Member State and the agreements, decisions or practices do not relate either to imports or to exports between Member States;

(2)

(a) the agreements or concerted practices are entered into by two or more undertakings, each operating, for the purposes of the agreement, at a different level of the production or distribution chain, and relate to the conditions under which the parties may purchase, sell or resell certain goods or services;

(b) not more than two undertakings are party thereto, and the agreements only impose restrictions on the exercise of the rights of the assignee or user of industrial property rights, in particular patents, utility models, designs or trade marks, or of the person entitled under a contract to the assignment, or grant, of the right to use a method of manufacture or knowledge relating to the use and to the application of industrial processes;

(3) they have as their sole object:

(a) the development or uniform application of standards or types; or

(b) joint research and development;

(c) specialisation in the manufacture of products, including agreements necessary for achieving this:

- where the products which are the subject of specialisation do not, in a substantial part of the common market, represent more than 15% of the volume of business done in identical products or those considered by consumers to be similar by reason of their characteristics, price and use, and
- where the total annual turnover of the participating undertakings does not exceed 200 million unit of account.

These agreements, decisions and practices may be notified to the Commission.

ARTICLE 5

Notification of existing agreements, decisions and practices

1. Agreements, decisions and concerted practices of the kind described in Article 85 (1) of the Treaty which are in existence at the date of entry into force of this Regulation and in respect of which the parties seek application of Article 85 (3) shall be notified to the Commission before 1 November 1962. However, notwithstanding the foregoing provisions, any agreements, decisions and concerted practices to which not more than two undertakings are party shall be notified before 1 February 1963.

2. Paragraph 1 shall not apply to agreements, decisions or concerted practices falling within Article 4 (2); these may be notified to the Commission.

ARTICLE 6

Decisions pursuant to Article 85 (3)

1. Whenever the Commission takes a decision pursuant to Article 85 (3) of the Treaty, it shall specify therein the date from which the decision shall take effect. Such a date shall not be earlier than the date of notification.

2. The second sentence of paragraph 1 shall not apply to agreements, decisions or concerted practices falling within Article 4 (2) and Article 5 (2), nor to those falling within Article 5 (1) which have been notified within the time limit specified in Article 5 (1).

ARTICLE 7

Special provisions for existing agreements, decisions and practices

1. Where agreements, decisions and concerted practices in existence at the date of entry into force of this Regulation and notified within the time limits specified in Article 5 (1) do not satisfy the requirements of Article 85 (3) of the Treaty and the undertakings or associations of undertakings concerned cease to give effect to them or modify them in such a manner that they no longer fall within the prohibition contained in Article 85 (1) or that they satisfy the requirements of Article 85 (3), the prohibition contained in Article 85 (1) shall apply only for a period fixed by the Commission. A decision by the Commission pursuant to the foregoing sentence shall not apply as against undertakings and associations of undertakings which did not expressly consent to the notification.

2. Paragraph 1 shall apply to agreements, decisions and concerted practices falling within Article 4 (2) which are in existence at the date of entry into force of this Regulation if they are notified before 1 January 1967.

ARTICLE 8

Duration and revocation of decisions under Article 85 (3)

1. A decision in application of Article 85 (3) of the Treaty shall be issued for a specified period and conditions and obligations may be attached thereto.

2. A decision may on application be renewed if the requirements of Article 85 (3) of the Treaty continue to be satisfied.

3. The Commission may revoke or amend its decision or prohibit specified acts by the parties:

(a) where there has been a change in any of the facts which were basic to the making of the decision;

(b) where the parties commit a breach of any obligation attached to the decision;

(c) where the decision is based on incorrect information or was induced by deceit;

(d) where the parties abuse the exemption from the provisions of Article 85 (1) of the Treaty granted to them by the decision.

In cases to which subparagraphs (b), (c) or (d) apply, the decision may be revoked with retroactive effect.

ARTICLE 9

Powers

1. Subject to review of its decision by the Court of Justice, the Commission shall have sole power to declare Article 85 (1) inapplicable pursuant to Article 85 (3) of the Treaty.

2. The Commission shall have power to apply Article 85 (1) and Article 86 of the Treaty; this power may be exercised notwithstanding that the time limits specified in Article 5 (1) and in Article 7 (2) relating to notification have not expired.

3. As long as the Commission has not initiated any procedure under Articles 2, 3 or 6, the authorities of the Member States shall remain competent to apply Article 85 (1) and Article 86 in accordance with Article 88 of the Treaty; they shall remain competent in this respect notwithstanding that the time limits specified in Article 5 (1) and in Article 7 (2) relating to notification have not expired.

ARTICLE 10

Liaison with the authorities of the Member States

1. The Commission shall forthwith transmit to the competent authorities of the Member States a copy of the applications and notifications together with copies of the most important documents lodged with the Commission for the purpose of establishing the existence of infringements of Articles 85 or 86 of the Treaty or of obtaining negative clearance or a decision in application of Article 85 (3).

2. The Commission shall carry out the procedure set out in paragraph 1 in close and constant liaison with the competent authorities of the Member States; such authorities shall have the right to express their views upon that procedure.

3. An Advisory Committee on Restrictive Practices and Monopolies shall be consulted prior to the taking of any decision following upon a procedure under paragraph 1, and of any decision concerning the renewal, amendment or revocation of a decision pursuant to Article 85 (3) of the Treaty.

information requested within the time limit fixed by the Commission, or supplies incomplete information, the Commission shall by decision require the information to be supplied. The decision shall specify what information is required, fix an appropriate time limit within which it is to be supplied and indicate the penalties provided for in Article 15 (1) (b) and Article 16 (1) (c) and the right to have the decision reviewed by the Court of Justice.

6. The Commission shall at the same time forward a copy of its decision to the competent authority of the Member State in whose territory the seat of the undertaking or association of undertakings is situated.

ARTICLE 12

Inquiry into sectors of the economy

1. If in any sector of the economy the trend of trade between Member States, price movements, inflexibility of prices or other circumstances suggest that in the economic sector concerned competition is being restricted or distorted within the common market, the Commission may decide to conduct a general inquiry into that economic sector and in the course thereof may request undertakings in the sector concerned to supply the information necessary for giving effect to the principles formulated in Articles 85 and 86 of the Treaty and for carrying out the duties entrusted to the Commission.

2. The Commission may in particular request every undertaking or association of undertakings in the economic sector concerned to communicate to it all agreements, decisions and concerted practices which are exempt from notification by virtue of Article 4 (2) and Article 5 (2).

3. When making inquiries pursuant to paragraph 2, the Commission shall also request undertakings or groups of undertakings whose size suggests that they occupy a dominant position within the common market or a substantial part thereof to supply to the Commission such particulars of the structure of the undertakings and of their behaviour as are requisite to an appraisal of their position in the light of Article 86 of the Treaty.

4. Article 10 (3) to (6) and Articles 11, 13 and 14 shall apply correspondingly.

ARTICLE 13

Investigations by the authorities of the Member States

1. At the request of the Commission, the competent authorities of the Member States shall undertake the investigations which the Commission considers to be necessary under Article 14 (1), or which it has ordered by decision pursuant to Article 14 (3). The officials of the competent authorities of the Member States responsible for conducting these investigations shall exercise their powers upon production of an authorisation in writing issued by the competent authority of the Member State in whose territory the investigation is to be made. Such authorisation shall specify the subject matter and purpose of the investigation.

2. If so requested by the Commission or by the competent authority of the Member State in whose territory the investigation is to be made, the officials of the Commission may assist the officials of such authorities in carrying out their duties.

ARTICLE 14

Investigating powers of the Commission

1. In carrying out the duties assigned to it by Article 89 and by provisions adopted under Article 87 of the Treaty, the Commission may undertake all necessary investigations into undertakings and associations of undertakings. To this end the officials authorised by the Commission are empowered:

(a) to examine the books and other business records;

(b) to take copies of or extracts from the books and business records;

(c) to ask for oral explanations on the spot;

(d) to enter any premises; land and means of transport of undertakings.

2. The officials of the Commission authorised for the purpose of these investigations shall exercise their powers upon production of an authorisation in writing specifying the subject matter and purpose of the investigation and the penalties provided for in Article 15 (1) (c) in cases where production of the required books or other business records is incomplete. In good time before the investigation, the Commission shall inform the competent authority of the Member State in whose territory the same is to be made of the investigation and of the identity of the authorised officials.

3. Undertakings and associations of undertakings shall submit to investigations ordered by decision of the Commission. The decision shall specify the subject matter and purpose of the investigation, appoint the date on which it is to begin and indicate the penalties provided for in Article 15 (1) (c) and Article 16 (1) (d) and the right to have the decision reviewed by the Court of Justice.

4. The Commission shall take decisions referred to in paragraph 3 after consultation with the competent authority of the Member State in whose territory the investigation is to be made.

5. Officials of the competent authority of the Member State in whose territory the investigation is to be made may, at the request of such authority or of the Commission, assist the officials of the Commission in carrying out their duties.

6. Where an undertaking opposes an investigation ordered pursuant to this Article, the Member State concerned shall afford the necessary assistance to the officials authorised by the Commission to enable them to make their investigation. Member States shall, after consultation with the Commission, take the necessary measures to this end before 1 October 1962.

ARTICLE 15

Fines

1. The Commission may by decision impose on undertakings or associations of undertakings fines of 100 to 5000 units of account where, intentionally or negligently:

(a) they supply incorrect or misleading information in an application pursuant to Article 2 or in a notification pursuant to Articles 4 or 5; or

(b) they supply incorrect information in response to a request made pursuant to Article 11 (3) or (5) or to Article 12, or do not supply information within the time limit fixed by a decision taken under Article 11 (5); or

(c) they produce the required books or other business records in incomplete form during investigations under Article 13 or 14, or refuse to submit to an investigation ordered by decision issued in implementation of Article 14 (3).

2. The Commission may by decision impose on undertakings or associations of undertakings fines of 1000 to 1 000 000 units of account, or a sum in excess thereof but not exceeding 10% of the turnover in the preceding business year of each of the undertakings participating in the infringement where, either intentionally or negligently:

(a) they infringe Article 85 (1) or Article 86 of the Treaty; or

(b) they commit a breach of any obligation imposed pursuant to Article 8 (1).

In fixing the amount of the fine, regard shall be had both to the gravity and to the duration of the infringement.

3. Article 10 (3) to (6) shall apply.

4. Decisions taken pursuant to paragraphs 1 and 2 shall not be of a criminal law nature.

5. The fines provided for in paragraph 2 (a) shall not be imposed in respect of acts taking place:

(a) after notification to the Commission and before its decision in application of Article 85 (3) of the Treaty, provided they fall within the limits of the activity described in the notification;

(b) before notification and in the course of agreements, decisions or concerted practices in existence at the date of entry into force of this Regulation, provided that notification was effected within the time limits specified in Article 5 (1) and Article 7 (2).

6. Paragraph 5 shall not have effect where the Commission has informed the undertakings concerned that after preliminary examination it is of opinion that Article 85 (1) of the Treaty applies and that application of Article 85 (3) is not justified.

ARTICLE 16

Periodic penalty payments

1. The Commission may by decision impose on undertakings or associations of undertakings periodic penalty payments of 50 to 1000 units of account per day,

calculated from the date appointed by the decision, in order to compel them:

(a) to put an end to an infringement of Article 85 or 86 of the Treaty, in accordance with a decision taken pursuant to Article 3 of this Regulation;

(b) to refrain from any act prohibited under Article 8 (3);

(c) to supply complete and correct information which it has requested by decision taken pursuant to Article 11 (5);

(d) to submit to an investigation which it has ordered by decision taken pursuant to Article 14 (3).

2. Where the undertakings or associations of undertakings have satisfied the obligation which it was the purpose of the periodic penalty payment to enforce, the Commission may fix the total amount of the periodic penalty payment at a lower figure than that which would arise under the original decision.

3. Article 10 (3) to (6) shall apply.

ARTICLE 17

Review by the Court of Justice

The Court of Justice shall have unlimited jurisdiction within the meaning of Article 172 of the Treaty to review decisions whereby the Commission has fixed a fine or periodic penalty payment; it may cancel, reduce or increase the fine or periodic penalty payment imposed.

ARTICLE 18

Unit of account

For the purposes of applying Articles 15 to 17 the unit of account shall be that adopted in drawing up the budget of the Community in accordance with Articles 207 and 209 of the Treaty.

ARTICLE 19

Hearing of the parties and of third persons

1. Before taking decisions as provided for in Articles 2, 3, 6, 7, 8, 15 and 16, the Commission shall give the undertakings or associations of undertakings concerned the opportunity of being heard on the matters to which the Commission has taken objection.

2. If the Commission or the competent authorities of the Member States consider it necessary, they may also hear other natural or legal persons. Applications to be heard on the part of such persons shall, where they show a sufficient interest, be granted.

3. Where the Commission intends to give negative clearance pursuant to Article 2 or take a decision in application of Article 85 (3) of the Treaty, it shall publish a summary of the relevant application or notification and invite all interested third parties to submit their observations within a time limit which it shall fix being not less than one month. Publication shall have regard to the legitimate interest of undertakings in the protection of their business secrets.

ARTICLE 20

Professional secrecy

1. Information acquired as a result of the application of Articles 11, 12, 13 and 14 shall be used only for the purpose of the relevant request or investigation.

2. Without prejudice to the provisions of Articles 19 and 21, the Commission and the competent authorities of the Member States, their officials and other servants shall not disclose information acquired by them as a result of the application of this Regulation and of the kind covered by the obligation of professional secrecy.

3. The provisions of paragraphs 1 and 2 shall not prevent publication of general information or surveys which do not contain information relating to particular undertakings or associations of undertakings.

ARTICLE 21

Publication of decisions

1. The Commission shall publish the decisions which it takes pursuant to Articles 2, 3, 6, 7 and 8.

2. The publication shall state the names of the parties and the main content of the decision; it shall have regard to the legitimate interest of undertakings in the protection of their business secrets.

ARTICLE 22

Special provisions

1. The Commission shall submit to the Council proposals for making certain categories of agreement, decision and concerted practice falling within Article 4 (2) or Article 5 (2) compulsorily notifiable under Article 4 or 5.

2. Within one year from the date of entry into force of this Regulation, the Council shall examine, on a proposal from the Commission, what special provisions might be made for exempting from the provisions of this Regulation agreements, decisions and concerted practices falling within Article 4 (2) or Article 5 (2).

ARTICLE 23

Transitional provisions applicable to decisions of authorities of the Member States

1. Agreements, decisions and concerted practices of the kind described in Article 85 (1) of the Treaty to which, before the entry into force of this Regulation, the competent authority of a Member State has declared Article 85 (1) to be inapplicable pursuant to Article 85 (3) shall not be subject to compulsory notification under Article 5. The decision of the competent authority of the Member State shall be deemed to be a decision within the meaning of Article 6; it shall cease to be valid upon expiration of the period fixed by such authority but in any event not more than three years after the entry into force of this Regulation. Article 8 (3) shall apply.

2. Applications for renewal of decisions of the kind described in paragraph 1 shall be decided upon by the Commission in accordance with Article 8 (2).

ARTICLE 24

Implementing provisions

The Commission shall have power to adopt implementing provisions concerning the form, content and other details of applications pursuant to Articles 2 and 3 and of notifications pursuant to Articles 4 and 5, and concerning hearings pursuant to Article 19 (1) and (2).

ARTICLE 25

1. As regards agreements, decisions and concerted practices to which Article 85 of the Treaty applies by virtue of accession, the date of accession shall be substituted for the date of entry into force of this Regulation in every place where reference is made in this Regulation to this latter date.

2. Agreements, decisions and concerted practices existing at the date of accession to which Article 85 of the Treaty applies by virtue of accession shall be notified pursuant to Article 5 (1) or Article 7 (1) and (2) within six months from the date of accession.

3. Fines under Article 15 (2) (a) shall not be imposed in respect of any act prior to notification of the agreements, decisions and practices to which paragraph 2 applies and which have been notified within the period therein specified.

4. New Member States shall take the measures referred to in Article 14 (6) within six months from the date of accession after consulting the Commission.

5. The provisions of paragraphs 1 to 4 above still apply in the same way in the case of the accession of the Hellenic Republic, the Kingdom of Spain and of the Portuguese Republic.

6. The provisions of paragraphs 1 to 4 still apply in the same way in the case of the accession of Austria, Finland and Sweden. However, they do not apply to agreements, decisions and concerted practises which at the date of accession already fall under Article 53 of the EEA Agreement.

This Regulation shall be binding in its entirety and directly applicable in all Member States.

REGULATION NO 19/65/EEC OF 2 MARCH OF THE COUNCIL ON APPLICATION OF ARTICLE 85 (3) OF THE TREATY TO CERTAIN CATEGORIES OF AGREEMENTS AND CONCERTED PRACTICES

REGULATION No 19/65/EEC OF THE COUNCIL of 2 March 1965 on application of Article 85 (3) of the Treaty to certain categories of agreements and concerted practices

THE COUNCIL OF THE EUROPEAN ECONOMIC COMMUNITY,

Having regard to the Treaty establishing the European Economic Community, and in particular Article 87 thereof;

Having regard to the proposal from the Commission;

Having regard to the Opinion of the European Parliament (1);

Having regard to the Opinion of the Economic and Social Committee (2);

Whereas Article 85 (1) of the Treaty may in accordance with Article 85(3) be declared inapplicable to certain categories of agreements, decisions and concerted practices which fulfil the conditions contained in Article 85 (3);

Whereas the provisions for implementation of Article 85 (3) must be adopted by way of regulation pursuant to Article 87;

Whereas in view of the large number of notifications submitted in pursuance of Regulation No 17(3) it is desirable that in order to facilitate the task of the Commission it should be enabled to declare by way of regulation that the provisions of Article 85 (1) do not apply to certain categories of agreements and concerted practices;

Whereas it should be laid down under what conditions the Commission, in close and constant liaison with the competent authorities of the Member States, may exercise such powers after sufficient experience has been gained in the light of individual decisions and it becomes possible to define categories of agreements and concerted practices in respect of which the conditions of Article 85 (3) may be considered as being fulfilled;

Whereas the Commission has indicated by the action it has taken, in particular by Regulation No 153, (4) that there can be no easing of the procedures prescribed by Regulation No 17 in respect of certain types of agreements and concerted practices that are particularly liable to distort competition in the common market;

Whereas under Article 6 of Regulation No 17 the Commission may provide that a decision taken pursuant to Article 85 (3) of the Treaty shall apply with retroactive effect; whereas it is desirable that the Commission be also empowered to adopt, by regulation, provisions to the like effect;

Whereas under Article 7 of Regulation No 17 agreements, decisions and concerted practices may, by decision of the Commission, be exempted from prohibition in particular if they are modified in such manner that they satisfy the requirements of Article 85 (3); whereas it is desirable that the Commission be enabled to grant like exemption by regulation to such agreements and concerted practices if they are modified in such manner as to fall within a category defined in an exempting regulation;

Whereas, since there can be no exemption if the conditions set out in Article 85 (3) are not satisfied, the Commission must have power to lay down by decision the conditions that must be satisfied by an agreement or concerted practice which owing to special circumstances has certain effects incompatible with Article 85 (3); (1) OJ No 81, 27.5.1964, p. 1275/64. (2) OJ No 197, 30.11.1964, p. 3320/64. (3) OJ No 13, 21.2.1962, p. 204/62 (Regulation No 17 as amended by Regulation No 59 – OJ No 58, 10.7.1962, p. 1655/62 – and Regulation No 118/63/EEC – OJ No 162, 7.11.1963, p. 2696/63. (4) OJ No 139, 24.12.1962, p. 2918/62.

HAS ADOPTED THIS REGULATION:

Article 1

1. Without prejudice to the application of Regulation No 17 and in accordance with Article 81(3) of the Treaty the Commission may by regulation declare that Article 81(3) shall not apply to:

(a) categories of agreements which are entered into by two or more undertakings, each operating, for the purposes of the agreement, at a different level of the production or distribution chain, and which relate to the conditions under which the parties may purchase, sell or resell certain goods or services,

(b) categories of agreements to which only two undertakings are party and which include restrictions imposed in relation to the acquisition or use of industrial property rights, in particular of patents, utility models, designs or trade marks, or to the rights arising out of contracts for the assignment of, or the right to use, a method of manufacture or knowledge relating to the use or to the application of industrial processes.

2. The regulation shall define the categories of agreements to which it applies and shall specify in particular:

(a) the restrictions or clauses which must not be contained in the agreements;

(b) the other conditions which must be satisfied.

3. Paragraphs 1 and 2 shall apply by analogy to categories of concerted practices.

Article 1a

A regulation pursuant to Article 1 may stipulate the conditions which may lead to the exclusion from its application of certain parallel networks of similar agreements or concerted practices operating on a particular market; when these circumstances are fulfilled the Commission may establish this by means of regulation and fix a period at the expiry of which the Regulation pursuant to Article 1 would no longer be applicable in respect of the relevant agreements or concerted practices on that market; such period must be shorter than six months.

Article 2

1. A regulation pursuant to Article 1 shall be made for a specified period.

2. It may be repealed or amended where circumstances have changed with respect to any factor which was basic to its being made; in such case, a period shall be fixed for modification of the agreements and concerted practices to which the earlier regulation applies.

Article 3

A regulation pursuant to Article 1 may stipulate that it shall apply with retroactive effect to agreements and concerted practices to which, at the date of entry into force of that regulation, a decision issued with retroactive effect in pursuance of Article 6 of Regulation No 17 would have applied.

Article 4

1. A regulation pursuant to Article 1 may stipulate that the prohibition contained in Article 85(1) of the Treaty shall not apply, for such period as shall be fixed by that regulation, to agreements and concerted practices already in existence on 13 March 1962 which do not satisfy the conditions of Article 85(3), where —

A regulation pursuant to Article 1 may stipulate that the prohibition contained in Article 85(1) of the Treaty shall not apply, for such period as shall be fixed by that regulation, to agreements and concerted practices already in existence at the date of accession to which Article 85 applies by virtue of accession and which do not satisfy the conditions of Article 85(3), where:

- within three months from the entry into force of the regulation, they are so modified as to satisfy the said conditions in accordance with the provisions of the regulation; and
- the modifications are brought to the notice of the Commission within the time limit fixed by the regulation.

The provisions of the preceding paragraph shall apply in the same way in the case of the accession of the Hellenic Republic, the Kingdom of Spain and of the Portuguese Republic.

The provisions of the preceding paragraph shall apply in the same way in the case of the accession of Austria, Finland and Sweden.

2. Paragraph 1 shall apply to agreements and concerted practices which had to be notified before 1 February 1963, in accordance with Article 5 of Regulation No. 17, only where they have been so notified before that date.

Paragraph 1 shall not apply to agreements and concerted practices to which Article 85(1) of the Treaty applies by virtue of accession and which must be notified before 1 July 1973, in accordance with Articles 5 and 25 of Regulation No. 17, unless they have been so notified before that date.

Paragraph 1 shall not apply to agreements and concerted practices to which Article 85(1) of the Treaty applies by virtue of the accession of the Hellenic Republic and which must be notified before 1 July 1981, in accordance with Articles 5 and 25 of Regulation No. 17, unless they have been so notified before that date.

Paragraph 2 shall not apply to agreements and concerted practices to which Article 85(1) of the Treaty applies by virtue of the accession of the Kingdom of Spain and of the Portuguese Republic and which must be notified before 1 July 1986, in accordance with Articles 5 and 25 of Regulation No. 17, unless they have been so notified before that date.

Paragraph 1 shall not apply to agreements and concerted practices to which Article 85(1) of the Treaty applies by virtue of the accession of Austria, Finland and Sweden and which must be notified within six months of accession, in accordance with Articles 5 and 25 of Regulation No. 17, unless they have been so notified within that period. The present paragraph shall not apply to agreements and concerted practices which at the date of accession already fall under Article 53(1) of the EEA agreement.

Article 5

Before adopting a regulation, the Commission shall publish a draft thereof and invite all persons concerned to submit their comments within such time limit, being not less than one month, as the Commission shall fix.

Article 6

1. The Commission shall consult the Advisory Committee on Restrictive Practices and Monopolies:

(a) without regard to a regulation pursuant to Article 1 before publishing a draft regulation and before adopting a regulation;

(b) with regard to a regulation pursuant to Article 1a before publishing a draft regulation if requested by a Member State, and before adopting a regulation.

2. Article 10 (5) and (6) of Regulation No 17, relating to consultation with the Advisory Committee, shall apply by analogy, it being understood that joint meetings with the Commission shall take place not earlier than one month after dispatch of the notice convening them.

Article 7

1. Where the Commission, either on its own initiative or at the request of a Member State or of natural or legal persons claiming a legitimate interest, finds that in any particular case agreements or concerted practices to which a regulation adopted pursuant to Article 1 of this Regulation applies have nevertheless certain effects which are incompatible with the conditions laid down in Article 85 (3) of the Treaty, it may withdraw the benefit of application of that regulation and issue a decision in accordance with Articles 6 and 8 of Regulation No 17, without any notification under Article 4 (1) of Regulation No 17 being required.

2. When in any particular case agreements or concerted practices to which a regulation adopted pursuant to Article 1 applies have certain effects which are incompatible with the conditions laid down in Article 81(3) of the Treaty in the territory of a Member State, or in part thereof, which has all the characteristics of a distinct market, the competent authority in the Member State may on its own initiative or at the request of the Commission or of natural of legal persons claiming a legitimate interest withdraw the benefit of application of that regulation.

Article 8

The Commission shall, before 1 January 1970, submit to the Council a proposal for a Regulation for such amendment of this Regulation as may prove necessary in the light of experience.

This Regulation shall be binding in its entirety and directly applicable in all Member States.

Done at Brussels, 2 March 1965.

For the Council
The President
M. COUVE DE MURVILLE

APPENDIX F

NOTICE ON AGREEMENTS OF MINOR IMPORTANCE WHICH DO NOT FALL WITHIN THE MEANING OF ARTICLE 85(1) OF THE TREATY ESTABLISHING THE EUROPEAN COMMUNITY (97/C 372/04)

(Text with EEA relevance)

I.

1. The Commission considers it important to facilitate cooperation between undertakings where such cooperation is economically desirable without presenting difficulties from the point of view of competition policy. To this end, it published the notice concerning agreements, decisions and concerted practices in the field of cooperation between enterprises[1] listing a number of agreements that by their nature cannot be regarded as being in restraint of competition. Furthermore, in the notice concerning its assessment of certain subcontracting agreements[2] the Commission considered that that type of contract, which offers all undertakings opportunities for development, does not automatically fall within the scope of Article 85(1). The notice concerning the assessment of cooperative joint ventures pursuant to Article 85 of the EC Treaty[3] describes in detail the conditions under which the agreements in question do not fall under the prohibition of restrictive agreements. By issuing this notice which replaces the Commission notice of 3 September 1986[4], the Commission is taking a further step towards defining the scope of Article 85(1), in order to facilitate cooperation between undertakings.

---

1 OJ C 75, 29. 7. 1968. p. 3, as corrected in OJ C 84, 28. 8. 1968, p. 14.

2 OJ C 1, 3. 1. 1979, p. 2.

3 OJ C 43, 16. 2. 1993, p. 2.

4 OJ C 231, 12. 9. 1986, p. 2.

2. Article 85(1) prohibits agreements which may affect trade between Member States and which have as their object or effect the prevention, restriction or distortion of competition within the common market. The Court of Justice of the European Communities has clarified that this provision is not applicable where the impact of the agreement on intra-Community trade or on competition is not appreciable. Agreements which are not capable of significantly affecting trade between Member States are not caught by Article 85. They should therefore be examined on the basis, and within the framework, of national legislation alone. This is also the case for agreements whose actual or potential effect remains limited to the territory of only one Member State or of one or more third countries. Likewise, agreements which do not have as their object or their effect an appreciable restriction of competition are not caught by the prohibition contained in Article 85(1).

3. In this notice the Commission, by setting quantitative criteria and by explaining their application, has given a sufficiently concrete meaning to the term 'appreciable' for undertakings to be able to judge for themselves whether their agreements do not fall within the prohibition pursuant to Article 85(1) by virtue of their minor importance. The quantitiative definition of appreciability, however, serves only as a guideline: in individual cases even agreements between undertakings which exceed the threshold set out below may still have only a negligible effect on trade between Member States or on competition within the common market and are therefore not caught by Article 85(1). This notices does not contain an exhaustive description of restictions which fall outside Article 85(1). It is generally recognized that even agreements which are not of minor importance can escape the prohibition on agreements on account of their exclusively favourable impact on competition.

4. The benchmarks provided by the Commission in this notice should eliminate the need to have the legal status of agreements covered by it established through individual Commission decisions; notification for this purpose will no longer be necessary for such agreements. However, if it is doubtful whether, in an individual case, an agreement is likely to affect trade between Member States or to restrict competition to any significant extent, undertakings are free to apply for negative clearance or to notify the agreement pursuant to Council Regulations No 17[5], (EEC) No 1017/69[6], (EEC) No 4056/86[7] and (EEC) No 3975/87[8].

---

5 OJ 13, 21. 2. 1962, p. 204/62.

6 OJ L 175, 23. 7. 1968, p. 1.

7 OJ L 378, 31. 12. 1986, p. 4.

8 OJ L 374, 31. 12. 1987, p. 1.

5. In cases covered by this notice, and subject to points 11 and 20, the Commission will not institute any proceedings either on application or on its own initiative. Where undertakings have failed to notify an agreement falling within the scope of Article 85(1) because they assumed in good faith that the agreement was covered by this notice, the Commission will not consider imposing fines.

6. This notice is likewise applicable to decisions by associations of undertakings and to concerted practices.

7. This notice is without prejudice to the competence of national courts to apply Article 85. However, it constitutes a factor which those courts may take into account when deciding a pending case. It is also without prejudice to any interpretation of Article 85 which may be given by the Court of Justice or the Court of First Instance of the European Communities.

8. This notice is without prejudice to the application of national competition laws.

II.

9. The Commission holds the view that agreements between undertakings engaged in the production or distribution of goods or in the provision of services do not fall under the prohibition in Article 85(1) if the aggregate market shares held by all of the participating undertakings do not exceed, on any of the relevant markets:

(a) the 5 % threshold, where the agreement is made between undertakings operating at the same level of production or of marketing ('horizontal' agreement);

(b) the 10 % threshold, where the agreement is made between undertakings operating at different economic levels ('vertical' agreement).

In the case of a mixed horizontal/vertical agreement or where it is difficult to classify the agreement as either horizontal or vertical, the 5 % threshold is applicable.

10. The Commission also holds the view that the said agreements do not fall under the prohibition of Article 85(1) if the market shares given at point 9 are exceeded by no more than one 10th during two successive financial years.

11. With regard to:

(a) horizontal agreements which have as their object

- to fix prices or to limit production or sales, or

- to share markets or sources of supply,

(b) vertical agreements which have as their object
  - to fix resale prices, or
  - to confer territorial protection on the participating undertakings or third undertakings,

the applicability of Article 85(1) cannot be ruled out even where the aggregate market shares held by all of the participating undertakings remain below the thresholds mentioned in points 9 and 10.

The Commission considers, however, that in the first instance it is for the authorities and courts of the Member States to take action on any agreements envisaged above in (a) and (b). Accordingly, it will only intervene in such cases when it considers that the interest of the Community so demands, and in particular if the agreements impair the proper functioning of the internal market.

12. For the purposes of this notice, 'participating undertakings' are:

(a) undertakings being parties to the agreement;

(b) undertakings in which a party to the agreement, directly or indirectly,
  - owns more than half of the capital or business assets, or
  - has the power to exercise more than half of the voting rights, or
  - has the power to appoint more than half of the members of the supervisory board, board of management or bodies legally representing the undertakings, or
  - has to the right to manage the undertaking's business;

(c) undertakings which directly or indirectly have over a party to the agreement the rights or powers listed in (b);

(d) undertakings over which an undertaking referred to in (c) has, directly or indirectly, the rights or powers listed in (b).

Undertakings over which several undertakings as referred to in (a) to (d) jointly have, directly or indirectly, the rights or powers set out in (b) shall also be considered to be participating undertakings.

13. In order to calculate the market share, it is necessary to determine the relevant market; for this, the relevant product market and the relevant geographic market must be defined.

14. The relevant product market comprises any products or services which are regarded as interchangeable or substitutable by the consumer, by reason of their characteristics, prices and intended use.

15. The relevant geographic market comprises the area in which the participating undertakings are involved in the supply of relevant products or services, in which the conditions of competition are sufficiently homogeneous, and which can be distinguished from neighbouring geographic areas because, in particular, conditions of competition are appreciably different in those areas.

16. When applying points 14 and 15, reference should be had to the notice (on the definition of the relevant market under Community competition law[9].

17. In the case of doubt about the delimitation of the relevant geographic market, undertakings may take the view that their agreement has no appreciable effect on intra-Community trade or on competition when the market share thresholds indicated in points 9 and 10 are not exceeded in any Member State. This view, however, does not preclude the application of national competition law to the agreements in question.

18. Chapter II of this notice shall not apply where in a relevant market competition is restricted by the cumulative effects of parallel networks of similar agreements established by several manufacturers or dealers.

III.

19. Agreements between small and medium-sized undertakings, as defined in the Annex to Commission recommendation 96/280/EC[10] are rarely capable of significantly affecting trade between Member States and competition within the common market. Consequently, as a general rule, they are not caught by the prohibition in Article 85(1). In cases where such agreements exceptionally meet the conditions for the application of that provision, they will not be of sufficient Community interest to justify any intervention. This is why the Commission will not institute any proceedings, either on request or on its own initiative, to apply the provisions of Article 85(1) to such agreements, even if the thresholds set out in points 9 and 10 above are exceeded.

---

9 OJ C 372, 9. 12. 1997, p. 5.

10 OJ L 107, 30. 4. 1996, p. 4.

APPENDIX G

NOTICE OF THE COMMISSION RELATING TO THE REVISION OF THE 1997 NOTICE ON AGREEMENTS OF MINOR IMPORTANCE WHICH DO NOT FALL UNDER ARTICLE 81(1) OF THE EC TREATY (2001/C 149/05)

(Text with EEA relevance)

The Commission invites all interested parties to submit their written observations on the following draft of a revised notice on agreements of minor importance. Observations should be sent in the two months following the date of the present publication to the following address:

European Commission
Directorate General for Competition
Unit A-2
J 70 – 5/203 Rue de la Loi/Wetstraat 200
B-1049 Brussels
Internet address: Lucas.Peeperkorn@cec.eu.int.

Draft Notice on agreements of minor importance which do not appreciably restrict competition under Article 81(1) of the Treaty establishing the European Community (de minimis)[1]

I

1. Article 81(1) prohibits agreements which may affect trade between Member States and which have as their object or effect the prevention, restriction or distortion of competition within the common market. The Court of Justice of the European Communities has clarified that this provision is not applicable where the impact of the agreement on intra-community trade or on competition is not appreciable.

---

1 This notice replaces the notice on agreements of minor importance published in OJ C 372, 9.12.1997.

2. In the present notice the Commission quantifies, with the help of market share thresholds, what is not an appreciable restriction of competition under Article 81 of the EC Treaty. This negative definition of appreciability does not imply that agreements between undertakings which exceed the thresholds set out in this notice appreciably restrict competition. Such agreements may still have only a negligible effect on competition within the common market and may therefore not be caught by Article 81(1).[2]

3. Agreements may also not be caught by Article 81(1) because they are not capable of appreciably affecting trade between Member States. This notice does not deal with this issue. It does not quantify what does or does not constitute an appreciable effect on trade.

4. In cases covered by this notice, and subject to point 11, the Commission will not institute proceedings either upon application or on its own initiative. Where undertakings assume in good faith that an agreement is covered by this notice, the Commission will not impose fines. Although not binding on them, this notice also intends to give guidance to the courts and authorities of the Member States in their application of Article 81.

5. This notice also applies to decisions by associations of undertakings and to concerted practices.

6. This notice is without prejudice to any interpretation of Article 81 which may be given by the Court of Justice or the Court of First Instance of the European Communities.

7. This notice is without prejudice to the application of national competition laws.

II

8. The Commission holds the view that agreements between undertakings which affect trade between Member States do not appreciably restrict competition within the meaning of Article 81(1):

---

2 See for instance the judgment of the Court of Justice in Joined Cases C-215/96 and C-216/96 Bagnasco (Carlos) v Banca Popolare di Novara and Casa di Risparmio di Genova e Imperia (1999) ECR I-135, points 34-35.

(a) if the aggregate market share held by all the parties to the agreement does not exceed 10 % on any of the relevant markets affected by the agreement, where the agreement is made between undertakings which are actual or potential competitors on any of the affected relevant markets (agreements between competitors)[3]; or

(b) if the market share held by each of the parties to the agreement does not exceed 15 % on any of the relevant markets affected by the agreement, where the agreement is made between undertakings which are not actual or potential competitors on any of the affected relevant markets (agreements between non-competitors).

In cases where it is difficult to classify the agreement as either an agreement between competitors or an agreement between non-competitors the 10 % threshold is applicable.

9. Where in an affected relevant market competition is restricted by the cumulative effect of parallel networks of agreements for the sale of goods or services established by several suppliers or distributors and which have similar effects on the market, the market share threshold under point 8 is reduced to 5 %, both for agreements between competitors and for agreements between non-competitors. The agreements of a supplier or distributor with a market share not exceeding 5 % are in general not considered to contribute significantly to a cumulative foreclosure effect resulting from agreements of several suppliers or distributors[4].

10. The Commission also holds the view that the said agreements are not restrictive of competition if the market shares given at point 8 and 9 are exceeded by no more than one percentage point during two successive calendar years.

---

3 On what are actual or potential competitors, see the Commission Notice 'Guidelines on the applicability of Article 81 of the EC Treaty to horizontal cooperation agreements', OJ C 3, 6.1.2001, p. 2, paragraph 9.

4 See also the Commission Notice 'Guidelines on vertical restraints', OJ C 291, 13.10.2000, in particular paragraphs 73, 142 and 189. While in the guidelines on vertical restraints in relation to certain restrictions reference is made not only to the total but also to the tied market share, in this notice the market share thresholds all refer to total market shares.

11. In order to calculate the market share, it is necessary to determine the relevant market. This consists of the relevant product market and the relevant geographic market. When defining the relevant market, reference should be had to the notice on the definition of the relevant market for the purposes of Community competition law[5].

12. Provided that the condition of effect on trade between Member States is fulfilled, agreements containing any of the following hardcore restrictions do not benefit from the thresholds set out in points 8, 9 and 10 and are unlikely to qualify for individual exemption:

(1) horizontal agreements (i.e. agreements between undertakings operating at the same level of the production or distribution chain) which, directly or indirectly, in isolation or in combination with other factors under the control of the parties, have as their object:
   - (a) the fixing of prices when selling the products to third parties;
   - (b) the limitation of output or sales;
   - (c) the allocation of markets or customers;

(2) vertical agreements (i.e. agreements between undertakings operating, for the purposes of the agreement, at a different level of the production or distribution chain) which, directly or indirectly, in isolation or in combination with other factors under the control of the parties, have as their object:
   - (a) the restriction of the buyer's ability to determine its sale price, without prejudice to the possibility of the supplier imposing a maximum sale price or recommending a sale price, provided that they do not amount to a fixed or minimum sale price as a result of pressure from, or incentives offered by, any of the parties;
   - (b) the restriction of the territory into which, or of the customers to whom, the buyer may sell the contract goods or services, except the following restrictions which are not hardcore:
     - the restriction of active sales into the exclusive territory or to an exclusive customer group reserved to the supplier or allocated by the supplier to another buyer, where such a restriction does not limit sales by the customers of the buyer,
     - the restriction of sales to end users by a buyer operating at the wholesale level of trade,

---

5 OJ C 372, 9.12.1997, p. 5.

- the restriction of sales to unauthorised distributors by the members of a selective distribution system, and
- the restriction of the buyer's ability to sell components, supplied for the purposes of incorporation, to customers who would use them to manufacture the same type of goods as those produced by the supplier;

(c) the restriction of active or passive sales to end-users by members of a selective distribution system operating at the retail level of trade, without prejudice to the possibility of prohibiting a member of the system from operating out of an unauthorised place of establishment;

(d) the restriction of cross-supplies between distributors within a selective distribution system, including between distributors operating at different levels of trade;

(e) the restriction agreed between a supplier of components and a buyer who incorporates those components, which limits the supplier's ability to sell the components as spare parts to end-users or to repairers or other service providers not entrusted by the buyer with the repair or servicing of its goods.

(3) vertical agreements entered into between actual or potential competitors if they contain any of the hardcore restrictions listed in paragraph (1) or (2) above.

The above hardcore restrictions may however escape the prohibition laid down in Article 81(1) in particular in cases where the agreement does not affect trade between Member States. Case-law has established, especially with regard to territorial protection in vertical agreements, that there is no violation of Article 81(1) in cases where the agreement has only an insignificant effect on the relevant markets due to the weak positions which the parties concerned have on the markets in question.[6] Agreements between small and medium-sized undertakings, as defined in the annex to Commission Recommendation 96/280/EC,[7] are rarely capable of affecting trade between Member States.

---

6 See the following judgments of the Court of Justice: Case 5/69 *Völck v Vervaecke* (1969) ECR 295; Case 1/71 *Cadillon v Höss* (1971) ECR 351; Case 19/77 *Miller International Schallplatten v Commission* (1978) ECR 131; Case C-70/93 *BMW AG v ALD Auto-Leasing D GmbH* (1995) ECR I-3439; Case C-306/96 *Javico International and Javico AG v Yves Saint Laurent Parfums SA* (1998) ECR I-1983.

7 OJ L 107, 30.4.1996, p. 4.

13.

(1) For the purposes of this notice, the terms 'undertaking', 'party to the agreement', 'distributor', 'supplier' and 'buyer' shall include their respective connected undertakings.

(2) 'Connected undertakings' are:

(a) undertakings in which a party to the agreement, directly or indirectly:
- has the power to exercise more than half the voting rights, or
- has the power to appoint more than half the members of the supervisory board, board of management or bodies legally representing the undertaking, or
- has the right to manage the undertaking's affairs;

(b) undertakings which directly or indirectly have, over a party to the agreement, the rights or powers listed in (a);

(c) undertakings in which an undertaking referred to in (b) has, directly or indirectly, the rights or powers listed in (a);

(d) undertakings in which a party to the agreement together with one or more of the undertakings referred to in (a), (b) or (c), or in which two or more of the latter undertakings, jointly have the rights or powers listed in (a);

(e) undertakings in which the rights or the powers listed in (a) are jointly held by:
- parties to the agreement or their respective connected undertakings referred to in (a) to (d), or
- one or more of the parties to the agreement or one or more of their connected undertakings referred to in (a) to (d) and one or more third parties.

(3) For the purposes of paragraph 2(e), the market share held by these jointly held undertakings shall be apportioned equally to each undertaking having the rights or the powers listed in paragraph 2(a).

APPENDIX H

:OMMISSION NOTICE ON THE DEFINITION OF RELEVANT MARKET FOR THE PURPOSES OF :OMMUNITY COMPETITION LAW (97/C 372/03)

with EEA relevance)

I. INTRODUCTION

: purpose of this notice is to provide guidance as to how the Commission s the concept of relevant product and geographic market in its ongoing ement of Community competition law, in particular the application of Council ation No 17 and (EEC) No 4064/89, their equivalents in other sectoral ations such as transport, coal and steel, and agriculture, and the relevant ;ions of the EEA Agreement[1]. Throughout this notice, references to Articles 1 86 of the Treaty and to merger control are to be understood as referring to uivalent provisions in the EEA Agreement and the ECSC Treaty.

rket definition is a tool to identify and define the boundaries of competition en firms. It serves to establish the framework within which competition policy ied by the Commission. The main purpose of market definition is to identify ystematic way the competitive constraints that the undertakings involved[2] The objective of defining a market in both its product and geographic dimen- ; to identify those actual competitors of the undertakings involved that are

---

: focus of assessment in State aid cases is the aid recipient and the industry/sector cerned rather than identification of competitive constraints faced by the aid recipient. en consideration of market power and therefore of the relevant market are raised in particular case, elements of the approach outlined here might serve as a basis for the essment of State aid cases.

the purposes of this notice, the undertakings involved will be, in the case of a centration, the parties to the concentration; in investigations within the meaning of icle 86 of the Treaty, the undertaking being investigated or the complainants; for estigations within the meaning of Article 85, the parties to the Agreement.

capable of constraining those undertakings' behaviour and of preventing them from behaving independently of effective competitive pressure. It is from this perspective that the market definition makes it possible inter alia to calculate market shares that would convey meaningful information regarding market power for the purposes of assessing dominance or for the purposes of applying Article 85.

3. It follows from point 2 that the concept of 'relevant market' is different from other definitions of market often used in other contexts. For instance, companies often use the term 'market' to refer to the area where it sells its products or to refer broadly to the industry or sector where it belongs.

4. The definition of the relevant market in both its product and its geographic dimensions often has a decisive influence on the assessment of a competition case. By rendering public the procedures which the Commission follows when considering market definition and by indicating the criteria and evidence on which it relies to reach a decision, the Commission expects to increase the transparency of its policy and decision-making in the area of competition policy.

5. Increased transparency will also result in companies and their advisers being able to better anticipate the possibility that the Commission may raise competition concerns in an individual case. Companies could, therefore, take such a possibility into account in their own internal decision-making when contemplating, for instance, acquisitions, the creation of joint ventures, or the establishment of certain agreements. It is also intended that companies should be in a better position to understand what sort of information the Commission considers relevant for the purposes of market definition.

6. The Commission's interpretation of 'relevant market' is without prejudice to the interpretation which may be given by the Court of Justice or the Court of First Instance of the European Communities.

II. DEFINITION OF RELEVANT MARKET

Definition of relevant product market and relevant geographic market

7. The Regulations based on Article 85 and 86 of the Treaty, in particular in section 6 of Form A/B with respect to Regulation No 17, as well as in section 6 of Form CO with respect to Regulation (EEC) No 4064/89 on the control of concentrations

having a Community dimension have laid down the following definitions, 'Relevant product markets' are defined as follows:

> 'A relevant product market comprises all those products and/or services which are regarded as interchangeable or substitutable by the consumer, by reason of the products' characteristics, their prices and their intended use'.

8. 'Relevant geographic markets' are defined as follows:

> 'The relevant geographic market comprises the area in which the undertakings concerned are involved in the supply and demand of products or services, in which the conditions of competition are sufficiently homogeneous and which can be distinguished from neighbouring areas because the conditions of competition are appreciably different in those area'.

9. The relevant market within which to assess a given competition issue is therefore established by the combination of the product and geographic markets. The Commission interprets the definitions in paragraphs 7 an 8 (which reflect the case-law of the Court of Justice and the Court of First Instance as well as its own decision-making practice) according to the orientations defined in this notice.

Concept of relevant market and objectives of Community competition policy

10. The concept of relevant market is closely related to the objectives pursued under Community competition policy. For example, under the Community's merger control, the objective in controlling structural changes in the supply of a product/service is to prevent the creation or reinforcement of a dominant position as a result of which effective competition would be significantly impeded in a substantial part of the common market. Under the Community's competition rules, a dominant position is such that a firm or group of firms would be in a position to behave to an appreciable extent independently of its competitors, customers and ultimately of its consumers[3]. Such a position would usually arise when a firm or group of firms accounted for a large share of the supply in any given market, provided that other factors analysed in the assessment (such as entry barriers, customers' capacity to react, etc.) point in the same direction.

---

3 Definition given by the Court of Justice in its judgment of 13 February 1979 in Case 85/76, Hoffmann-La Roche [1979] ECR 461, and confirmed in subsequent judgments.

11. The same approach is followed by the Commission in its application of Article 86 of the Treaty to firms that enjoy a single or collective dominant position. Within the meaning of Regulation No 17, the Commission has the power to investigate and bring to an end abuses of such a dominant position, which must also be defined by reference to the relevant market. Markets may also need to be defined in the application of Article 85 of the Treaty, in particular, in determining whether an appreciable restriction of competition exists or in establishing if the condition pursuant to Article 85(3) (b) for an exemption from the application of Article 85(1) is met.

12. The criteria for defining the relevant market are applied generally for the analysis of certain types of behaviour in the market and for the analysis of structural changes in the supply of products. This methodology, though, might lead to different results depending on the nature of the competition issue being examined. For instance, the scope of the geographic market might be different when analysing a concentration, where the analysis is essentially prospective, from an analysis of past behaviour. The different time horizon considered in each case might lead to the result that different geographic markets are defined for the same products depending on whether the Commission is examining a change in the structure of supply, such as a concentration or a cooperative joint venture, or examining issues relating to certain past behaviour.

Basic principles for market definition

Competitive constraints

13. Firms are subject to three main sources or competitive constraints: demand substitutability, supply substitutability and potential competition. From an economic point of view, for the definition of the relevant market, demand substitution constitutes the most immediate and effective disciplinary force on the suppliers of a given product, in particular in relation to their pricing decisions. A firm or a group of firms cannot have a significant impact on the prevailing conditions of sale, such as prices, if its customers are in a position to switch easily to available substitute products or to suppliers located elsewhere. Basically, the exercise of market definition consists in identifying the effective alternative sources of supply for the customers of the undertakings involved, in terms both of products/services and of geographic location of suppliers.

14. The competitive constraints arising from supply side substitutability other then those described in paragraphs 20 to 23 and from potential competition are in general

less immediate and in any case require an analysis of additional factors. As a result such constraints are taken into account at the assessment stage of competition analysis.

Demand substitution

15. The assessment of demand substitution entails a determination of the range of products which are viewed as substitutes by the consumer. One way of making this determination can be viewed as a speculative experiment, postulating a hypothetical small, lasting change in relative prices and evaluating the likely reactions of customers to that increase. The exercise of market definition focuses on prices for operational and practical purposes, and more precisely on demand substitution arising from small, permanent changes in relative prices. This concept can provide clear indications as to the evidence that is relevant in defining markets.

16. Conceptually, this approach means that, starting from the type of products that the undertakings involved sell and the area in which they sell them, additional products and areas will be included in, or excluded from, the market definition depending on whether competition from these other products and areas affect or restrain sufficiently the pricing of the parties' products in the short term.

17. The question to be answered is whether the parties' customers would switch to readily available substitutes or to suppliers located elsewhere in response to a hypothetical small (in the range 5 % to 10 %) but permanent relative price increase in the products and areas being considered. If substitution were enough to make the price increase unprofitable because of the resulting loss of sales, additional substitutes and areas are included in the relevant market. This would be done until the set of products and geographical areas is such that small, permanent increases in relative prices would be profitable. The equivalent analysis is applicable in cases concerning the concentraiton of buying power, where the starting point would then be the supplier and the price test serves to identify the alternative distribution channels or outlets for the supplier's products. In the application of these principles, careful account should be taken of certain particular situations as described within paragraphs 56 and 58.

18. A practical example of this test can be provided by its application to a merger of, for instance, soft-drink bottlers. An issue to examine in such a case would be to decide whether different flavours of soft drinks belong to the same market. In practice, the question to address would be whether consumers of flavour A would switch to other flavours when confronted with a permanent price increase of 5 %

to 10 % for flavour A. If a sufficient number of consumers would switch to, say, flavour B, to such an extent that the price increase for flavour A would not be profitable owing to the resulting loss of sales, then the market would comprise at least flavours A and B. The process would have to be extended in addition to other available flavours until a set of products is identified for which a price rise would not induce a sufficient substitution in demand.

19. Generally, and in particular for the analysis of merger cases, the price to take into account will be the prevailing market price. This may not be the case where the prevailing price has been determined in the absence of sufficient competition. In particular for the investigation of abuses of dominant positions, the fact that the prevailing price might already have been substantially increased will be taken into account.

Supply substitution

20. Supply-side substitutability may also be taken into account when defining markets in those situaitons in which its effects are equivalent to those of demand substitution in terms of effectiveness and immediacy. This means that suppliers are able to switch production to the relevant products and market them in the short term[4] without incurring significant additional costs or risks in response to small and permanent changes in relative prices. When these conditions are met, the additional production that is put on the market will have a disciplinary effect on the competitive behaviour of the companies involved. Such an impact in terms of effectiveness and immediacy is equivalent to the demand substitution effect.

21. These situations typically arise when companies market a wide range of qualities or grades of one product; even if, for a given final customer or group of consumers, the different qualities are not substitutable, the different qualities will be grouped into one product market, provided that most of the suppliers are able to offer and sell the various qualities immediately and without the significant increases in costs described above. In such cases, the relevant product market will encompass all products that are substitutable in demand and supply, and the current sales of those products will be aggregated so as to give the total value or volume of the market. The same reasoning may lead to group different geographic areas.

---

4 That is such a period that does not entail a significant adjustment of existing tangible and intangible assets (see paragraph 23).

22. A practical example of the approach to supply-side substitutability when defining product markets is to be found in the case of paper. Paer is usually supplied in a range of different qualities, from standard writing paper to high quality papers to be used, for instance, to publish art books. From a demand point of view, different qualities of paper cannot be used for any given use, i.e. an art book or a high quality publication cannot be based on lower quality papers. However, paper plants are prepared to manufacture the different qualities, and production can be adjusted with negligible costs and in a short time-frame. In the absence of particular difficulties in distribution, paper manufacturers are able therefore, to compete for orders of the various qualities, in particular if orders are placed with sufficient lead time to allow for modification of production plans. Under such circumstances, the Commission would not define a separate market for each quality of paper and its respective use. The various qualities of paper are included in the relevant market, and their sales added up to estimate total market galue and volume.

23. When supply-side substitutability would entail the need to adjust significantly existing tangible and intangible assets, additional investments, strategic decisions or time delays, it will not be considered at the stage of market definition. Examples where supply-side substitution did not induce the Commission to enlarge the market are offered in the area of consumer products, in particular for branded beverages. Although bottling plants may in principle bottle different beverages, there are costs and lead times involved (in terms of advertising, product testing and distribution) before the products can actually be sold. In these cases, the effects of supply-side substitutability and other forms of potential competition would then be examined at a later stage.

Potential competition

24. The third source of competitive constraint, potential competition, is not taken into account when defining markets, since the conditions under which potential competition will actually represent an effective competitive constraint depend on the analysis of specific factors and circumstances related to the conditions of entry. If required, this analysis is only carried out at a subsequent stage, in general once the position of the companies involved in the relevant market has already been ascertained, and when such position gives rise to concerns from a competition point of view.

III. EVIDENCE RELIED ON TO DEFINE RELEVANT MARKETS

The process of defining the relevant market in practice

Product dimension

25. There is a range of evidence permitting an assessment of the extent to which substitution would take place. In individual cases, certain types of evidence will be determinant, depending very much on the characteristics and specificity of the industry and products or services that are being examined. The same type of evidence may be of no importance in other cases. In most cases, a decision will have to be based on the consideration of a number of criteria and different items of evidence. The Commission follows an open approach to empirical evidence, aimed at making an effective use of all available information which may be relevant in individual cases. The Commission does not follow a rigid hierarchy of different sources of information or types of evidence.

26. The process of defining relevant markets may be summarized as follows: on the basis of the preliminary information available or information submitted by the undertakings involved, the Commission will usually be in a position to broadly establish the possible relevant markets within which, for instance, a concentration or a restriction of competition has to be assessed. In general, and for all practical purposes when handling individual cases, the question will usually be to decide on a few alternative possible relevant markets. For instance, with respect to the product market, the issue will often be to establish whether product A and product B belong or do not belong to the same product market. it is often the case that the inclusion of product B would be enough to remove any competition concerns.

27. In such situations it is not necessary to consider whether the market includes additional products, or to reach a definitive conclusion on the precise product market. If under the conceivable alternative market definitions the operation in question does not raise competition concerns, the question of market definition will be left open, reducing thereby the burden on companies to supply information.

Geographic dimension

28. The Commission's approach to geographic market definition might be summarized as follows: it will take a preliminary view of the scope of the geographic market on the basis of broad indications as to the distribution of market shares between the parties and their competitors, as well as a preliminary analysis of

Market integration in the Community

32. Finally, the Commission also takes into account the continuing process of market integration, in particular in the Community, when defining geographic markets, especially in the area of concentrations and structural joint ventures. The measures adopted and implemented in the internal market programme to remove barriers to trade and further integrate the Community markets cannot be ignored when assessing the effects on competition of a concentration or a structural joint venture. A situation where national markets have been artifically isolated from each other because of the existence of legislative barriers that have now been removed will generally lead to a cautious assessment of past evidence regarding prices, market shares or trade patterns. A process of market integration that would, in the short term, lead to wider geographic markets may therefore be taken into consideration when defining the geographic market for the purposes of assessing concentrations and joint ventures.

The process of gathering evidence

33. When a precise market definition is deemed necessary, the Commission will often contact the main customers and the main companies in the industry to enquire into their views about the boudaries of product and geographic markets and to obtain the necessary factual evidence to reach a conclusion. The Commission might also contact the relevant professional associations, and companies active in upstream markets, so as to be able to define, in so far as necessary, separate product and geographic markets, for different levels of production or distribution of the products/ services in question. It might also request additional information to the undertakings involved.

34. Where appropriate, the Commission will address written requests for information to the market players mentioned above. These requests will usually include questions relating to the perceptions of companies about reactions to hypothetical price increases and their views of the boundaries of the relevant market. They will also ask for provision of the factual information the Commission deems necessary to reach a conclusion on the extent of the relevant market. The Commission might also discuss with marketing directors or other officers of those companies to gain a better understanding on how negotiations between suppliers and customers take place and better understand issues relating to the definition of the relevant market. Where appropriate, they might also carry out visits or inspections to the premises of the parties, their customers and/or their competitors, in order to better understand

the demand of a product, tests based on similarity of price movements over time, the analysis of causality between price series and similarity of price levels and/or their convergence. The Commission takes into account the available quantitative evidence capable of withstanding rigorous scrutiny for the purposes of establishing patterns of substitution in the past.

40. Views of customers and competitors. The Commission often contacts the main customers and competitors of the companies involved in its enquiries, to gather their views on the boundaries of the product market as well as most of the factual information it requires to reach a conclusion on the scope of the market. Reasoned answers of customers and competitors as to what would happen if relative prices for the candidate products were to increase in the candidate geographic area by a small amount (for instance of 5 % to 10 %) are taken into account when they are sufficiently backed by factual evidence.

41. Consumer preferences. In the case of consumer goods, it may be difficult for the Commission to gather the direct views of end consumers about substitute products. Marketing studies that companies have commissioned in the past and that are used by companies in their own decision-making as to pricing of their products and/or marketing actions may provide useful information for the Commission's delineation of the relevant market. Consumer surveys on usage patterns and attitudes, data from consumer's purchasing patterns, the views expressed by retailers and more generally, market research studies submitted by the parties and their competitors are taken into account to establish whether an economically significant proportion of consumers consider two products as substitutable, also taking into account the importance of brands for the products in question. The methodology followed in consumer surveys carried out ad hoc by the undertakings involved or their competitors for the purposes of a merger procedure or a procedure pursuant to Regulation No 17 will usually be scrutinized with utmost care. Unlike pre-existing studies, they have not been prepared in the normal course of business for the adoption of business decisions.

42. Barriers and costs associated with switching demand to potential substitutes. There are a number of barriers and costs that might prevent the Commission from considering two prima facie demand substitutes as belonging to one single product market. It is not possible to provide an exhaustive list of all the possible barriers to substitution and of switching costs. These barriers or obstacles might have a wide range of origins, and in its decisions, the Commission has been confronted with regulatory barriers or other forms of State intervention, constraints arising in

downstream markets, need to incur specific capital investment or loss in current output in order to switch to alternative inputs, the location of customers, specific investment in production process, learning and human capital investment, retooling costs or other investments, uncertainty about quality and reputation of unknown suppliers, and others.

43. Different categories of customers and price discrimination. The extent of the product market might be narrowed in the presence of distinct groups of customers. A distinct group of customers for the relevant product may constitute a narrower, distinct market when such ha group could be subject to price discrimination. This will usually be the case when two conditions are met: (a) it is possible to identify clearly which group an individual customer belongs to at the moment of selling the relevant products to him, and (b) trade among customers or arbitrage by third parties should not be feasible.

Evidence for defining markets – geographic dimension

44. The type of evidence the Commission considers relevant to reach a conclusion as to the geographic market can be categorized as follows:

45. Past evidence of diversion of orders to other areas. In certain cases, evidence on changes in prices between different areas and consequent reactions by customers might be available. Generally, the same quantitative tests used for product market definition might as well be used in geographic market definition, bearing in mind that international comparisons of prices might be more complex due to a number of factors such as exchange rate movements, taxation and product differentiation.

46. Basic demand characteristics. The nature of demand for the relevant product may in itself determine the scope of the geographical market. Factors such as national preferences or preferences for national brands, language, culture and life style, and the need for a local presence have a strong potential to limit the geographic scope of competition.

47. Views of customers and competitors. Where appropriate, the Commission will contact the main customers and competitors of the parties in its enquiries, to gather their views on the boundaries of the geographic market as well as most of the factual information it requires to reach a conclusion on the scope of the market when they are sufficiently backed by factual evidence.

48. Current geographic pattern of purchases. An examination of the customers'

current geographic pattern of purchases provides useful evidence as to the possible scope of the geographic market. When customers purchase from companies located anywhere in the Community or the EEA on similar terms, or they procure their supplies through effective tendering procedures in which companies from anywhere in the Community or the EEA submit bids, usually the geographic market will be considered to be Community-wide.

49. Trade flows/pattern of shipments. When the number of customers is so large that it is not possible to obtain through them a clear picture of geographic purchasing patterns, information on trade flows might be used alternatively, provided that the trade statistics are available with a sufficient degree of detail for the relevant products. Trade flows, and above all, the rationale behind trade flows provide useful insights and information for the purpose of establishing the scope of the geographic market but are not in themselves conclusive.

50. Barriers and switching costs associated to divert orders to companies located in other areas. The absence of trans-border purchases or trade flows, for instance, does not necessarily mean that the market is at most national in scope. Still, barriers isolating the national market have to identified before it is concluded that the relevant geographic market in such a case is national. Perhaps the clearest obstacle for a customer to divert its orders to other areas is the impact of transport costs and transport restrictions arising from legislation or from the nature of the relevant products. The impact of transport costs will usually limit the scope of the geographic market for bulky, low-value products, bearing in mind that a transport disadvantage might also be compensated by a comparative advantage in other costs (labour costs or raw materials). Access to distribution in a given area, regulatory barriers still existing in certain sectors, quotas and custom tariffs might also constitute barriers isolating a geographic area from the competitive pressure of companies located outside that area. Significant switching costs in procuring supplies from companies located in other countries constitute additional sources of such barriers.

51. On the basis of the evidence gathered, the Commission will then define a geographic market that could range from a local dimension to a global one, and there are examples of both local and global markets in past decisions of the Commission.

52. The paragraphs above describe the different factors which might be relevant to define markets. This does not imply that in each individual case it will be necessary to obtain evidence and assess each of these factors. Often in practice the evidence

provided by a susbset of these factors will be sufficient to reach a conclusion, as shown in the past decisional practice of the Commission.

IV. CALCULATION OF MARKET SHARE

53. The definition of the relevant market in both its product and geograhic dimensions allows the identification the suppliers and the customers/consumers active on that market. On that basis, a total market size and market shares for each supplier can be calculated on the basis of their sales of the relevant products in the relevant area. In practice, the total market size and market shares are often available from market sources, i.e. companies' estimates, studies commissioned from industry consultants and/or trade associations. When this is not the case, or when available estimates are not reliable, the Commission will usually ask each supplier in the relevant market to provide its own sales in order to calculate total market size and market shares.

54. If sales are usually the reference to calculate market shares, there are nevertheless other indications that, depending on the specific products or industry in question, can offer useful information such as, in particular, capacity, the number of players in bidding markets, units of fleet as in aerospace, or the reserves held in the case of sectors such as mining.

55. As a rule of thumb, both volume sales and value sales provide useful information. In cases of differentiated products, sales in value and their associated market share will usually be considered to better reflect the relative position and strength of each supplier.

V. ADDITIONAL CONSIDERATIONS

56. There are certain areas where the application of the principles above has to be undertaken with care. This is the case when considering primary and secondary markets, in particular, when the behaviour of undertakings at a point in time has to be analysed pursuant to Article 86. The method of defining markets in these cases is the same, i.e. assessing the responses of customers based on their purchasing decisions to relative price changes, but taking into account as well, constraints on substitution imposed by conditions in the connected markets. A narrow definition of market for secondary products, for instance, spare parts, may result when compatibility with the primary product is important. Problems of finding compatible secondary products together with the existence of high prices and a long lifetime

of the primary products may render relative price increases of secondary products profitable. A different market definition may result if significant substitution between secondary products is possible or if the characteristics of the primary products make quick and direct consumer responses to relative price increases of the secondary products feasible.

57. In certain cases, the existence of chains of substitution might lead to the definition of a relevant market where products or areas at the extreme of the market are not directly substitutable. An example might be provided by the geographic dimension of a product with significant transport costs. In such cases, deliveries from a given plant are limited to a certain area around each plant by the impact of transport costs. In principle, such an area could constitute the relevant geographic market. However, if the distribution of plants is such that there are considerable overlaps between the areas around different plants, it is possible that the pricing of those products will be constrained by a chain substitution effect, and lead to the definition of a broader geographic market. The same reasoning may apply if product B is a demand substitute for products A and C. Even if products A and C are not direct demand substitutes, they might be found to be in the same relevant product market since their respective pricing might be constrained by substitution to B.

58. From a practical perspective, the concept of chains of substitution has to be corroborated by actual evidence, for instance related to price interdependence at the extremes of the chains of substitution, in order to lead to an extension of the relevant market in an individual case. Price levels at the extremes of the chains would have to be of the same magnitude as well.

INTERNATIONAL COMPETITION LAW SERIES

1. Ignacio De León, *Latin American Competition Law and Policy: A Policy in Search of Identity* (2001)
(ISBN 90-411-1542-0)

2. Wim Dejonghe and Wouter Van de Voorde, *M & A in Belgium* (2001)
(ISBN 90-411-1594-3)

3. Yang-Ching Chao, Gee San, Changfa Lo, Jiming Ho, *International and Comparative Competition Law and Policies* (2001)
(ISBN 90-411-1643-5)

4. Martin Mendelsohn and Stephen Rose, *Guide to the EC Block Exemption for Vertical Agreements* (2002)
(ISBN 90-411-9813-X)

www.ingramcontent.com/pod-product-compliance
Lightning Source LLC
LaVergne TN
LVHW020000031026
849161LV00021B/784
* 9 7 8 9 0 4 1 1 9 8 1 3 6 *